Praise for the Second Edition of
Product Management in Practice

"Just get this book, OK? From start to finish it teaches hard-won lessons from the real-world challenges facing product people today, remote or in person. If you make products for a living, the answers you've been looking for throughout your career are here waiting for you."

—*Scott Berkun, Author of* Making Things Happen
and The Myths of Innovation

"Product management is one of the most sought-after roles of the 21st century. It is also one of the most poorly understood and widely variable in its expectations. This book examines the requirements, expectations, and realities of the role, beautifully illustrated with real-life examples. It challenges the myth that product management is only available to a select few, and shapes it into a 'practice' that is accessible to everybody. I recommend the book as a desk reference for all current and future product managers irrespective of where they are in their career trajectory."

—*Praneeta Paradkar, Director,*
Product Management, Broadcom Software

""This is an indispensable guide to navigating the daily ambiguity and compromise that define product management once you realize there is no one right way to do the job. In these pages Matt leads you past the theory to how to really get the job done in the real world, underlining each insight with stories from practicing product managers."

—*Martin Eriksson, Cofounder of Mind the Product*
and Coauthor of Product Leadership

"This book embraces all the complexity and ambiguity that product people navigate every day. It does *not* try to oversimplify product management into a handful of frameworks. Instead, it is a practical, hands-on guide full of real-world stories about how other product people are approaching their work. *Product Management in Practice* recreates the experience of learning directly from senior product managers across industries and organizations—and captures those learnings in concise summaries and easy-to-use checklists."

—*Petra Wille, Author of* Strong Product People
and Product Leadership Coach

"Matt's book is a must-read for any junior and more experienced PM, for engineers who often don't have much understanding of the PM world, and for executives interested in exploring better ways to enable their product teams and drive greater innovation. The book shares compelling stories anchored in today's reality, and contains a myriad of pragmatic tips and checklists. Far from a dry and stuffy manual, this book focuses on the real-world complexity of the role, the true conditions and constraints in which product managers operate today. It beautifully captures the human, connective, and messy nature of the PM role. A must-add to any product organization's book club!"

—*Shaaron A Alvares, Senior Manager,*
Agile Delivery and Transformation, Salesforce

"Matt is one of the brightest product people I know, and our conversations clarify the art of product management. This book makes those conversations available to the broader product community, enriching the reader with both Matt's experience and one of his best skills: the ability to extend and open new paths to think about everyday challenges."

—*Adam Thomas, Principal, Approaching One*

"Matt LeMay is a guiding force in the demystification of product management. This book is a reflection of his pragmatic approach to the many complexities and uncertainties that traverse one's entire career in product management. Matt understands that this is difficult work that heightens the complexity of having shared goals to attain while maintaining your humanity. He gives us actionable steps to manage those waters. As Matt says, 'Step into the discomfort.' I highly recommend all of Matt's writings and am excited to see an updated edition that speaks to the evolution of our craft and discipline."

—*Cliff Barrett, VP of Product, ChowNow*

Praise for the First Edition of *Product Management in Practice*

"It can seem impossible to learn the nuances of day-to-day product work without doing it yourself. Matt LeMay weaves together case studies from experienced product managers and frameworks to help teach and reinforce key dimensions of the product management job."

—*Ellen Chisa*

"This is an outstanding practical primer on the day-to-day job of product management. What Matt does here is break down product management into specific responsibilities and actions that new PMs can take to outline, plan, build, and monitor a smooth product development process. This should be a first-stop resource for any new product manager."

—*Blair Reeves, Author of* Building Products for the Enterprise

"What makes this book unique is how it goes beyond the jargon and zeroes in on the practical challenges of product management, with super actionable tips. I was smiling and nodding as I read chapter after chapter—I highly recommend this for all product managers."

—*Pradeep GanapathyRaj, VP of Product, Sinch, and former Head of Product Management, Yammer*

"*Product Management in Practice* is a bold and honest playbook by someone who's truly done the job and understands the real challenges PMs face every day. Matt LeMay's actionable advice should be required reading for both experienced and aspiring PMs."

—*Ken Norton*

"If you want to be a great product manager, you need to go beyond frameworks and tools. *Product Management in Practice* does just that with an honest, humble, and insightful look at the realities of life as a PM. Rich with real-world stories of success, failure, and common misconceptions that face every product manager, Matt reminds us that, above all, building great products is about building great relationships. A must-read for practicing and aspiring product managers or anyone who is interested in building great products."

—*Craig Villamor, Principal Design Architect,*
Stash, and former VP of Product, Salesforce

Product Management in Practice

SECOND EDITION

A Practical, Tactical Guide for Your First Day and Every Day After

Matt LeMay

Beijing · Boston · Farnham · Sebastopol · Tokyo

Product Management in Practice

by Matt LeMay

Copyright © 2022 Matt LeMay LLC. All rights reserved.

Published by O'Reilly Media, Inc., 1005 Gravenstein Highway North, Sebastopol, CA 95472.

O'Reilly books may be purchased for educational, business, or sales promotional use. Online editions are also available for most titles (*http://oreilly.com*). For more information, contact our corporate/institutional sales department: 800-998-9938 or *corporate@oreilly.com*.

Acquisitions Editor: Amanda Quinn	**Indexer:** nSight, Inc.
Development Editor: Angela Rufino	**Interior Designer:** Monica Kamsvaag
Production Editor: Elizabeth Faerm	**Cover Designer:** Susan Thompson
Copyeditor: Paula L. Fleming	**Cover Illustration:** Jose Marzan Jr.
Proofreader: Piper Editorial Consulting, LLC	**Illustrators:** Jose Marzan Jr. and Kate Dullea

November 2017:   First Edition

May 2022:   Second Edition

Revision History for the Second Edition

2022-05-16:   First Release

See *http://oreilly.com/catalog/errata.csp?isbn=9781098119737* for release details.

The O'Reilly logo is a registered trademark of O'Reilly Media, Inc. *Product Management in Practice*, the cover image, and related trade dress are trademarks of O'Reilly Media, Inc.

The views expressed in this work are those of the author and do not represent the publisher's views. While the publisher and the author have used good faith efforts to ensure that the information and instructions contained in this work are accurate, the publisher and the author disclaim all responsibility for errors or omissions, including without limitation responsibility for damages resulting from the use of or reliance on this work. Use of the information and instructions contained in this work is at your own risk. If any code samples or other technology this work contains or describes is subject to open source licenses or the intellectual property rights of others, it is your responsibility to ensure that your use thereof complies with such licenses and/or rights.

978-1-098-11973-7

[LSI]

Contents

Foreword

I remember one of the first times I wondered if I was good enough to be a product manager. I can't remember where I put my keys five seconds ago, but this experience has been burned indelibly into my brain. It was 2011, and I had flown into my company's San Francisco office. I was sitting in a conference room in the Monadnock Building on Market and Kearny, with its lime-green accent wall, gray couches, and wall-to-wall whiteboard. I was discussing the merits of my business case with two other product managers I really admired for the way they presented their business cases so charmingly and effortlessly. They could easily recite any statistic for our industry or company and could answer questions like "How many piano tuners are there in the entire world?" if asked on the spot. I wanted to be like them even though they, in a blaccent, would greet me with "Whut up, sista," and put their back-from-vacation skin against mine and say, "I'm almost as dark as you!" I admired them because I thought that was what a good product manager was—someone who was so knowledgeable and confident that they could be forgiven for being an asshole by the people they were being an asshole to.

I was seeking tacit approval from these product managers on a business case I was preparing. Instead, they interrogated the hell out of me:

"The NPV seems pretty low to get approved by Greg—what were your assumptions?"

"The COGS line isn't the number I use—where did you get this from?"

"Did you do a complete pro forma for this? How many versions?"

"What are your epics?"

"You mentioned that you worked on this with the support team. You do realize that they are a cost center for us—anything with them involved is going to increase your expense line?"

"This is an inward-facing capability. I don't think this is going to help us dominate our competition. How is this not just a race to the bottom?"

The questions were coming too fast to answer, and at some point, the other product managers omitted me from the conversation entirely. I thought, "S***, if you can't get these answers out fast enough for these two, how are you going to get through defending your position when Greg starts asking questions?" I felt the blood drain from my face, saw the smug look of my peers, and admitted defeat. "Oh, I'm late for my next meeting," I said, and walked out of the conference room as fast as I possibly could.

I *could* answer the questions being asked—but I was much more excited to discover and solve for what I saw as a major fault line in our experience. The support team was an important source of validation because they were the first line of defense with our customers and could connect customer feedback to this issue. I wanted to talk about why this would be a great win for our customers and, in turn, for our business. However, the prevailing definition of a good product manager was someone who could socialize a fresh and clean financial model with a company-centric BHAG (big, hairy, audacious goal). My peers and I were speaking different languages.

Product management is a challenging job because it can look different from company to company. It's certainly looked different over my career. Two companies ago, an analytical product manager was highly valued—we had targets we needed to hit, and leadership favored product managers who knew how to create "big rock" ideas with financial models that neatly laddered up topline sales goals. My last company valued relationship development and saw the team as a unit that was led by the product/design/engineering triad. Being able to develop a product-led growth strategy will be an important measure for my next company.

There are, however, universal truths in product management that you will experience across any digital organization. Product managers don't make the product but are accountable for it, from release to results. Product managers work with research and analytics to develop a vision, and they must socialize that vision with *everyone*, get buy-in from executives, get buy-in from the product team, and remove roadblocks.

This role requires chutzpah. And patience. And humility. And resilience. The job is challenging but so rewarding. It's such a great feeling to see your product launch, especially when you can validate your idea as quickly as possible. You get to work across the company with all levels of the organization. You get to talk with customers and partners in co-creating product with the team. Product management can build your confidence and make it easy to connect what you do with the success of your customer and company.

But as my vivid memory from 11 years ago illustrates, product management can also bring out the worst in people. Building product is not a heroic mission—which can be tough for people who seek status and recognition. Many people enter the field thinking that they will be the "mini-CEO" of the product, or that their job is to tell other people what to do. Others, like the product managers I once admired, poke holes in other people's ideas rather than working with them to make those ideas better.

I wish I could have read *Product Management in Practice* back when I wanted to be more like those product managers. With humor and generosity, Matt LeMay breaks down what actually makes a good product manager (communication, collaboration, learning from users) and what actually makes a bad product manager (defensiveness, arrogance, sucking up to executives). More than anything else I've read about product management, *Product Management in Practice* speaks to the messy reality of our work, beyond catchy acronyms and oversimplified frameworks.

During my tenure as chief product officer at Mailchimp, I had the pleasure of working directly with Matt to level up our product management practice throughout the organization. Reading through the second edition of *Product Management in Practice*, I see so many echoes of the challenges my team navigated as we worked to adapt quickly and stay customer focused during an unprecedented global pandemic. For product managers who have been struggling with burnout and exhaustion—as so many of us have—I think this second edition will provide much-needed comfort and guidance.

I have learned in my 20 years of product experience that being able to break down a financial model is a great skill but, honestly, one that doesn't matter if you can't earn the trust of your team or solve a problem for your customers. We need to get rid of territoriality and defensiveness in our discipline. *Product Management in Practice* shows us a better path forward.

Happy reading!

—*Natalia Williams*
March 2022

Author's Foreword to the Second Edition

The first edition of this book was written in spring of 2017. Thankfully, not much has changed since then.

All kidding aside, I am extraordinarily grateful for the opportunity to revise and expand this book. Reading back through the first edition, I'm struck by how thoroughly my own thinking has changed over the last four years. As you read this book, I hope you find yourself navigating similar moments of uncertainty and brow furrowing; being confident enough in your own perspective and experiences to disagree with something you read in a book is a good sign that your product management practice is maturing.

To that end, I was struck by how many of the people I interviewed for this edition have become deeply and justifiably skeptical toward any suggestion that there is a single "right way" to do product management. If I could sum up this round of interviews in a single paraphrased sentence, it would be "I wish I hadn't stressed out so much about how 'the company I work for isn't doing product management right' and had just focused on doing the best work I could."

I suspect that much of this has to do with the fact that many of us have now worked at enough organizations to know that nobody has all of this figured out. I also suspect that, after the last two years, any declarations of "If you just do these things, then everything will work out for you" ring much hollower than they did in the years before. The idea that the world is fast changing and unpredictable used to be a handy, nod-along-able platitude, but it is now a deeply felt experiential reality.

And from that position, I believe that we have the opportunity to reclaim some of the joy of product management. For there is a tremendous upside in the irresolvable ambiguity of this role and the irreducible complexity of this world:

there are always new things to learn, new stories to share, new situations to navigate, new mistakes to make, new frustrations to work through, new depths of resilience and adaptability to find in ourselves and each other. Here's to whatever comes next.

—Matt LeMay
Portland, Oregon
March 2022

Preface

Why I Wrote This Book: My First Day as a Product Manager

I never felt more prepared for anything than I did for my first day as a product manager. Ever the eager student, I had made a point of reading up on the basic tenets of user experience, sharpening my programming skills, and learning about software development methodologies. I knew the Agile Manifesto by heart and could drop terms like *minimum viable product* and *iterative development* into casual conversation. After settling in at my new workstation, I approached my boss—who was not a product manager himself but had worked with enough of them to know the type—with the overconfident swagger of a young person who had read a lot of books very quickly.

"I'm so excited to really dig into this work," I told him. "Where's the latest version of the product roadmap? What are our quarterly goals and KPIs? And who should I be talking to if I want to better understand the needs of our users?"

He gave me a weary look and took a deep breath. "You're smart," he said. "Figure it out."

Though this was far from the response I had hoped for, it taught me something very important about the world of product management: real-world guidance would be very, very hard to come by. For all the books I had read and all the "best practices" I had studied, the only thing I was left with when I sat back down at my desk was "What the hell am I supposed to *do* all day?" If there was no roadmap, how was I supposed to manage the roadmap? If there was no product development process, how was I supposed to oversee the product development process?

Early on in my career, I chalked much of this up to the fast pace and loose job definitions that come with working at a startup. But as I began to do more consulting and training work at organizations of different sizes and types, similar patterns began to emerge. Even in highly process-driven enterprise organizations, much of the actual work of product management seemed to be taking place on the margins and in the shadows. Product ideas were being hashed out over coffee breaks, not in planning meetings. Highly prescriptive scaled Agile frameworks were being bypassed by savvy politicking. Messy human communication reigned supreme over neatly structured frameworks and processes. And those same questions I had asked myself on my first day as a product manager were still being asked by product managers at organizations large and small, at cutting-edge technology startups and slow-moving enterprises, by new and experienced product managers alike.

Product management in theory is very different from product management in practice. In theory, product management is about building products that people love. In practice, product management often means fighting for incremental improvements on products that are facing much more fundamental challenges. In theory, product management is about triangulating business goals with user needs. In practice, product management often means pushing relentlessly to get any kind of clarity about what the business's "goals" actually are. In theory, product management is a masterfully played game of chess. In practice, product management often feels like a hundred simultaneous games of checkers.

To that end, this book is not a step-by-step guide to building great products, nor is it a list of frameworks and technical concepts guaranteed to bring you Product Management Success™. This book is intended to help you through the challenges that no tool, framework, or "best practice" can prepare you for. This book is about the day-to-day *practice* of product management with all its ambiguity, contradictions, and grudging compromises. Simply put, this is the book I needed on my first day as a product manager—and many, many days thereafter.

Who This Book Is For

Product management is a uniquely connective role, requiring its practitioners to bridge user needs with business goals, technical viability with user experience, and vision with execution. The connective nature of product management means that the role will look very different depending on the people, perspectives, and roles that you are connecting.

To that end, even defining what is and is not "product management" can be quite challenging. For the purposes of this book, *product management* refers to the entire nexus of product and product-adjacent connective roles—which might be "product manager," "product owner," "program manager," "project manager," or even "business analyst," depending on where you work and what you do. At some organizations, a "product manager" is the person responsible for defining a product's strategic vision, whereas a "project manager" oversees day-to-day tactics. At other organizations, people with "project manager" or "program manager" titles are informally expected to fill in the strategic gaps left open by the business at large. I worked with one organization in which a team of "business analysts" woke up to find themselves magically transformed into "product managers" by executive fiat, with no clear sense of how their day-to-day responsibilities had changed, or why.

Titles, like software tools and product development methodologies, are one way to provide some kind of structure and certainty to a role that offers precious little of either. Successful product management is much less a question of titles, tools, or processes than it is of *practice*. I use this word the same way one might refer to a yoga practice or a meditation practice—it is something that is built up with time and experience and cannot be learned from examples and instructions alone.

This book is for anybody who wants to better understand the real-world practice of product management. For folks who are new to product management, I hope that this book will present a clear and accurate picture of what you can expect from the day-to-day realities of the job. For folks who are more experienced in the practice of product management, I hope that this book will provide guidance for working through the challenges and roadblocks that somehow seem to keep presenting themselves time after time, year after year. And for everybody else, I hope this book will help you understand why the product managers in your life are so stressed out all the time—but really good to have around when you're trying to make a plan or solve a problem.

How This Book Is Organized

Each chapter of this book is organized around a particular theme, but these themes necessarily blur and blend into one another. Some of the concepts introduced in the first chapters of this book are referenced in later chapters, and some of the ideas explored at length in the later chapters of this book are set up toward the beginning. In practice, product management often feels more like a series of interrelated novellas than it does a neatly organized textbook.

Note that this book does not get into great detail about any particular roadmapping tools, Agile software development methodologies, or product life cycle frameworks. There is no shortage of very useful information out there about choosing a platform for bug tracking, a development methodology for product teams at medium-sized startups, or a framework for estimating user stories. The goal of this book is not to address the specific tools you might choose in your product management practice but rather to help you build a practice that can effectively incorporate whatever tools you encounter along the way.

Also note that this book does not get into great detail about what makes an entire organization more or less "good at doing product management" (or, if you prefer, "product led"). Most working product managers don't have much influence over how their organizations think about product development more broadly. More often than you'd probably imagine, even C-suite product leaders don't have nearly as much influence as they'd like over how their organizations think about product development more broadly. As we will discuss at length later in this book, hand-wringing about how your organization "doesn't do product right" is more often than not a huge waste of time—and a stressful one at that.

For simplicity's sake, I have generally described the people for whom you are building products as "users" and occasionally as "customers." Not every product is paid for directly by the people who use it, but every product is used by someone or something. In some cases, such as enterprise B2B software sales, you might have a "customer" who is different from your "user," and you can find yourself having to understand and connect the needs of both. If you're interested in reading more about this distinction and the ramifications it can have on product design, I would recommend checking out Blair Reeves's article "Product Management for the Enterprise" (*https://oreil.ly/i3Jk7*).

Finally, this book is not intended to be a high-level introductory glossary of product management terminology. If you encounter an idea, a concept, or an acronym that is new to you, take a moment to look it up.

STORIES FROM WORKING PRODUCT MANAGERS

There's often a knowing, conspiratorial tone to conversations shared between working product managers—like we're all in on the same secret. That secret, for those of you who are wondering, is that our job is widely misunderstood and really, really, really hard. Product managers are much more likely to share "war stories" than "best practices" and are more likely to talk about the mistakes they've made than the meteoric successes they've achieved.

In the hopes of bringing this kind of conversation to people who might bene-fit from it, I have included stories from working product managers in this book. Most of these stories started with the question, "What is one story from your work that you wish somebody had told you on your first day as a product manager?" As you will see, most of these stories are about people—not frameworks, tools, or methodologies. Several of the product managers I spoke to provided multiple stories that, taken together, paint a more comprehensive picture of the distinct but related challenges a product manager is likely to encounter over the course of their career.

Some of these stories are directly attributed to the folks who told them, some are anonymized, and some are composited from multiple sources. But they all represent the messy, complex realities of product management in the field. I have learned—and continue to learn—a lot from these stories, and I hope that you will too.

"YOUR CHECKLIST"

Every chapter of this book ends with an actionable to-do list called "Your Checklist." Product management can be heady and abstract stuff, and my primary goal with this book is for it to prove useful to working product managers. Each item on "Your Checklist" serves as an action-oriented summary of an idea that was explored at more length within that chapter.

O'Reilly Online Learning

 For more than 40 years, *O'Reilly Media* has provided technology and business training, knowledge, and insight to help companies succeed.

Our unique network of experts and innovators share their knowledge and expertise through books, articles, and our online learning platform. O'Reilly's online learning platform gives you on-demand access to live training courses, in-depth learning paths, interactive coding environments, and a vast collection of text and video from O'Reilly and 200+ other publishers. For more information, visit *https://oreilly.com*.

How to Contact Us

Please address comments and questions concerning this book to the publisher:

O'Reilly Media, Inc.

1005 Gravenstein Highway North

Sebastopol, CA 95472

800-998-9938 (in the United States or Canada)

707-829-0515 (international or local)

707-829-0104 (fax)

We have a web page for this book, where we list errata, examples, and any additional information. You can access this page at *https://oreil.ly/prod-mgmt-in-practice-2e*.

Email *bookquestions@oreilly.com* to comment or ask technical questions about this book.

For news and information about our books and courses, visit *https://oreilly.com*.

Find us on LinkedIn: *https://linkedin.com/company/oreilly-media*

Follow us on Twitter: *https://twitter.com/oreillymedia*

Watch us on YouTube: *https://youtube.com/oreillymedia*

Acknowledgments

Thanks to Mary Treseler, Angela Rufino, Laurel Ruma, Meg Foley, and everybody at O'Reilly Media for turning a pitch about a "very voicey and opinionated book about product management" into a real thing.

Thanks to Amanda Quinn, Suzanne McQuade, and again to Angela Rufino for shepherding this second edition into existence.

Thanks to everybody who provided both formal and informal feedback along the way.

Thanks to Natalia Williams for the chutzpah, patience, humility, and resilience.

Thanks to Mikhail Pozin for helping me ask better questions.

Thanks to Tim Casasola for helping me find better words.

Thanks to Ken Norton for bringing the donuts.

Thanks to Martin Eriksson for minding the community.

Thanks to Roger Magoulas for bringing me into the fold.

Thanks to every product manager who shared their stories with me. And, special thanks to those who helped me streamline the process of gathering these stories. (Product managers, amirite?)

Thanks to everybody I have had the pleasure of working with through the ups, downs, and literal and figurative tears of my own product management career. Your patience and generosity will always mean the world to me.

Thanks to Josh Wexler for the best coffee meetings ever.

Thanks to Andy Weissman for taking a chance on me way back when.

Thanks to Sarah Milstein for getting this all started.

Thanks to Jodi Leo for an exceptionally well-timed gift of encouragement.

Thanks to Tricia Wang and Sunny Bates for showing me the power of true partnership.

Thanks to Mom for not obfuscating the message.

Thanks to Dad for a grudging but unshakeable love of learning.

Thanks to Joan for everything, every day.

The Practice
of Product Management

I recently asked Pradeep GanapathyRaj, VP of product at Sinch and former head of product management at Yammer, what he wished that every new product management hire understood about their responsibilities. Here are his answers:

- Bring out the best in the people on your team.
- Work with people outside of your immediate team, who are not directly incentivized to work with you.
- Deal with ambiguity.

To his third point, he added, "The skill of actually figuring out what you need is probably as important as what you do after you figure it out."

Perhaps the most striking thing about these answers is that none of them are about product, per se. Many people are drawn to product management by the promise of "building products that people love." And, sure enough, delivering products that provide real value to real people is one of the most important (and rewarding!) aspects of product management. But the day-to-day work of delivering those products usually involves less *building* than it does communicating, supporting, and facilitating. No matter how much expertise a product manager might have in software development, data analytics, or go-to-market strategy, their success can only be realized through the shared efforts of the people around them—people who each carry their own complex and oft-inscrutable needs, ambitions, doubts, and limitations.

In this chapter, we discuss the real-world practice of product management, addressing a few common traps that product managers fall into when their expectations of the role don't line up with the reality.

What Is Product Management?

These days, it can seem like there are as many working definitions of product management as there are actual product managers. All of these definitions are helpful for understanding how particular individuals and organizations think about product management. Many of these definitions contradict each other in subtle but appreciable ways. And not a single one of these definitions even begins to capture the breadth of day-to-day experiences that a single product manager is likely to encounter over the course of their career.

In a sense, product management is best understood not by a single "correct" definition but rather by the very impossibility of such a definition. In navigating the ever-growing discourse around product management, I've found it helpful to think less about "definitions" than about *descriptions*, with the understanding that any descriptive text about product management will be rooted in its author's unique perspective and experiences.

One description of product management that I find particularly instructive comes from Melissa Perri's excellent book *Escaping the Build Trap* (O'Reilly). In this book, Perri describes product managers as the stewards of a *value exchange* between a business and its customers. When you think about just how large, important, and complex a task that is, you start to get a good sense of why product management can be so challenging.

So what exactly is the day-to-day work of delivering on that challenge?

The answer to that question depends on a lot of things. At a small startup, you might find a product manager cobbling together product mock-ups, scheduling check-in points with contract developers, and conducting informal interviews with prospective users. At a medium-sized technology company, you might find a product manager running planning meetings with a team of designers and developers, negotiating product roadmaps with senior executives, and working with colleagues in sales and customer service to understand and prioritize user needs. At a large enterprise organization, you might find a product manager rewriting feature requests as "user stories," requesting specific data from colleagues who work in analytics or insights, and attending a whole lot of meetings.

In other words, if you are working as a product manager, you will probably find yourself doing lots of different things at different times—and what exactly those things are can change at a moment's notice. However, there are a few consistent themes that unite the work of product management across job titles, industries, business models, and company sizes:

You have lots of responsibility but little authority.

Did your team miss a launch deadline? That is your responsibility. Did the product you manage fail to meet its quarterly goals? That's also your responsibility. As a product manager, you are the person who is ultimately responsible for the success or failure of your product—regardless of how well the rest of the organization supports that product.

Working in a position of high responsibility is challenging enough, but to further complicate matters, product managers rarely have any direct organizational authority. Is there a designer on your team who strongly disagrees with the direction of the product? An engineer whose attitude is proving toxic to the team at large? These are your problems to solve, but you can't solve them with threats or orders—nor can you solve them by yourself.

If it needs to get done, it's part of your job.

"But—that's not my job!" is a phrase rarely uttered by successful product managers. Regardless of whether it falls neatly into the boundaries of your written job description, you are responsible for doing *whatever needs to get done* to ensure the success of your team and your product. This might mean coming in early to bring coffee and breakfast to an overworked product team. It might mean navigating tense conversations with a senior executive to resolve ambiguity around your team's goals. And it might mean calling in a favor from elsewhere in the organization if your team simply doesn't have the capacity to do what's needed on its own.

If you work as a "product manager" at a very early-stage startup, you might find yourself spending most of your time doing work that feels like it has very little to do with "product management" at all. Product managers I've known at early-stage startups have found themselves working as ad hoc community managers, HR leads, UX designers, and office managers. If it needs to be done, and it isn't anyone else's job, then—surprise!—it's your job. Even at large enterprise companies, there will almost certainly be times when you need to step up and do something that is not officially part of your job. And, because you are held responsible for the performance of your team and your product, "That wasn't my job," plays as well at a Fortune 500 corporation as it does at a five-person startup.

To make this even more challenging, most of the things you will need to get done as a product manager are not things you can do alone. You do not have the luxury of disappearing for a few weeks, reading a bunch of books, and returning fully skilled up and ready to singlehandedly deliver a product. You will need to ask for support, guidance, and hard work from the people around you—often people outside of your immediate team, who might have no obvious reason to help you out.

You are in the middle.

Product managers tend to find themselves in the middle of everything—translating between business needs and user goals, mediating conflicts between engineers and designers, and connecting high-level company strategy with day-to-day product decisions. Successful product management expresses itself in hundreds of daily interactions with the people who represent these far-flung perspectives, skill sets, and objectives. You must learn to navigate their communication styles, their sensitivities, and the differences between what they say and what they mean.

Even at organizations that are highly structured and systematized, or that claim to be impartial and "data driven," it is inevitable that at some point you will find yourself navigating a tangled web of unspoken resentment and unresolved conflict. Others might be able to keep their heads down and "just do their work," but making connections between messy, real-world people *is* your work.

What Is Not Product Management?

Product management can be many different things, but it is not everything. Here are a few consistent—and for some people, consistently disappointing—realities of what product management is not:

You are not the boss.

I've often seen the role of product manager described as the "mini-CEO" of a product. Unfortunately, most of the product managers I've seen act like a "mini-CEO" are more interested in the status of this honorary distinction than they are in its responsibility. Yes, as a product manager, you are responsible for the success or failure of your product. But, for you to meet this responsibility, you are entirely dependent upon the trust and hard work of your team. That trust can be easily squandered if you carry yourself like a big important boss.

You are not actually building the product yourself.

For some people, product management evokes visions of brilliant inventors and tinkerers, toiling away to bring their game-changing ideas to the masses. If you like to be the person actually *building* things with your hands, you might find yourself deeply frustrated by the connective and facilitative nature of product management. Furthermore, what feels like a good-natured wish to get into the weeds of technical and design decisions might come off as infuriating micromanagement to the people who *are* tasked with building the product you manage.

This absolutely does not mean that you should take zero interest in your product team's technical and design decisions. Taking a genuine interest in the work of your colleagues is one of the most important things you can do as a product manager. But product management often poses a particular challenge to those who come from the "Never mind, I'll just go do it myself," school of problem solving. If you, like me, are the kind of person who absolutely hated group projects in school and sought to take on as much work as possible for yourself, product management is likely to teach you difficult yet important lessons about trust, collaboration, and delegation.

You can't wait around until somebody tells you what to do.

As I learned on my first day as a product manager, it's exceptionally rare that you will be given clear guidelines and instructions in this role. Larger companies, especially those that have a longer history with product management, are more likely to have well-defined expectations around the product manager role. But even at those companies, you will have your work cut out for you figuring out what you should do, who you should talk to, and how you can effectively communicate with the specific people on your team.

If you're unclear about a directive coming down from senior leadership, you can't sit around waiting for them to clarify it. If you see something in a mock-up that you think will be a problem, you can't wait until somebody else catches it. It is your job to identify, evaluate, prioritize, and address anything that might affect your team's ability to deliver on its goals —whether or not you're explicitly told to do so.

What Is the Profile of a Great Product Manager?

Some organizations are well-known for favoring a certain profile among product management candidates. Amazon, for example, has historically preferred MBAs. Google, on the other hand, has been known for preferring candidates with a computer science degree from Stanford. (The extent to which either of these companies still harbors these preferences is the subject of frequent debate.) Generally speaking, the "classic" profile for a product manager is either a technical person with some business savvy, or a business-savvy person who will not annoy the hell out of developers.

Although there are plenty of product managers who fit this profile to some degree, some of the very best product managers I've met—including product managers who cut their teeth at Amazon and Google—don't fit any "classic" profile. The truth is, great product managers can come from anywhere. Some of the best product managers I've met have backgrounds in music, politics, nonprofits, theater, marketing—you name it. They are people who like to solve interesting problems, learn new things, and work with smart people.

Great product managers are the sum of their experiences, the challenges they've faced, and the people they've worked with. They are constantly evolving and adapting their own practice to meet the specific needs of their current team and organization. They are humble enough to recognize that there will always be new things to learn and curious enough to constantly learn new things from the people around them.

When I consult with organizations that are looking to identify internal candidates for PM roles, I often ask a few people to draw out a diagram of how information travels within the company—not a formal org chart, just an informal sketch of how people communicate with each other. Without fail, a few people continuously show up smack in the middle. These people are the information brokers, the connectors, the expansive thinkers who are actively seeking out new perspectives. They rarely fit the "traditional" profile of a product manager, and, in many cases, they are entirely nontechnical. But these are the people who have already proven that they have the interest and the inclination to do the challenging connective work that is key to successful product management.

What Is the Profile of a Bad Product Manager?

Although great product managers rarely fit a single profile, bad product managers are quite consistent. There are some bad product manager archetypes that seem to show up in nearly every kind of organization:

The Jargon Jockey

The Jargon Jockey wants you to know that the approach you're describing might make sense if you were working in a hybrid Scrumban methodology but is simply unacceptable to a certified PSM III Scrum Master. (If you had to look any of that up, the Jargon Jockey is shocked by your incompetence—how did you even get this job?) The Jargon Jockey defines words you haven't heard with other words you haven't heard and seems to use those words more and more when there's a high-stakes disagreement playing out.

The Steve Jobs Acolyte

The Steve Jobs Acolyte Thinks Differently™. The Steve Jobs Acolyte likes to lean back in chairs and ask big, provocative questions. The Steve Jobs Acolyte would like to remind you that people didn't know that they wanted the iPhone either. The Steve Jobs Acolyte doesn't want to build a faster horse. The Steve Jobs Acolyte wouldn't say that your users are stupid—at least, not exactly—but they are definitely not visionaries like the Steve Jobs Acolyte.

The Hero Product Manager

Have no fear, the Hero Product Manager is here with an amazing idea that will save the whole company. The Hero Product Manager is not particularly interested in hearing why this idea might not work, or that it's already been discussed and explored a million times. Did you hear about what the Hero Product Manager did at their last company? They pretty much built the whole thing single-handedly, or at least the good parts. And yet, the people at *this* company just never seem to give the Hero Product Manager the resources or support they need to deliver on all those amazing promises.

The Overachiever

The Overachiever *gets s*** done*. Did you know that the Overachiever's team shipped *fifty* features last year? And did you hear about the time that the Overachiever led their team through three consecutive all-nighters to keep a major product release on schedule? The Overachiever is revered by company leadership as a go-getter who can deliver *lots of stuff*, but it's not entirely clear what that stuff actually achieved for the business or its users. And you can't help but notice that the folks on the Overachiever's team seem pretty stressed out...that is, the folks on the Overachiever's team who haven't already quit.

The Product Martyr

Fine! The Product Martyr (Figure 1-1) will do it. If the product didn't launch on time or didn't meet its goals, the Product Martyr takes complete and unequivocal responsibility for screwing everything up (again). The Product Martyr says it's no big deal that they pick up coffee for the whole team every morning, but the way they place the Starbucks tray down on their desk seems just a liiiiiiiittle more emphatic than it needs to be. The Product Martyr says repeatedly that they've put this job ahead of everything else in their life, and yet they seem outraged and overburdened every time you come to them with a new question or concern.

Figure 1-1. The Product Martyr, in the wild

These patterns are shockingly easy to fall into—I've definitely fallen into all of them at one point or another in my career. Why? Because by and large they are driven not by malice or incompetence but by insecurity. Product management can be a brutal and relentless trigger for insecurity, and insecurity can bring out the worst in all of us.

Because product management is a connective and facilitative role, the actual value product managers bring to the table can be very difficult to quantify. Your developer wrote 10,000 lines of code. Your designer created a tactile, visual universe that wowed everybody in the room. Your CEO is the visionary who led the team to success. Just what did *you* do, exactly?

This question—and the urge to defensively demonstrate value—can lead to some epic acts of unintentional self-sabotage. Insecure product managers might begin speaking in gibberish to prove that product management is a real thing that is really complicated and important (the Jargon Jockey). They might (and often do) lead their teams down a path of exhaustion and burnout just to prove how much stuff they did (the Overachiever). They might even start to make big, awkward public displays of just how much they are personally sacrificing in order to do all that stuff (the Product Martyr).

For product managers, the value you create will be largely manifest in the work of your team. The best product managers I've met are those who truly believe that their team's success *is* their own success. These are the product managers whose teams use phrases like "I would trust that person with my life" and "That person makes me feel excited to show up for work in the morning." If you're starting to feel insecure about your work, talk to your team and see what you can do to better contribute to their success. But don't let insecurity turn you into a bad product manager.

No, You Don't Have to Work 60 Hours a Week to Be a Product Manager

In the last six months, a number of people have told me, "I'd love to be a product manager, but I've heard you need to work sixty hours a week to do that job well." Early in my career I would have vehemently agreed with this sentiment, maybe even offering an obnoxious addendum like "Sixty hours if you're lucky!" But I have matured past that belief, and I believe that our discipline has largely matured past it as well.

When I reflect on my time as a 60-hour-a-week product manager, the truth is that most of those hours were driven by inexperience, insecurity, and the inability to prioritize my time effectively. I had no idea what I was doing, and I was afraid that *other people* would see that I had no idea what I was doing, so I set about doing as much as I could as loudly and visibly as I could (hence, my journey from wide-eyed newbie to Overachiever to Product Martyr). Not only was this approach disastrous for my mental health, it was also profoundly harmful to my team, who were left wondering if *they* should still be in the office at 8 p.m. while I was still there loudly sighing and clacking away at my keyboard.

During my most effective and impactful years as a product manager, I was working from 10 to 4 most days—and yes, this was at a fast-paced, high-growth startup. With the help of some extremely talented colleagues (and an extremely good therapist), I was able to prioritize the tasks that were helping my team achieve its goals and stop worrying so much about whether my colleagues thought I was working hard enough. It turns out that nobody (aside from myself) was keeping meticulous tabs on how late I stayed in the office on a given Friday night or how quickly I responded to a Sunday morning Slack message.

Anybody who has done the hard work of learning to set boundaries and prioritize their time will be, and should be, put off by the idea that any job will require them to work an unreasonable and unhealthy number of hours. And the field of product management desperately needs more people who have done the hard work of learning to set boundaries and prioritize their time. The idea that long hours are an inextricable part of the job discourages talented people from entering the field, and it discourages those already in the field from learning how to prioritize their time and set reasonable and healthy expectations for their teams. Let's get over it.

What About Program Managers? Product Owners?

Nearly every time I teach a workshop about product management, the first question I get asked is some version of "What's the difference between a product manager and a (program manager/product owner/solution manager/project manager)?"

It's not hard to understand why this question is top-of-mind for so many people. As the constellation of similar-sounding product and product-related titles continues to grow, clarity around role and purpose can be harder and harder to find. If you're a product manager on a team that's suddenly hiring a program manager—what does that mean for you? Is your job being rendered obsolete? Is somebody else going to be doing the same work as you? And, not to be tacky but, hey, who's getting paid more?

When I started doing product coaching and training, I did my best to definitively answer these questions using a combination of past experience and frantic googling. I would say with great confidence, "Well, in most situations, the product manager is the person who's accountable for the business outcomes the team delivers, and the product owner is the person who's in charge of managing the team's day-to-day activities." Nods of recognition! Sweet relief! A specific, concrete answer!

It only took a couple of weeks for me to find myself working with an organization that defined these roles in the exact opposite way. As I started to give my boilerplate answer to this very same question, an executive interrupted me and said, "Um, we actually define it kind of the opposite here. After all, why would we call the person who manages the team's activities the product *owner*, and the person who owns the product's outcomes the product *manager*?" Needless to say, "Because that's what it said when I googled it" was not a great answer.

Since that fateful day, I have found myself providing a very different, much less immediately satisfying answer: "It varies enormously from organization to organization and from team to team. Some organizations define the difference one way, and others define it the exact opposite way. Talk with the folks at your organization to find out how they think about the role and what their specific expectations are for you." Fewer nods, less relief.

I've started thinking about the ever-expanding list of "pro**** ******er" titles as Ambiguously Descriptive Product Roles (ADPRs), in the interest of having a banner concept to encompass the myriad job titles that likely won't tell you all that much about your day-to-day activities and responsibilities. For ADPRs whose teams include other ADPRs, I find myself offering the following, similarly disappointing advice: "Sit down with your fellow ADPRs, figure out what needs to be done, and figure out how you're going to do it together. Focus on your shared efforts, rather than trying to establish absolute nonoverlapping clarity around your titles." As an ADPR, you will likely never have absolute clarity about what exactly your job entails. Ask lots of questions, work closely with your team, and stay focused on doing the most impactful work you can.

I find myself offering the same advice when asked about specialized ADPR titles such as "growth product manager" or "technical product manager." I have deeply mixed feelings about the increasing specialization of product manager roles. At best, this trend could help create a little more clarity around what is expected of people working in a specific role at a specific company. At worst, it could become another source of false certainty that obscures the inherent generalism of product roles. (I've already overheard my first "Well, that person has only worked as a *growth* product manager—do you think they'd be able to cut it as a regular product manager?" conversation, and I fear there are many more to come.)

Long story short: every single product job on every single team at every single company is a little different. The sooner you truly embrace this, the sooner you can get to the hard work of doing *your* specific product job as best you, specifically, can.

Summary: Sailing the Seas of Ambiguity

No matter how many books you've read (including this one), how many articles you've scrolled through, or how many conversations you've had with working product managers, there will always be new and unexpected challenges in this line of work. Do your best to remain open to these challenges and, if possible, enjoy the fact that the ambiguity around your role means that you are likely to learn lots of entirely new things.

Your Checklist

- Accept that being a product manager means that you are going to have to do lots of different things. Don't become upset if your day-to-day work is not visionary and important seeming, so long as it is contributing to the goals of your team.

- Be proactive about seeking out ways that you can help contribute to the success of your product and your team. Nobody is going to tell you exactly what to do all the time.

- Get out ahead of potential miscommunications and misalignments, no matter how inconsequential they might seem in the moment.

- Don't get too hung up on the "typical profile" of a successful product manager. Successful product managers can come from anywhere.

- Don't let insecurity turn you into the caricature of a bad product manager! Resist the urge to defensively show off your knowledge or skills.

- Measure your success by the impact you're having on your business, your users, and your team—not how many hours you're working.

- Stop looking for a single "correct" definition of any Ambiguously Descriptive Product Role (such as product manager, product owner, or program manager). Acknowledge the uniqueness of each product role on each team and ask a lot of questions to understand what's expected of you specifically.

- If your team has multiple Ambiguously Descriptive Product Roles (say, a product manager and a product owner), work with your fellow ADPRs to align on your shared goals and figure out how best to work together toward achieving those goals.

2

The CORE Skills
of Product Management

Given the vast variability of product management roles between teams and organizations, the actual *skills* of product management can prove very hard to pin down. This often results in product management being described as a mishmash of the skills used in other, easier-to-define roles. A little bit of coding, a pinch of business acumen, some user experience design, and—voilá!—you're a product manager.

As we discuss in this chapter, the connective work of product management requires its own set of skills. Defining this set of skills helps carve out a place for product management as a unique and valuable role and provides much-needed day-to-day guidance for how product managers can excel at their work.

The Hybrid Model: UX/Tech/Business

Insofar as there is a commonly accepted visual representation of product management, it is a three-way Venn diagram (Figure 2-1) that positions product management at the intersection of business, tech, and UX (user experience).

I have seen a number of variations on this—sometimes *UX* is replaced with *design* or *people*. Sometimes *business* is replaced with *statistics* or *finance*. I recently saw a job listing from a major bank that asked for candidates who are proficient in "business, technology, and human"—which in no way sounds like a job listing written by and for sentient robots.

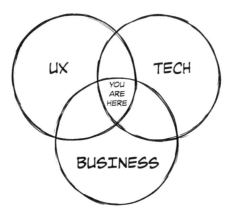

Figure 2-1. The hybrid product management Venn diagram, from Martin Eriksson's "What, Exactly, Is a Product Manager?" (https://oreil.ly/K6MZ3)

Earlier this year, I had the pleasure of chatting with Martin Eriksson, the creator of the Venn diagram, in a fireside chat (*https://oreil.ly/cBEds*) with the Mind the Product community that Eriksson helped build. In this conversation, Eriksson shared how the Venn diagram stemmed not from a desire to definitively pin down the role of product management for generations to come, but rather from a desire to share his own particular perspective on the role:

> It was never intended to be the ultimate definition in any way, shape, or form—just a story I was telling about the job I was doing, and what I thought about it, and why I thought it was a pretty great job to have. [The Venn diagram emerged from] looking at the team I was trying to build at the time. I was working at a startup as a VP of product—basically the first real product person in the business. We were experimenting a lot with "How do we build cross-functional autonomous teams?" though we didn't quite call it that at the time....I was thinking about, "What are the things that we need in our teams to be successful and build great products?" And the most important things are those three elements—some sense of the customer, the user experience, some sense of the business aspect. How do you make that valuable and capture that value, and how do you work with engineering to actually deliver that and make sure it's something that's feasible to build?

This team-level definition serves as a tremendously helpful and succinct description of the product management role. Indeed, you will rarely encounter a product manager whose work doesn't involve some element of understanding their users and/or customers, some element of understanding their business, and some element of understanding whatever it is they need to understand to help their team actually *deliver* something that enhances the value exchange between the business and its customers. When I started out as a product manager, this visual helped me understand that I had a unique place in the world. Not as an engineer, a designer, or a business analyst, but as a different kind of person who connects and aligns these disparate roles to help my team succeed.

This is, of course, just one person's interpretation—and there are many other interpretations of this Venn diagram, some of which are...appreciably less helpful than others. One unhelpful interpretation I often encounter is the Venn-diagram-as-flat-circle fallacy: the mistaken belief that a single product manager must possess *all the skills and knowledge* of a developer, a designer, and a business analyst. If you've ever been overwhelmed by a product management job listing that appears to be calling for the skills and experience of an entire team—or even an entire company—you may have seen this fallacy in action. Here, again, Eriksson is quick to clarify: "Product is at the intersection of those three things, but that doesn't mean we have to have all the answers or be experts in any one or all three of those."

Indeed, the skills required to *be* a designer, a developer, or a business analyst can be very different from the skills required to *create alignment among* designers, developers, and business analysts. This Venn diagram can help describe where you are as a product manager, but—as with any single model or description—it can't tell you everything about what you're supposed to *do* there. Indeed, when I asked Eriksson for one caveat he wished could travel along with the Venn diagram, he answered: "One size does not fit all."

The CORE Skills of Product Management: Communication, Organization, Research, and Execution

In the most textbook-perfect version of product management, you may very well be sitting on a classic "product triad" with a designer and an engineer, while regularly interfacing with business stakeholders outside of your immediate team. But in nearly all cases, you will also need to find yourself connecting and aligning stakeholders who fall outside of *any* three-way Venn diagram. At a large, regulated enterprise, a product manager might spend most of their time connecting and aligning between lawyers and account managers. At a new startup, a product manager might spend most of their time connecting and aligning between the company's founder and an external vendor who has been hired to build the initial version of the company's product.

When I host product management workshops that are open to people from multiple companies, the first question I usually ask them is "What are the top five roles in your company *you* must connect and align to achieve your goals?" To say that the answers vary widely would be an understatement. Some do, in fact, start by listing developers, designers, and business stakeholders. Others start by listing marketers, salespeople, data scientists, and compliance officers. Some list roles I've never heard of before, and others just write the word "CUSTOMERS" in all caps and leave it at that.

As product management becomes a more ubiquitous and farther-reaching role, the Venn diagram being navigated by any product manager is only going to get more unwieldy and less predictable. Given the reality that product managers must connect and align a wide-reaching range of stakeholders, the question becomes "What are the specific skills that product managers need, across organizations and teams and industries, to successfully connect and align *whoever* they work with on a day-to-day basis?"

When I began researching this book, I set out to develop a new skill model for product managers that could better speak to the *connective* skills that make product management a unique and exciting role. In my interviews with product managers across industries and organizations, I found that the fundamental skills required to succeed are often quite similar (Figure 2-2). A product manager must be able to:

- *Communicate* with stakeholders
- *Organize* the product team for sustainable success
- *Research* the needs and goals of the product's users
- *Execute* the day-to-day tasks required for the product team to meet its goals

This CORE skills model constitutes a new framing of product management that better reflects the day-to-day realities of the role across organizations and industries.

Figure 2-2. The CORE skills of product management

What follows is a breakdown of the CORE skills of product management, with a guiding principle for each skill that speaks to the real-world behaviors that put these skills into action.

COMMUNICATION

Clarity over comfort.

Communication is far and away the most important skill for a product manager to develop and nurture. If you cannot communicate effectively with your team, your stakeholders, and your users, you will not succeed as a product manager. Great product managers not only tolerate, but actively enjoy, the challenge of creating alignment and understanding between different people with different experiences and perspectives.

The guiding principle for communication is "clarity over comfort." The choice between clarity and comfort is a real one, and one that we are often faced with at the most important moments of our career. For example, you might find yourself attending a meeting in which an executive makes a passing reference to a feature that your team chose to de-prioritize weeks ago. Not wanting to create an uncomfortable situation, you might decide to let it pass, figuring that the feature in question is just a small part of the overall product launch and probably isn't a big deal. But from the executive's perspective, your silence might be interpreted as a tacit agreement that the small feature in question will *definitely* be part of the product launch. The consequences of this lack of clarity could be trivial—or cataclysmic.

It is no accident that uncomfortable moments like this are often the ones that prove most impactful. Discomfort is often the manifestation of a lack of clarity. It is a valuable signpost indicating that people are not on the same page or that expectations have not been clearly set. As a product manager, you cannot fear discomfort; you must actively work through it to get clarity for yourself and your team. We will discuss specific strategies for achieving clarity over comfort in Chapter 4, "The Art of Egregious Overcommunication".

I want to emphasize here that good communication does not mean "choosing fancy words and speaking in an impressive manner." Many of the product managers I talk to—especially those who self-identify as introverts or who are working in a language that is not their first—fear that they are operating at an intrinsic disadvantage when it comes to developing communication skills. In fact, I've found that these product managers often have a head start when it comes to cultivating clarity over comfort, as they are more practiced in working through some degree of uncertainty or discomfort to achieve clarity for themselves and their teams.

Regardless of where you're starting from, there are always steps you can take to become a better communicator. Here are a few questions you can ask yourself to evaluate your communication skills:

- Am I asking the necessary questions and facilitating the necessary conversations to make sure my team has clarity on what we are doing and why?

- Am I proactively reaching out to other product teams and managers if I believe that coordination will help deliver better user and business outcomes?

- Am I responding promptly and thoughtfully to stakeholders who reach out to me?
- When exploring potential solutions, am I consistently presenting multiple options and walking stakeholders through the trade-offs of each one?

ORGANIZATION

Make yourself obsolete.

Beyond using their own personal communication skills, product managers must organize their teams to work well together. If communication skills come down to managing personal interactions, organization is about operationalizing and scaling those interactions.

Not all individuals who excel as individual communicators are naturally gifted organizers. Product managers who lack organization skills, no matter how knowledgeable and charismatic they are, often become a bottleneck for their teams. They run around giving directions, unblocking team members, and resolving conflicts, but their teams are incapable of functioning without their direct and constant intervention. Product managers who lack organization skills are happy to hear questions like "What should we be working on right now?" because these questions put the product manager in the utterly indispensable role of guiding the team's day-to-day priorities and decisions.

By contrast, product managers who excel at organization see the question "What should we be working on right now?" as a sign that something is broken. They strive to ensure that everybody on their team will always know what they should be working on and why, without having to ask them personally. When something goes wrong, organization-minded product managers don't just ask, "How can I solve this problem right now?" but also, "How can I make sure this doesn't happen again?"

The guiding principle for organization is "Make yourself obsolete." Product managers who excel at organization work with their teams to organize people, processes, and tools into self-sustaining systems that do not require their moment-to-moment participation or oversight. The drive to make oneself obsolete is counterintuitive to many product managers, especially those who seek recognition for their individual efforts. But the best product managers are secure in the understanding that those individual efforts are most impactful when they empower the entire team.

Here are a few questions you can ask yourself to evaluate your organization skills:

- If I were to go on vacation for a month, would my team have the information and processes in place to prioritize and deliver without my day-to-day participation?

- If I were to ask anybody on my team, "What are you working on and why?" would they all have immediate and consistent answers?

- If somebody on any other team wanted to know what my team was working on, would they be able to easily access that information in an up-to-date, understandable format?

- If a particular process or system (or lack thereof) is not working for my team, am I proactively working with my team to change that process or system? Or, if we are not in a position to directly change that process or system, am I proactively working with my team to change how we interact with that process or system?

RESEARCH

Live in your user's reality.

Research is how product managers stay connected to the complex and chaotic world around them, even as they navigate the exhausting minutiae of their day-to-day work. The practice of research includes both formalized activities, such as user interviews, and informal conversations, Google searches, and social media rabbit holes that help product managers stay up-to-date with their users. If curiosity is the key mindset of the product manager, research is how that curiosity is actualized and extended beyond the walls of the organization.

Product managers who lack research skills tend to lead their team steadfastly down a predetermined path without taking the time to ask *why* they are pursuing that path or seeking out new information that might compel them to adjust course. These product managers might be able to hit their deadlines, but they are constantly playing catch-up with their market and their users.

The guiding principle for research is "Live in your user's reality." Every product has a user—whether it's a consumer, another business, or an engineer utilizing an API. The things that matter to you, such as hitting project deadlines, managing the product backlog, or balancing the profit and loss statement, do not matter at all to them. Your users have their own set of priorities, needs, and concerns, the most critical of which might not be directly related to their interactions with your product at all. The most successful product managers I've met understand not only how users interact with their product but also how the product fits into users' broader *reality*. When these product managers evaluate a competitor's product, they ask, "What might this product mean to our users," not, "How can we achieve feature parity?" We'll talk more about learning directly from our users in Chapter 6, "Talking to Users (or, "What's a Poker Game?")".

Here are a few questions you can ask yourself to evaluate your research skills:

- Is my team learning *directly* from our users/customers *at least* once a week? (This is Teresa Torres's most excellent definition (*https://oreil.ly/iOYm4*) of continuous discovery.)

- Is every product decision my team makes informed by both business goals *and* user needs?

- Is my team regularly using both our product and competing/adjacent products to better understand our users' needs and behaviors?

- Do the user needs and goals articulated by my team *actually* reflect the needs and goals of our users, or just what the business *wants* those needs and goals to be?

EXECUTION

All efforts in service of outcomes.

Product managers are, of course, still responsible for making sure that stuff gets done. This often means stepping up to do whatever work is needed for your team to achieve its goals, even if that work is not technically part of your job description. Execution-minded product managers *start* by understanding the business and user outcomes for which their teams are responsible, then ruthlessly prioritize their time, resources, and activities to deliver against those outcomes.

Product managers who lack execution skills fail to connect their day-to-day efforts with the actual purpose of their team's work. They get bogged down in the sheer volume of stuff they have to do, focusing on effort *without* outcomes. Or they get distracted by chasing the perfect product to build or metric to measure, focusing on outcomes *without* effort. (We'll get into more depth about the relationship between outcomes and output in Chapter 10, "Vision, Mission, Objectives, Strategy, and Other Fancy Words".)

Because execution-minded product managers prioritize their efforts against goals and outcomes, they are willing to take on work that might not be seen as particularly heroic or high status. An execution-minded product manager, for example, will happily go on an early morning coffee run if that is an important step toward getting a product out the door. As Ken Norton says, "Always bring the donuts" (*https://oreil.ly/BN9Ak*).

When I started working as a product manager, I was prepared to do my share of donut and coffee runs. What I was not expecting was how many times I would need to step into conversations that felt *above* my proverbial pay grade. During one particularly tumultuous moment early in my career, I was made "VP for a day" so that I could lead a mission-critical negotiation with a major platform partner. Embarrassingly, I was much more focused on the fact that I had not been given a real promotion than I was on successfully leading this important negotiation. An execution-minded product manager is willing to step into critical, high-level conversations for the sake of clarifying and achieving organizational goals, not for personal glory.

Here are a few questions you can ask yourself to evaluate your execution skills:

- Is my team *starting* with the customer and business impact we seek to drive and *then* evaluating and prioritizing multiple ways to achieve that impact, as opposed to starting with features and retroactively justifying them by estimating impact?

- Are my team's strategic goals and objectives front and center during tactical conversations and activities (like sprint planning, story writing, etc.)?

- Am I prioritizing my own time in a way that reflects the goals and priorities of my team?

- If I do not have the capacity to do the work that my team needs without burning myself out, am I communicating that directly to my manager?

Taken together, these CORE skills are critical for the fundamental activities of product management across industries and organizations: research to uncover customer needs, communication to articulate and socialize those needs, organization to prioritize effective solutions, and execution to deliver those solutions.

...But What About Hard Skills?

The skills I have outlined in this chapter could be described as "soft skills." Generally speaking, soft skills are considered the squishy, subjective, interpersonal skills that are difficult to quantify or measure. "Hard skills," on the other hand, are considered fixed, objective, and measurable. For example, communication and time management skills are often considered soft skills, whereas computer programming and statistical analysis are considered hard skills.

In some contexts, hard skills are considered the absolute essentials to perform a job, whereas soft skills are considered a "nice to have." And for some roles, there is a bar of hard skills that must be met—after all, you wouldn't hire a computer programmer who had never written a line of code or a dentist who had never attended dental school. But the absolute distinction between "hard" and "soft" skills is often deployed in a way that feels reductive, imbalanced, and unfair to both types of skills. Hard skills like programming require nuance and craft, and soft skills like communication and time management can be learned, practiced, and evaluated.

When it comes to product management, though, the distinction between soft and hard skills can be particularly harmful. To put it bluntly, far too many people and organizations hire product managers based on hard skills that have precious little to do with the day-to-day work that those product managers will be expected to perform. I've seen fantastic product managers fail job interviews because they couldn't whiteboard an algorithm or solve a code challenge, even if their day-to-day work would require them to do neither of these things.

For most software product managers, the particular "hard skills" that cause the most anxiety and consternation are *technical skills*. To this day, one of the most common questions I am asked by aspiring product managers is "Just how technical do I have to be?"

In an article titled "Getting to Technical Enough as a Product Manager" (*https://oreil.ly/9xWpa*), Lulu Cheng provides a swift and definitive take on this issue:

> The day-to-day responsibilities [of a product manager], and technical bar, vary widely depending on the industry and size of the company, as well as the part of the product you work on. At the same time, the qualities that make someone a universally respected PM rarely have to do with technical expertise.

Indeed, if you are working on a highly technical product, having a basic knowledge of the systems with which you are working will soften the learning curve and give you a head start. But any assessment of the required hard skills for a specific product management role should begin with the specific work that a product manager will be expected to accomplish in that role—not a generic list of programming, data analysis, and general number-crunching skills.

So why does this focus on hard skills (and technical skills in particular) persist? Here are a few myths I've encountered and would like to debunk:

You need hard skills to win the respect of technical folks.

The idea that technical folks can respect only somebody who shares their skill set is, frankly, insulting to technical folks. If anything, I've seen product managers who "play" developer initially win over their technical counterparts, only to alienate them later by micromanaging implementation details. As we will discuss in Chapter 3, communication skills will help you learn hard skills in a way that respects the expertise of your colleagues and the specific context of your organization.

You need hard skills to challenge technical folks.

There is a kernel of truth here: if you have no idea how technical systems work, your developers could tell you that something relatively easy to build will take a million years. But if your team is flat-out lying to you about how long things will take, you have a more fundamental problem on your hands. Product managers with excellent execution skills inspire their teams to get impactful stuff out the door quickly, and they don't do it by playing "gotcha" with technical specificities.

You need hard skills to stay interested and engaged with technical work.

It is absolutely true that a product manager who is uninterested in the work of their colleagues is likely to fail. But knowledge and interest are two very different things, and I've found that many of the most technically knowledgeable product managers are also those least interested in learning new things and engaging deeply with the work of their colleagues. The best product managers, regardless of their technical skills, are able to take a genuine interest in the technical work of their colleagues and draw compelling connections between technical work, user needs, and business goals.

You need hard skills to do things like query databases, write documentation, and push minor changes.

> In many cases, this is actually 100% true. In keeping with the idea that "If it needs to get done, it's part of your job," product managers often find themselves faced with tasks that do require some specific knowledge of programming languages, version control systems, or database logic. For example, at a small company, a product manager might be asked to make minor code changes (such as updates to website copy) without enlisting the help of a developer. This will likely require the product manager to develop some basic familiarity with the programming language used by their team, as well as the tools that their team uses to deploy code.

The challenge here is not to be an expert in technical concepts but rather to be comfortable exploring and learning about technical as well as nontechnical concepts. I have seen nontechnical product managers excel in highly technical organizations when they approach technical challenges with openness and curiosity, and I have seen nontechnical product managers falter in relatively nontechnical organizations because they see technical work as either uninteresting or unapproachable. The best product managers are just as curious about technical concepts as they are about nontechnical concepts. We discuss this more in Chapter 3, "Showing Up Curious".

Summary: Changing the Conversation About Product Management

Because product management is a relatively new discipline and because the role can vary so much from organization to organization, it is tempting to describe product management as a hybrid of other roles. Unfortunately, this approach often results in a mismatch between what makes a product manager look good on paper (e.g., "a designer who knows some code" or "a developer with an MBA") and what makes a product manager successful in their day-to-day work. I hope that the CORE skills model will change the conversation about product management in theory to something that better aligns with the day-to-day work of product management in practice.

Your Checklist

- Embrace the uniqueness of the product manager role. Don't try to be a designer, a developer, or a business analyst—and don't confuse the skills needed to excel at those roles with the skills needed to excel at product management.

- Remember that being a great communicator doesn't mean "using fancy words and talking in a way that seems to impress people."

- Recognize that creating clarity for yourself and your team will require navigating a lot of uncomfortable conversations. Learn to treat discomfort as a valuable signal of potential misalignment, not as something to be avoided or minimized.

- Seek out opportunities to solve organizational problems on the systemic level rather than the individual level.

- Don't let the day-to-day demands of your work pull you out of your user's reality. Remember that what your company cares about and what your users care about are different things, and be a relentless advocate for the latter.

- Remember that there is no work beneath you and no work above you. Be willing to do whatever it takes to help your team and your organization succeed.

- Prioritize all your efforts against the outcomes your team is responsible for delivering.

- Even if you don't self-identify as a "technical" person, avoid saying things like "I'm not a technical person, so I could never understand that!" Trust in your own ability to learn and grow.

3

Showing Up Curious

When I started working as a product manager, I was incredibly intimidated by data scientists. I've never been a "math person," and these folks were writing up complex equations on whiteboards and making nerdy in-jokes that I desperately wanted to understand. I spent the first year or so of my career as a product manager tiptoeing deferentially around the data scientists in my orbit, never really understanding what they did and assuming that they had no interest in explaining it to me. After all, these were, like, actual geniuses. Why would they want to waste their time taking me to data-science preschool?

After a year or so, it became clear to me that this approach was making it much more difficult for me to do my job. Even though they weren't on my immediate team, our data scientists had a lot to offer, and I didn't even know what to ask for. So, in a moment of caffeine-fueled anxious desperation, I emailed somebody on the data-science team to see if he would be willing to chat. It was a short email that went something like this:

Subj: Coffee?

Hey! Hope your week is off to a great start. I'm really curious to learn a little bit more about what you're working on—are you free to grab a quick coffee this week? Maybe Thursday morning?

Thanks!

I hit Send and logged out of my inbox in an attempt to distract myself from creeping anxiety and embarrassment. Had I just done something totally weird?

Within a few hours, I got a straightforward response that included none of the overcompensatory enthusiasm of my original message. And that Thursday, we had our coffee—I'm hesitant to even call it a "meeting." It was a great conversation that revealed both some mutual interests (we're both guitarists with a fondness for Fender Jazzmasters!) and some important insights about our work together. It turned out that this data scientist felt just as alienated from the product team as I did from the data-science team. It was difficult to admit, but this disconnect was entirely of my own making. In assuming that other people had no interest in what I was doing, I had created the impression that I had no interest in what *they* were doing. Oops.

In this chapter, we discuss the single most important dimension of a successful product manager's attitude and approach: curiosity.

Taking a Genuine Interest

When people ask me how product managers can earn the trust of developers, or data scientists, or compliance officers, or any other person with a specialized and distant-seeming expertise, my answer is: take a genuine interest in the work that they do. "I'm curious to learn more about the work that you do" is the most powerful sentence at your disposal as a product manager, whether it's your first day or you've been working in the field for decades.

A simple gesture of curiosity can have an enormous and immediate positive impact on your work as a product manager. Here are three critical things you can accomplish by reaching out to your colleagues from a place of openness and genuine curiosity:

Understand "hard skills" contextually.

No matter how much time you spend trying to learn "hard skills" such as data science or programming, you will never keep pace with the people whose actual job is to use those skills. You will learn more by asking those people about their work than you will by reading a book about data science or Python and then showing up to work trying to "talk the talk." Learning about hard skills from the people tasked with applying those skills ensures that you will learn about the specific hard skills that are most important to your organization right now—and that you're doing so in a way that directly strengthens your bond with technical folks.

Note that this approach applies equally to nontechnical specialized skills. For example, I've seen this strategy work very well for product managers who need to work with compliance experts at financial services companies. As a product manager, it is exceptionally unlikely that you will become an expert in compliance, but getting to know and understand the folks who *are* experts in compliance will help you make better-informed decisions and work more closely with their teams.

Build bridges before you need something.

If you only talk to people when you need something from them, nobody will be particularly happy to hear from you. Build relationships with people *before* you need something from them, and those relationships will be there for you when you need them.

Expand your network of trust.

The people you reach out to each have their own networks of trust—people they talk with "off the record" and from whom they are willing to call in favors when needed. By reaching out to folks in your organization beyond the people you are working with every day, you're building a far-reaching network that might lead you to places you never expected.

In my experience, it has been exceptionally rare that "I'm curious to learn more about the work that you do" has been met with anything other than gratitude and some sense of relief. And while reaching out to schedule your first meeting with somebody might feel awkward in the moment (especially when that meeting is to take place over video chat rather than coffee), it is always worthwhile.

So, take a moment and reach out to somebody who is not an immediate member of your team. Maybe it's somebody whose team you have worked with in the past, but you are not working with at the moment. Maybe it's somebody whose role you don't fully understand, but you think could have an impact on your work sometime in the future. Maybe it's somebody from a far-off corner of the organization who made a particularly thoughtful comment in a shared Slack channel. There is no wrong person to reach out to—any step toward expanding your network of knowledge and trust is a step in the right direction.

Peeling Back the Layers of an Enterprise Organization

Amelia S.
Product Manager, enterprise media company

When I moved from a small technology startup to a large media company, I fully expected that a company of such scale and size would completely have their act together when it came to product management. But I found out very quickly that this is not exactly the case. Large companies have a veneer of formality that startups usually don't, but that doesn't mean that things are linear or predictable. Startups are often much more candid about their challenges: "This is messed up; let's fix it." At a large company, it can take months to get people to open up and speak candidly about the challenges they're facing.

Building that kind of trust involves using a lot of classic product manager tricks: having coffee with people, getting drinks with them, getting to know their work and their problems. Starting from a place of openness: "I'm new; I don't know anything. Tell me your problems and we'll figure something out." Nothing transactional, no quid pro quo, no "You'll scratch my back...." No expectations. People appreciate that kind of candor.

Part of the challenge at a big company is that the higher-ups usually aren't the people who understand what's really going on. They get reports from people who do the work. But I realized that in order for me to be successful, I needed to have core partnerships with folks within editorial, design, engineering—these very established orgs within the bigger organization. They have the organizational knowledge and history that I just don't. If you have a meeting with marketing, you need someone who can tell you, "Here's what's actually happening." You need to make sure that the human connection is there, and active.

I was genuinely surprised by how much of my on-the-ground work as a product manager at a large organization happened through back channels. I thought that all the action would be taking place in a big conference room—but really, it's all about getting people's buy-in outside of those formal settings, which I didn't expect.

Cultivating a Growth Mindset

In her pioneering work on learning and success, Stanford psychology professor and author Carol Dweck posits that people operate with either a "growth" or a "fixed" mindset. When operating with a growth mindset, people see failures and setbacks as learning opportunities. When operating with a fixed mindset, people see failures and setbacks as negative reflections of their intrinsic worth. People operating with a growth mindset are able to approach skills and subject matter that are new to them as an opportunity to, well, grow. People operating with a fixed mindset feel threatened by skills and subject matter that are new to them.

If you have spent most of your life being an overachiever, as many product managers have, it is quite likely that you are operating with a fixed mindset.

Why? Because many overachievers find success not by growing their skills in areas where they struggle but rather by avoiding these areas altogether. Fixed-mindset overachievers dismiss as useless, irrelevant, or counterproductive the things at which they do not immediately excel. By way of self-incriminating example, I avoided taking any music theory courses in college because "Formal training takes the soul out of music." But in reality, I avoided these courses because reading music was something I found really challenging. It was easier to create a self-serving lie around a kernel of defensible half-truth than it was to simply admit that there were areas where I could stand to grow my knowledge and skills—or, even worse, that I would need to get better at things that did not come easily or naturally to me.

As a product manager, you likely cannot succeed if you are operating with a fixed mindset. There are simply too many new things that you will need to learn, and you will not even know what these things *are* until it is too late for you to give yourself an overachiever-y head start. Like it or not, you will need to acknowledge and address the limits of your own personal knowledge and skills if you want to do right by your team and your organization.

For example, imagine two product managers are facing the same challenge. They have spent the last couple months working on new mobile products for a large financial institution. The week before launch, both product managers receive a letter from their compliance department that their projects are not approved to move forward.

The first product manager is operating with a fixed mindset. He receives the letter and turns red with embarrassment and anger. He whispers furiously under his breath, "My team is going to hate me for this." But he also knows that his team has been through this before and will probably be more than willing to lay the blame squarely on those jerks in compliance. The next day, he gathers his team together. "Well, guess what? Those jerks in compliance have done it again. Say good-bye to the last six months of work." The team is crushed. The product never launches.

The second product manager is operating with a growth mindset. She receives the same letter and immediately sends an email to the compliance department. In a nicely worded message, this product manager explains that she wants to make sure that she understands *why* exactly the compliance department could not approve this product. The next day, she has a meeting with the compliance officer who wrote the letter. The product manager—who has no legal background—asks the compliance officer to walk her through the exact process by which compliance evaluated the product. In the course of this walkthrough, the compliance officer reveals that there was one specific user interaction that compelled them to reject the entire product. The product manager proposes an alternate approach, and both parties agree. The team learns an important new consideration for developing future products. And the product launches the following week.

If you are going to succeed as a product manager, you must be willing to engage deeply with people whose knowledge and expertise in a specific area greatly exceed your own. If you want to be the smartest person in the room, you probably will not succeed as a product manager. (In fact, you're much more likely to succeed as a product manager if you stop trying to figure out who the "smartest person" might be in *any* room.)

The Gift of Being Wrong

Truly cultivating a growth mindset means being open not just to the unknown but also to being flat-out wrong. The most rewarding compliment I ever received as a product manager immediately followed one of the most difficult and contentious meetings I've ever attended. "You know," said a senior leader as we walked out of the conference room, "you walked into that meeting advocating for one path forward, and by the end of it, you were open to something totally different. I'm really impressed by how you let yourself be convinced by the other people in the room."

Just a few years prior, this comment would have infuriated me. I had gone into a meeting with senior leaders to present my vision for the product, and by the end of the meeting, I was effectively advocating for someone else's vision. In a very real sense, I abdicated any claim I might have had to being the company's "product visionary." But I also demonstrated to senior leadership that I was willing to go with the idea that seemed best for the company, even if it wasn't my own. For one of the very first times in my career, I had accepted the gift of being wrong.

This is not to say that product managers should just defer to what other people want. For being wrong to be a gift, you need to know exactly *why* you're wrong—and choose to value the overall goals you are working toward above your own plan for achieving those goals. If somebody else suggests an approach that better reflects what you are collectively working toward, aligning with that plan gives you a chance to reinforce the entire group's commitment to your shared goals.

Staying Off the Defensive

So if curiosity is the single most important quality for product managers to demonstrate, what is the *opposite* of curiosity? The answer I keep coming back to is, quite simply, defensiveness.

Given the ambiguous and connective nature of product management, it is easy to find yourself on the defensive—whether that means defending your team against executive interference, defending your decisions against probing questions, or defending yourself against the sneaking suspicion that nobody understands or appreciates all the hard work you're doing.

Perhaps the hardest single lesson I've learned in my product career is that literally every single attempt I've made to defend something has actually wound up harming that thing. When I have sought to defend my team against executive interference, I've created a dangerous divide between their work and the business's goals (we'll talk about this more in Chapter 5). When I have sought to defend my decisions against probing questions, I have missed out on critical information that would have made those decisions better. And when I have sought to defend myself against the feeling—real or imagined—that I am under-recognized or underappreciated by my colleagues, it has made me appreciably worse at my actual job.

In the day-to-day work of product management, it is impossible to avoid situations that will trigger an impulse to go on the defensive. But there are a few concrete things you can do to help manage that impulse. Here are some practical tips for staying off the defensive:

Provide options, not arguments.

Getting into a yes–no battle of wills is a surefire path to a defensive position. But giving stakeholders multiple options gives you the opportunity to evaluate and explore several different pathways without feeling like you are in a position to "win" or "lose" an argument. There's been a lot of talk about how saying no is key to product management, but the best product managers I work with never have to say no—they just provide a set of options and help their teams (and especially their team and company leadership) choose the best one according to their goals and objectives.

If you feel compelled to do something out of anxiety or defensiveness, write it down and reapproach it the next day.

We all have those "Oh s***" moments where we realize that we could have handled a situation better, communicated something more clearly, or asked a question that we forgot to ask. But actions driven by anxiety don't always make these situations better, and we are rarely able to thoughtfully prioritize our efforts when we are surfing a wave of adrenaline. More than once, I have sent a frantic message to colleagues, only to realize that this message actually made the thing I was worried about worse, or distracted my colleagues from more important tasks. Over the last year or so, I've gotten into the habit of taking a deep breath and writing down any anxiety-fueled actions I feel compelled to take, then revisiting them the next morning. After a decent night of sleep, about 90% of those actions tend to feel *extremely not worth taking* the next day.

Say, "OK, great," and then figure out the rest.

Sometimes, staying off the defensive is as simple as getting in the habit of saying, "OK, great," to nearly any defensiveness-inducing question or statement you receive...and then figuring out the rest. Those few moments between the word "great" and whatever words come next may very well defuse a tense situation and set you up for an easier path forward. I've found this strategy particularly helpful when navigating tense moments in large meetings. For example, I once sat in on a meeting where a product manager presented his team's work to a large group of key stakeholders, only for one of the engineers on his own team to chime in and say, "Um, excuse me, I still don't fully understand why we're building this." The product manager froze. "OK, great!" he said, "I'll make sure to take some time at the end of this presentation to walk through our prioritization criteria again. Thanks for bringing that up!" This approach not only gave the product manager an opportunity to stop the meeting from getting totally derailed, but it also gave the engineer an opportunity to cool down and gather their thoughts before getting into a high-stakes public disagreement.

Ask for help.

One of the most profound and meaningful ways to stay off the defensive is to proactively ask for help from people around you. This approach can be particularly meaningful when you ask for help from somebody who has proven stubborn, combative, arrogant, or otherwise challenging to work with. I've been truly shocked at the extent to which I have been able to improve my relationship with such people simply by reaching out and asking them to share their expertise with me or help me work through a problem I'm struggling to solve. I often encourage product managers to start the week by listing the people they are most afraid will undermine or misunderstand their work, then reach out to those people and schedule one-on-one time for an open and curious conversation.

Even the most experienced and even-keeled product managers will still sometimes find themselves digging into a yes–no argument or refusing input and feedback from stakeholders who possess mission-critical information. The challenge is to get to a place where you can recognize your own defensive reactions, acknowledge that they are unlikely to lead to better outcomes for yourself or your team, and bring yourself back to a place of openness and curiosity as best you can.

Separating Product Failure from Personal Failure

Susana Lopes
Director of Product, Onfido

The first product I ever worked on out of university was the iOS app for a growing startup. At the time, this company required product teams to commit to a set of features they would deliver each quarter. This was a way for our sales team to be able to sell things we didn't have in the product yet. Missing the end-of-quarter deadline meant breaking promises to clients, which was a big no-no. In this first phase of my career, my mantra was "Failure is not an option." This was ingrained in me from an early age; I grew up with a magnet sporting those exact words staring at me every time I opened the fridge door! And in this role, success for me was delivering committed features on time.

In practice, this meant I tortured my colleagues by locking them in rooms for hours to break down months of work into small stories that we could estimate. I cut scope as the deadline approached. I drove our designer mad, as I relentlessly butchered her designs to make them easier to implement, to make the deadline, to not fail. And then, when our company Secret Santa rolled around in December, I was confronted with the harsh reality of my behavior by way of a passive-aggressive Secret Santa gift: one of my teammates gifted me a mug with the word "DICTATOR" emblazoned across its surface.

A year or so into being a product manager, I was asked if I wanted to take on our Android app. By this time, I was keen to show I had learned all the things and grown beyond my dictator mug. "Failure is not an option" had begrudgingly been set aside for "Fail fast, fail early." It wasn't yet clear to me how to do it in practice, but all the thought leaders and blog posts pointed to this as the way to build successful products, so I was keen to give it a go. Release schedules were replaced by objectives and key results. I was ready to fail fast and early, de-risking as many aspects of the product as possible.

We kept shipping and we kept growing and always failing first before shipping, validating usability along the way, and things were great. Until...the numbers stalled. We kept iterating, trying to serve more complex use cases that we believed would unlock a new set of users, but nothing worked. We had failed early, but now we were failing late. Our product simply wasn't meeting its growth targets, and I couldn't understand why. The engineers were doing the right thing, shipping almost every week in a company used to shipping every month. The designers had iterated and talked to end users. It must be me. My product was failing. I was failing. I experienced sleepless nights, cried once in a bathroom, and once escaped to a church to cry...and I'm not even religious.

I was crying not because my product had failed, but because I felt I had failed. My sense of self-worth and the value of my product were one and the same. **I was conflating product failure with personal failure...and I was burning out.** Even now, some of the products I work on see slower adoption and growth than I would like. But I no longer feel like I personally am a failure. To foster emotional distance, I am my product's worst critic. I can list out in excruciating detail why every single product that I currently manage sucks. I can recognize that even the most successful products I work on are not perfect—and, more importantly, that they are not me. My products serve a purpose, and they succeed at certain things and fail at others. And that's OK.

Note: This story was adapted from a phenomenal talk delivered at the Jam! London conference in 2019, which you can and should watch in its entirety here: *https://oreil.ly/wJdgE*.

Asking Why Without Asking "Why"

In your quest to work with and learn from the people around you, you are certain to find yourself in a few situations where you trigger *other people's* insecurity and defensiveness. In my experience, this occurs most often when you ask somebody a question to which they don't know the answer. And those defensive reactions tend to be most pronounced when you utter the word that is both most strategically important and most reflexively challenging: *why?*

In a very real sense, it is a product manager's job to always understand "why." But, as many product managers have learned the hard way, you are not likely to generate much goodwill by being the person who goes around asking everybody, "WHY ARE YOU DOING THAT?" More than once, I've asked an innocuous-seeming "Huh, why did you choose to work on that right now?" question only to be met with a frustrated, blustery response that I *know* will harm my long-term relationship with the person to whom I posed the question. And, perhaps even more frequently, I've responded to an innocuous-seeming "Huh, why did you choose to work on that right now?" with my own blustery and evasive response.

Tactically speaking, I've found it helpful to reframe "Why?" questions as open and genuine "Could you show me how?" questions. For example, I tend to have much better conversations when I say something like "That looks awesome! Could you show me how your team came up with the idea?" as opposed to "Why are you building that?" This framing puts the asker in the position of a student, not an inquisitor. And it gives the person *being* asked a little more time and space to provide an honest and thoughtful answer—even if that answer is "Gee, to tell you the truth, I don't really know how we came up with that idea" or even "We didn't really come up with that idea—our boss just kinda handed it to us."

Spreading Curiosity

Good product managers minimize defensiveness and cultivate curiosity. Great product managers turn curiosity into a core value for their team and their organization. Genuine curiosity can be contagious, and it naturally encourages people to collaborate more closely and better understand each other's perspectives. In a curious organization, negotiations between stakeholders feel expansive rather than combative, and deep conversations about goals and outcomes feel like an important part of your work rather than an impediment to doing the "real" work. Curiosity makes everything seem more interesting and less transactional.

The first key to spreading curiosity is to model it yourself, relentlessly. "I'm too busy right now" is a very dangerous sentence for product managers. If your colleagues are taking the time to come to you with questions and thoughts, however trivial those questions and thoughts might seem, encourage that behavior. Similarly, if you're interested in something that a colleague is doing, don't feel bad about asking for some of that person's time—be confident in the knowledge that time spent learning from your colleagues is time well spent. And when you do need some time to go heads-down on a project and work in relative isolation, avoid saying things like "I just need a tiny bit of time to myself so that I can actually get something done." Remember, the time you spend communicating with your colleagues *is* time spent getting things done.

Another great way to spread curiosity is to cross-pollinate knowledge and skills among your colleagues. If you're working with a team of designers and developers, ask them what other skills they'd like to learn. Maybe you have a designer who wants to learn more about frontend development. Or a web developer who wants to better understand the UX patterns of mobile apps. Make it as easy as possible for people to learn from one another as part of their day-to-day job. I've seen some product managers go so far as to declare one day a week "cross-functional pairing day," in which designers and developers (or developers working in different technical systems) pair with each other for the explicit purpose of expanding their knowledge and skills. Formal practices like this make it clear that you are explicitly valuing curiosity and knowledge sharing among your team.

Finally, organizing "demo days" and other opportunities for product teams to present their work to the organization at large is an incredibly valuable way to spread curiosity far and wide. I've been truly amazed to see how a team's work transforms when they are tasked with presenting to their colleagues once a week—people work harder, collaborate more closely, and begin asking questions about their own work in anticipation of those they will receive from their colleagues. The assumption that, for example, people in marketing couldn't possibly care about a highly technical product is replaced by the question "How can we present this highly technical product to all of our colleagues in a way that seems interesting?"

Summary: Curiosity Is Key

Every organization is different, every team is different, and every individual is different. As a product manager, it is your responsibility to communicate, align, and translate between people who might have wildly diverging skill sets, goals, and agendas. The only way to do this is by taking an open, genuine, and curious interest in the work that they do. Learning about specialized skills directly from the people who use those skills within your organization is always more valuable than learning about them from a book or a Wikipedia page. Indeed, every single channel of open and curious communication that you can establish is an important step toward the success of your team. We'll discuss this more in the next chapter, "The Art of Egregious Overcommunication."

Your Checklist

- Reach out to folks in your organization and say, "I'm curious to learn more about the work that you do."

- Be vigilant about getting to know people outside of your immediate team. Take the time to understand their goals and motivations before you need something from them.

- Be particularly vigilant about reaching out to the folks who you are most afraid will undermine or misunderstand your work.

- Cultivate a growth mindset and open yourself up to learning from people whose skills and knowledge exceed your own.

- Embrace "the gift of being wrong" by choosing the plan that best meets your organization's goals, even if it is not your plan.

- Present multiple options to avoid locking horns in a yes–no battle of wills.

- If you find yourself getting defensive in a meeting or conversation, buy yourself some time by saying, "OK, great," and then thinking through your next steps.

- If you feel compelled to take an action that might be motivated by defensiveness or anxiety, write down that action and revisit it the next day.

- Be willing to take a clear-eyed look at your product's limitations and recognize that they are not your personal limitations.

- Consider reframing the "why" questions as "could you show me how" questions.

- Avoid saying, "I'm too busy to deal with that right now" and other things that might implicitly discourage your team from asking open and curious questions.

- Encourage your colleagues to learn from one another and pair up folks who want to learn about one another's skills.

- Organize "demo days" and other opportunities for product teams to share and discuss their work with the organization at large.

4

The Art of Egregious Overcommunication

The title of this chapter is in many ways a joke. But for working product managers, it is also deadly serious. The biggest mistakes I've made as a product manager, and the biggest mistakes I've heard about from many other product managers, involve failing to communicate things that seem either too politically dangerous or too inconsequential to openly address.

Sometimes, things can seem both dangerous and inconsequential. For example, suppose that you're in a meeting with your team and a developer rattles off a detail about a product that feels ever so slightly different from something you discussed in a separate conversation with executive leadership. You start to fidget in your seat. You're *pretty sure* that the developer on your team just misspoke. After all, your team has been working off the same product spec that you walked through with the executive leadership team. In any case, it's just a minor difference. And the last thing you want to do in this moment is to pause the conversation, put a developer on your own team in an uncomfortable position, and draw attention to your own potential mistakes. It's just a tiny thing. Nobody will notice. It would make *no sense* if this turned out to be a big deal! It's fine.

Cut to two weeks later. Your team is presenting a demo of this product, and a member of the executive leadership team begins to make a sour face. Her nose scrunches up and her eyes narrow. She mouths the words "What is that?" juuuuuust distinctly enough for your heart to completely stop. Head shaking back and forth, she interrupts your developer midsentence: "I'm sorry, but this looks *very* different from what I signed off on. I'm very confused right now." Your team stops in its tracks. Everyone's eyes turn to you. After the string of expletives in your head concludes, you say to yourself, "You were afraid this was a big deal, it is a big deal, and now it's too late."

For most working product managers, this scenario is not hypothetical. It happens all the time, and it keeps happening, even when you swear a million times over that you will never let it happen again. The potential downside of undercommunicating is cavernous and terrifying. The potential downside of overcommunicating is, realistically, a few eye rolls and maybe some snarky comments. Since you can never be sure of the exact right amount of communication called for in any situation, you are always better off erring on the side of overcommunicating. In theory, at least, this is an easy one.

In practice, however, the day-to-day work of comprehensive communication can prove very difficult. Choosing to communicate in the moment is much more challenging than choosing to communicate in the abstract. This chapter provides some tactical guidance for making egregious overcommunication a part of your product management practice.

Asking the Obvious

If there's such a thing as a Ten Commandments of product management, it is Ben Horowitz's "Good Product Manager/Bad Product Manager" (*https://oreil.ly/ z3688*), a document Horowitz composed as a kind of ad hoc training for Netscape product managers way back in the days of the first internet boom. "Good Product Manager/Bad Product Manager" is a short and simple document, but it accomplishes something very important: it lays out in exceptionally clear terms the day-to-day expectations for product managers at that particular organization at that particular time. "Do this, not that." Every company should have a document like "Good Product Manager/Bad Product Manager" that spells out the responsibilities of the job in clear, instructive, behavioral terms—and explicitly names the behaviors that are to be avoided.

My very favorite part of "Good Product Manager/Bad Product Manager" says quite simply: "Good product managers err on the side of clarity versus explaining the obvious. Bad product managers never explain the obvious."

When I began working as a product manager, I wondered what exactly this meant—why would explaining "the obvious" be important? The answer, it turns out, is that the things that seem obvious to *you* might not be obvious to anybody else. In fact, other people might have drawn vastly different conclusions that seem equally "obvious" to them. For that reason, things that seem obvious often carry the most potential for disastrous miscommunication.

Being the first person to call into question something that seems obvious or self-explanatory can feel deeply uncomfortable. It takes courage to chime in and say, for example, "Just to make sure we're all on the same page, when we talk about the 'launch date' next week, our current plan is to do a small, closed beta launch to a group of about fifty users so we can gather some data before rolling anything out to a broader group." Even if the response you get is a unified chorus of "Yes, of course, we all knew that," I guarantee that at least one other person is quietly thinking, "Whew, I sure am glad somebody spoke up, because I *definitely did not know that.*"

When we orient ourselves toward our team's business and user goals, the upside of asking the obvious seems...well, obvious. If it turns out everybody was already aligned in the first place, we can move forward even more secure in our shared understanding. And if it turns out everybody was *not* aligned, we can openly address any miscommunications before they become a much bigger problem.

Bringing Uncomfortable Information to a Big Meeting

Julia G.
Senior Product Manager, midsized startup

A few years ago, I found myself sitting in a big meeting with about 50 of my market-facing colleagues: our entire sales, customer success, and marketing leadership team. During this meeting, a question got brought up about a particular functionality that our customers had been wanting. Our CEO chimed in on our company chat to share that we had recently shipped this exact functionality and to encourage us to spread the word.

There was only one problem—this functionality had been shipped for *some* of our channels—but not for the one we were actually discussing. This was a major "uh-oh" moment: do I actually jump in during this huge meeting and point out that this functionality—which had just been celebrated by our CEO—was actually *not* ready for the customers who were asking for it?

Having lived through the consequences of *not* bringing these things up in the past, I made the decision to speak up: "Actually, that feature isn't live on that channel yet, but we have it roadmapped for Q4." Silence. Was I about to get in trouble? And then, a new message from our CEO on the company chat: "OK, great, thanks for letting me know."

In that moment, I felt a degree of safety I had never really felt before as a product manager. I had recently joined this company after working at a series of early-stage startups where things were often expected "yesterday." I had developed a tendency to hear every question as an accusation. If somebody asked me, "Hey, do we support this?" I would hear it as "Why don't we support this yet?" I always wanted to be ahead of expectations, so if somebody even *asked* a question, I felt like I had already failed. Informing the CEO that a feature wasn't ready in the middle of a large meeting definitely felt high risk. His response made me feel trusted and empowered.

I used to trip myself up thinking, "If I tell people this will take a long time, or isn't a priority, they'll think that I'm doing a bad job." Now, I make a point of getting out ahead of these conversations and telling people what's actually going on, not what they want to hear. I'm not sure how much of it is natural maturation as a product manager and how much of it is working in environments where folks are generally thoughtful and supportive. But I feel like, even if I were to find myself at a place that was *less* thoughtful and supportive, I would bring this newfound confidence with me. It can be uncomfortable, but at the end of the day, it makes me more impactful.

Don't Deflect, Be Direct

Several years ago, I received an unexpected text message from my manager at about 9 p.m. on a Thursday night. It read, "Hey, would be really great if we could get that new release of the iPhone app submitted to the App Store tonight!"

I was confused. Was this an urgent demand? A friendly but low-priority request? Was I being asked to do something *right now*? Or was I simply being shown a 113-character window into this person's vision of a better world? In most situations, I probably would have just dragged my Product Martyr-y self to my computer, grumpily submitted the app, and sent back a tellingly overenthusiastic message like "OF COURSE—NO PROBLEM!!"

But this time, I was actually out at a concert, a solid hour away from my computer. (And yes, shame on me for checking my phone during a concert.) Unable to fall back into my usual routine of passive-aggressive overwork, I stepped out and called my manager.

"Hey, I'm really sorry, but I'm actually at a concert right now. If you need me to go home and submit the app, though, I can totally do it."

The voice on the other end of the line was hesitant.

"Oh, umm, yeah, I mean, it would be really great to get it into the store tonight!" A pause. "But if you're out at a concert...I mean...you know what, don't worry about it, we can talk about it in the morning."

I let out a cheery "Sounds good, thanks," and was immediately overcome by a deep sense of dread. Had I just overstepped some invisible line of work-life balance? Had I done something bad for the company for my own selfish purposes? Was I, as I had long suspected, a terrible, selfish person?

The next morning, I prepared to receive my punishment. My manager, though, seemed remarkably nonchalant. "Oh, yeah, I mean, I realized last night that it would have been nice to submit the app right away, but it's totally fine to submit it today, it's not like it's going to make all that much of a difference with the final timing."

In an uncharacteristic moment of directness, I said, "OK, can I ask you a favor? In the future, can you be very, very clear when you are actually asking me to do something *right now*? When I got your message, it was hard for me to tell how urgent the situation really was. If you ever urgently need me to do something, then I will do everything in my power to make sure it gets done. But if it's more like a 'nice to have,' could you just be as clear as possible about that?"

For about 10 seconds, I felt deeply proud of myself for being so direct. I then realized that most of the requests I was making to my colleagues still started with some version of "It would be great if..." or "Hey! Do you think you could, maybe, perhaps..." or "HEY NICE DAY HOW'S THE WEATHER I LIKE SANDWICHES DO YOU LIKE SANDWICHES anyways I was just wondering if you maybe had time to..."

Because product managers rarely have direct organizational authority, it can be tempting to couch any requests in the "nicest" possible terms—especially requests for things like staying late to release a product or redoing work that was already completed. But being ambiguous about what you're asking for (and whether you're asking at all) is not nice. It is a deflection of responsibility, a passive-aggressive attempt to get the result you want without being the "bad guy."

The pull toward any and all kinds of deflection, overwrought apologies, and general self-deprecation is strong for product managers. But it is also damaging and dangerous, both to you and to your team. For many years, I used self-deprecation to slither out of situations in which I felt like people might be mad at me. When I was coming to my team with a tough deadline or a request for new work, I would often say something like "Guess what, here comes the PRODUCT MANAGER with another FUN DEADLINE FOR EVERYBODY!" It felt like a good way to alleviate the tension and to show that I was "one of the team." And most of the time, it got at least a little chuckle.

But the long-term effect it had on the team was neither good nor particularly funny. By using self-deprecation to spare my own feelings, I was doing absolutely nothing to communicate to my team *why* I was asking them to meet a tough deadline or revisit something that they thought was already finished. My goal was not to get the team aligned around our purpose but rather to end the conversation as quickly as I possibly could. I was communicating, intentionally or not, that the work I was asking for was meaningless—because if I took responsibility for conveying its meaning, I would be the person asking for the work. And nobody likes the person asking for the work.

When you are a product manager, there will be times when you need to ask people to do things that they don't want to do. If these things are mission critical for your team's success, help your team understand *why* and work with them to figure out what other tasks can be deprioritized. And if they are not mission critical for your team's success, ask yourself whether you are thoughtfully prioritizing your team's time or just saying yes to anything that seems vaguely important.

Not Everything Is Your Fault, and Outcomes Matter More Than Intentions

Product managers are often counseled to take full and unequivocal responsibility for anything that goes wrong on their team. "If something goes wrong," I was told earlier in my career, "it's your fault—whether or not it's really your fault."

I took this counsel firmly to heart and embraced my Product Martyrdom. And, in a funny way, it felt like a relief. If something went wrong on my team, I could simply declare, "YUP, MY FAULT, I'M THE WORST," and get on with my day. This was actually much easier than initiating and facilitating an honest conversation about how the entire team may have contributed to a subpar outcome and what steps we could take to deliver better outcomes in the future.

Yes, as a product manager, you are ultimately responsible for the outcomes delivered by your team. But this is not a responsibility you can bear alone. If you take everything that goes wrong as your own personal failure, you are depriving your team of a critical opportunity to learn and grow. Nothing runs more counter to our guiding principle of making yourself obsolete than casting yourself as the sole personal receptacle for all your team's missteps, rather than working with your team to address the *systemic challenges* that may have contributed to those missteps.

The line between addressing systemic challenges and flinging around personal recriminations can be a very thin one. Over the last several years, I've often heard the directive "assume positive intent" deployed in the service of reinforcing this line and depersonalizing difficult conversations. And sure enough, "assume positive intent" is certainly a healthier directive than "Assume personal blame for anything that goes wrong, even if you don't really believe it's your fault."

But as "assume positive intent" has reached the point of ubiquity, it has also revealed some limitations. In the last year or so, I have unfortunately heard the phrase used as a kind of passive-aggressive challenge to the very conversations it was supposed to facilitate: "*How dare you* suggest that something is wrong with my team? Don't you know that I'm *doing the best I can*? What happened to 'assume positive intent'?"

As this nightmarish emotional Rube Goldberg machine of projections and deferrals suggests, the very idea of focusing on "intentions" can lead us into weird, murky emotional territory. For better or worse, people with good intentions can do a lot of harm, and people with bad intentions still stumble into positive actions from time to time. Broadly speaking, I have found it helpful to focus these conversations on *outcomes* as opposed to *intentions*.

In practice, this has often meant mediating conversations about interpersonal or team-level challenges with the question "Did this situation deliver the desired outcome?" For example, when a product manager comes to me upset that their counterpart in engineering feels left out of the decision-making process (a common dynamic on cross-functional product teams), I have gotten into the habit of asking, "Was the desired outcome of this situation for the engineering manager to be excluded from the decision-making process?" If the answer is "Yes, I did not have the time to involve them," or even "Yes, I don't trust them to participate in our team decision-making process," then we can take the conversation from there. And if the answer is "No, I was doing my best to involve everybody, and I'm not sure why they feel left out," then the product manager can initiate a follow-up conversation with their engineering counterpart to understand what happened and work toward a better outcome next time around.

If we take ourselves out of the picture as individuals and look at the whole system, we see that our *intentions* are often largely irrelevant. Our job is to improve *systems* in the hopes of delivering consistently better outcomes for our business and our users. When confronted with a colleague's frustrations or hurt feelings, I've found it helpful to respond with a statement like "OK, thank you for sharing that with me. It sounds like this didn't result in the outcome we wanted. How can we change things moving forward to get a better outcome?" This shift from emotions to outcomes can help redirect conversations that would otherwise deteriorate into passive-aggressive finger-pointing (or unabashed Product Martyrdom).

Turning Away from Self-Deprecation

M.L.

Product Manager, 100-person startup

I'll never forget the moment when I realized that self-deprecation was no longer a justifiable part of my approach to product management. I was about a month into a particularly challenging project that had involved a lot of late nights and last-minute rework. I felt genuinely guilty about putting my team through all that and did my best to alleviate the tension with overwrought apologies and dramatic self-effacing comments like "I know, I know, I am the very worst," and "Yup, this is all my fault, but y'all are the best for cleaning up the mess I made."

And then, out of the blue, I got an email from a developer on my team that genuinely surprised me. He was concerned about the way I had been talking about my own work. He wanted to know, did I really feel that bad about my job? Did I really think that I had nothing to offer? Had he done anything to make me feel like my contributions weren't valued by the team?

As I started to compose a response, it occurred to me: I *didn't* really think that I had nothing to offer, nor did I really think that everything that was happening was my fault. Without even realizing it consciously, I had been deploying self-deprecation as a passive-aggressive and not-entirely-sincere way to say, "Please don't challenge me on the stuff I'm asking you to do." I simply wasn't confident or mature enough as a product manager to have an open conversation with my team about *why* we were working late nights and redoing things we had already done. And I certainly wasn't confident or mature enough as a product manager to have an open conversation with company leadership about the downsides and trade-offs that went into those late nights and last-minute changes. It was easier for me to simply tell company leadership, "YUP, WHATEVER YOU WANT," and then tell my own team, "SORRY, I SUCK."

Here's a thought exercise I've been using to help train myself out of this behavior. If I feel the urge to make a self-deprecating comment, I ask myself: "If somebody on my team interrupted me to say, 'Hey, no need for that. You're doing a great job, and we respect your opinion,' would I be *relieved* or *annoyed*?" If the answer is "relieved," then I try to facilitate an open retrospective with my team to see if there are some other underlying issues that might be causing me to feel a lack of confidence in my work. If the answer is "annoyed," then I ask myself what difficult question or conversation I might be trying to deflect through self-deprecation, and I try to muster the courage to proactively bring that question or conversation to my team.

A few years into the practice of avoiding self-deprecation, I've had to get much better at facilitating open conversations with my team about what's really going on and what we can actually do about it. I certainly find myself fielding more challenging questions about *why* we're doing what we're doing or how I made a particular decision. But my experience answering these questions has helped me become a better product manager and, hopefully, a less defensive person as well.

The Two Most Dangerous Words in Product Management: "Looks Fine"

Early in my product management career, I genuinely believed that I could keep myself out of trouble by making sure that every step I took received perfunctory "approval" from somebody in a position of authority. Before finalizing my team's quarterly roadmap, I would make sure to present it in a meeting to company leadership. And before turning design mocks into working software, I would send those mocks to any stakeholders who I thought might be particularly opinionated about the look and feel of our product. While I was ostensibly seeking feedback from these stakeholders, I was *really* looking for a simple gesture of approval—a checked-off box that would effectively cover my ass in the event that things went sideways later.

More often than not, this gesture of approval took the form of a brief, passive acknowledgment like "Got it," or "Thanks for sending." And, really, that was all I needed—and, at the time, all I *wanted*. I figured that if anybody took issue with my team's work later on, I'd be able to throw that "Got it," right back in their face and emerge vindicated and victorious: "I SENT THIS TO YOU A MONTH AGO AND YOU DIDN'T HAVE ANY FEEDBACK, WHICH MEANS YOU CAN'T CHANGE IT NOW!!"

I quickly discovered that "no backsies" is not a binding corporate policy. As we will discuss in Chapter 5, stakeholders—especially executive stakeholders—are very busy people, and that quick nod in a meeting or "Got it, thanks," email doesn't necessarily mean they were paying attention to your point of view, let alone meaningfully engaging with it. In the world of product management, anything short of affirmative and specific buy-in is incredibly dangerous. And no two words better embody disengaged, ambiguous, and vague non-buy-in buy-in than "Looks fine."

The best product managers make it more or less impossible for people to react with "Looks fine." They always show up with open-ended questions to ask—even if those questions are awkward and nerve-wracking. And, as we discussed in Chapter 3, they provide options, not arguments, requiring active participation from their stakeholders rather than passive, glassy-eyed nods or two-word email responses.

I've found it helpful to include at least one meaningful choice or one open-ended question in any meeting or email where you are asking for feedback or approval. An email that says, "Attached, please find our roadmap for next quarter. Let me know if you have any questions," might create the outward appearance of transparency and collaboration, but it doesn't protect you from any "What the hell is that and why haven't I seen it before?" responses when you actually start *delivering* against that roadmap. By contrast, you are much more likely to get engaged responses from an email that says, "Attached, please find our roadmap for the next quarter. As you will see, we are considering two different options for sprints 6–8. Could you please let us know by the end of day Friday which one you believe would be more relevant to your team's goals?" (We'll discuss the importance of sending specific and time-bound asks via email and chat in Chapter 13, "Try This at Home: The Trials and Tribulations of Remote Work".)

A Tactical Approach to Move Past "Looks Fine": Disagree and Commit

In conversations with multiple stakeholders, the center of gravity around "Looks fine" grows all the more compelling and irresistible. As awkward as it is to disagree with one person in a one-on-one conversation, it can be exponentially more awkward to disagree with 10 people in a 10-person conversation. "Looks fine" will always be the path of least resistance—unless you do the difficult work of adding a whole lot of resistance to that very path.

Thankfully, the good folks at Intel pioneered a technique called "disagree and commit" that is designed to do this very thing. The idea behind disagree and commit is pretty simple: any decision made in a group setting should conclude with *affirmative commitment to a path forward from everybody involved*. And the process of getting to that commitment should necessitate bringing forward questions, concerns, and *disagreements* that would have otherwise gone unspoken.

By way of example, let's imagine two different meetings, each held with the purpose of deciding whether a new feature should be included in the free or paid tier of a freemium product. The first meeting operates under the traditional rules of implicit consensus: if everybody agrees (or, at least, nobody disagrees), the decision is made and you move forward. As the product manager on the team building this feature, you've been tasked with making your case to a group of about 10 director-level stakeholders. After thoughtfully walking through competitive analysis, usage projections, and revenue goals, you conclude with a strong recommendation that the feature be included in the free tier. "Does anybody have any questions? Does this sound like a good approach?" A few tepid nods, but general silence. You breathe a sigh of relief. "OK, great!"

Your team gets right back to work and begins implementing an exciting new free feature. Technical details are negotiated, marketing copy is written, and everything seems well on track. Then, two weeks after the meeting, you receive an email from one of the directors who had nodded along to your proposed direction: "Sorry, we need to put a hold on this—there are a few hiccups around the pricing tier decision we need to address." Wait, *what*? You thought everybody had agreed! You quickly shoot back an email, trying your best to suppress your rage and frustration: "Thanks for the note. Sorry, I'm a bit confused here—I thought we had all agreed that this would be a free feature?" A few hours later, you receive a response: "Yes, our VP of revenue is reevaluating the pricing strategy and isn't sure another free feature makes sense right now. I'll have more information for you next week."

You shake your head and let out a deep sigh. Now you have to go back to your team and tell them that the company's entire pricing strategy is in flux *and* that two weeks of their hard work is now in limbo because of it. You know this is going to be a big hit to morale and a big setback for your team's timeline, but, at this point, you're not sure what you can really do about it other than hope, wait, and vent.

Now, let's imagine a second meeting that operates under the rules of "disagree and commit": each person in the meeting must provide *specific, affirmative commitment* before a decision is made, and each person is responsible for raising any questions or disagreements that might stop them from providing that commitment. After thoughtfully walking through competitive analysis, usage projections, and revenue goals, you conclude with a strong recommendation that the feature be included in the free tier. "OK," you tell the assembled stakeholders, "we're going to try doing something a little bit different this time. This is a big decision for the team, and I want to make sure that we've gotten all the information that y'all have out on the table. So I'm going to go around and ask each of you, one by one, to say 'I commit' if you're committed to moving forward with the approach we've outlined. And if you *can't* commit, tell me why, and we'll figure out what to do from there."

You turn to the director of product marketing. "Do you commit to us moving forward with a free feature?" They seem a little taken aback and scramble to blurt out an "Um, sure, yes, I commit." "OK, great," you say. You pause for a moment and then continue: "Just to be clear, the goal here is to get any questions or concerns out on the table so that we can make the best decision possible. You don't *have* to say yes if you're not sure!" A few nervous laughs, and they chime back in with "Ha, no, thank you, yes, I commit! I think this makes a lot of sense."

You move on to the director of revenue operations. Right off the bat, they don't seem quite so sure. "Actually," they say, "I'm not sure if I can commit to this right now. Our VP of revenue is reevaluating our pricing strategy, and I wouldn't want to give you a definitive yes before we get that all sorted out." You pause. "OK great, thank you for that. When do you think we could get more clarity on this?" They respond, "Uh, let me get back with you next week."

In the week that follows, you're able to have several follow-up conversations with the revenue team and get a better sense of how and why the company's pricing strategy is changing. Meanwhile, your team moves forward with work that does *not* require a firm commitment to either pricing approach. Soon, you are able to reconvene the stakeholders from the original meeting and, with the full support of the director of revenue operations, explain how the company's pricing strategy has shifted toward putting more features in the paid tier. The back-and-forth is frustrating, but you're deeply relieved that you were able to navigate this change in full view of your team and your stakeholders.

As this example illustrates, disagree and commit doesn't resolve all the disconnects and miscommunications that can occur in an organization, but it can help surface those disconnects and miscommunications in a more timely and productive manner.

As with any best practice, the way you implement disagree and commit will change based on your team and your organization. Here are some tips for trying it out:

Introduce disagree and commit before you use it.
Because disagree and commit is a formalized best practice—and one with the likes of Intel and Amazon behind it—you can introduce it as an agreed-upon procedural experiment. This is important because it will help avoid any situations in which people might feel like you are implementing disagree and commit as a kind of passive-aggressive personal criticism directed toward any particularly noncommittal members of your team.

Interpret silence as disagreement.
In most meetings, silence is interpreted as implicit agreement. Somebody suggests a path forward, concludes their pitch with "Any questions?" and if nobody responds, it's more or less a done deal. With disagree and commit, nothing short of affirmative commitment is accepted, which means that silence amounts to disagreement. Be very clear with participants: "If you are silent, I am going to assume that you are disagreeing with me. Let's go through and have each person share their thoughts and concerns." The first time you try this, it might be one of the most uncomfortable moments of your product management career, but you'll be amazed at the insights that can emerge from the quietest people in the room.

In larger meetings, try doing a quick pulse check.
In larger meetings—especially large meetings held over video chat—I've often found it helpful to move toward the conclusion of a meeting with a quick "Can everybody who's committed to this approach give me a thumbs-up?" Even if only one or two people respond tentatively, this gives you a chance to dig in deeper and quickly demonstrate that dissenting opinions will be welcomed and taken seriously.

Set goals, test, and learn.

So, what if people simply won't commit to a path forward? This is, believe it or not, a great sign. It means that the people in the room are engaged enough that they will not commit to something that they think is wrong. One way to move this conversation forward is to establish success criteria and plan to revisit the decision later. Then you can validate whether the approach you chose is working and make adjustments accordingly.

For example, suppose that you are in a meeting with your engineering team and there is a disagreement about whether your product development cycle should be two weeks or six weeks. Rather than trying to get everybody to reach consensus, you could say, "What if we commit to trying two-week development cycles, then touch base in a month to see whether this decision is helping us meet our team goals or we want to try something else?" This ensures that a decision happens, and it creates a shared sense of accountability for measuring its success and adjusting course moving forward.

Don't completely misinterpret the entire point of this and say, "Well, it doesn't matter if you agree because we're doing disagree and commit!"

I almost can't believe I have to write this, but in a few cases, people have taken the idea of disagree and commit to the ridiculous extreme of flat-out barking at their colleagues, "IT DOESN'T MATTER IF YOU AGREE WITH ME—WE ARE DOING DISAGREE AND COMMIT." Remember that the purpose of disagree and commit is to surface hesitations, concerns, and questions that might otherwise go unspoken. If your implementation of disagree and commit berates would-be dissenters into submission, you are doing it wrong.

Using Disagree and Commit to Uncover Better Solutions
J.A.
Product Management Consultant

I was working with a small consultancy in California that builds products for media conglomerates. We were having a meeting to discuss internal processes, and the question came up of how to handle client emails that come in after working hours. This had clearly been a source of tension among the team, and most people fell silent when the question was posed directly.

Finally, one of the more senior people in the company chimed in with "Well, it's important that we respond to our clients in a timely manner. So if you happen to see the email, then I guess you should just respond to it." Somebody else asked, "But what if two people are on the thread?" A third person volunteered, "Maybe what we can do is, if you see an email come in after hours and you plan to respond to it, first send a Slack message to the other people cc'ed on the message, tell them you've got it, and THEN send a response to the client." There were a few nods from around the table. A collaborative solution had been reached, and we had a path forward.

But the faces around the table were still tense, and a few people were still suspiciously quiet. I had just learned about disagree and commit, and this seemed like a good moment to try it. I told everybody in the meeting that they would need to affirmatively commit to this approach— and that if they were silent, I would assume that they disagreed with the approach. As we went around the table, most people offered a commitment to the tune of "Yes, I'm willing to try this for a while and see what happens." But one person—the person who had been quietest for most of the meeting—volunteered, "Yeah, I mean, this plan seems fine...but I don't see why we need to email them back that night. When a client emails me at night, I write back to them the next morning. And over time, those clients are kind of trained out of the behavior. They email me at the start of the workday rather than late at night, and everything usually works out better since I'm not rushing to get back to them."

The energy in the room shifted so dramatically in that moment—it was like a window blew open or something. People who had been willing to make a lukewarm commitment to the previous approach started sharing stories of late-night emails gone awry, bad decisions made in haste, and dinner plans ruined by unclear client management expectations. **The entire team committed—enthusiastically—to a new path forward, and that path would never have emerged at all if we hadn't taken a "disagree and commit" approach.**

Accounting for Different Communication Styles

For many product managers, overcommunication comes naturally—that's part of what drew them to product management in the first place. From this perspective, people who are less inclined to ask a lot of questions, speak up in meetings, or provide detailed written responses can often seem like "bad" communicators.

In my career as a product manager, I have often become frustrated with people who don't share my penchant for extensive written communication and spur-of-the-moment "riffing" in meetings. (For those of you reading that last sentence and thinking, "Both of those things sound horrible," *I see you and I appreciate you.*) It's taken me a long time to realize that this is not an issue of "good communication" versus "bad communication," but rather a reflection of the many different communication styles you are likely to encounter in your career.

As a product manager, it is critical for you to remember that not everybody is going to share your style of communication. Be open and curious with those who might initially strike you as bad communicators. Here are a few general styles of communication I've often encountered, to help you start from a place of understanding and empathy:

Visual communicators

Some people cannot grasp a concept until they have seen it visualized. As a person who primarily uses words to communicate, it took me a long time to accept this. I would often become frustrated and just find myself using *more* words when my meticulously composed messages were met with blank stares. If you are not a visual communicator, visual communicators on your team can offer you a great opportunity to refine and focus your own thinking by quickly sketching out or visually prototyping your ideas.

Offline communicators

On numerous occasions, I have had somebody confront me after a meeting because they feel like I put them on the spot when I was simply trying to involve them in the conversation. Initially, I wrote this off as a kind of juvenile defensiveness. But I've come to accept that some people need to think things through before they talk them out. Whenever possible, give offline communicators on your team a heads-up, letting them think through a particular question or challenge before sharing their thoughts.

Also make sure that they know in advance if they will be asked to speak or present in a meeting.

Confrontation-averse communicators

In the day-to-day work of product management, receiving an uncomplicated "Yes" or "Looks good to me" can feel like a rare and precious moment of pure positivity and encouragement. But these encouraging yes answers are not always motivated by a thorough and nuanced evaluation of the question at hand. As a product manager, putting clarity over comfort is part of your job, but it is not everybody else's job, nor is it their inclination. If you need feedback from somebody whose first reaction always seems to be yes, ask for that feedback in a way that does not allow for a yes-or-no answer. Accept that person's implicit challenge to be both more precise and more open in the way that you ask for feedback, and it will likely help you gather better feedback from everybody in your organization.

The more you can learn about the specific people on your team and appreciate their individual communication styles, the better you can facilitate communication for your team and your organization. I've found that the easiest way to learn about somebody's communication style is often to see how *they* communicate things to *you*. People generally convey information in the way that they most easily absorb information, and you can create a lot of good will by meeting people where they are.

Communication Is Your Job—Don't Apologize for Doing Your Job

Effective product management requires asking lots of different people for lots of time, which can leave product managers feeling like the annoying jerks who drag everybody away from their "real" work and force them to attend meeting after meeting after meeting or answer email after email after email. Early on in my career as a product manager, I did my best to defuse this by insisting to my colleagues that I would do everything in my power to make sure that they had to attend as few (ugh) meetings as humanly possible. When I *did* have to schedule a meeting, I treated it like a necessary inconvenience, rather than an exciting opportunity for the team to solve important problems together.

It did not occur to me until much later that I had effectively created a self-fulfilling prophecy: every one of my team's meetings would be treated like a waste of time and would, in turn, *become* a waste of time. In his book *Death by Meeting* (Jossey-Bass), Patrick Lencioni makes a great point about meetings:

if people approach them with a bad attitude, no amount of procedural tweaking is likely to make them better. The same holds true for email and other forms of asynchronous communication. If you train your colleagues to think of your emails as a nuisance, they will treat your emails like a nuisance. If you complain about being "overwhelmed" with incoming messages, your colleagues will probably think twice before looping you into a conversation that may prove critical for your team's success.

If your team feels like they are wasting time in meetings, ask them about the best and most productive meetings they've recently attended. Then work together to craft a clear and achievable vision for what a "good" meeting looks like. If your team is overwhelmed with email or chat messages, work with them to set clearer expectations around the communication channels you use. (We'll discuss this more in Chapter 13.) Don't downplay the value of the time your team spends communicating with each other—instead, make sure that time is spent well.

Understanding Goals and Motivations Beyond Your Immediate Team
A.G.
Product Manager, 500-employee publishing company

When I was younger, I often became frustrated when I felt folks— usually in other parts of the company—weren't doing the right thing. I thought they were either morons or jerks, wielding power for fun and games. If there is one piece of advice I can give to people struggling with politics at work, it's this: assume people are smart and assume the best intentions. This is not some warm and fuzzy kumbaya mantra; rather, it's tactical, practical advice to help you survive and thrive as a product manager.

When I was working at a publishing company, I was tasked with building a product reliant on a large volume of content. Meanwhile, the VP on the content side was going out of his way to restrict the content we could use. I was livid. "This is a disgusting power play, and he should be ashamed." My very wise manager advised me to talk to the VP. I did (calmly, surprisingly), and he indulged me with an explanation of how content acquisition actually works. If he gave me what I wanted, there was a high probability it would piss off our content partner. It might actually put them out of business. He was protecting his relationship and the long-term viability of that source. Well then.

He wasn't a jerk. Not even a moron. I still didn't agree with the decision, but I understood why he made it and I definitely didn't have to get mad about it. His goals and, more importantly, his customers, were different from mine. It was a very humbling experience.

Since then, I've worked in many other industries—retail, social media, food and drink—and this dynamic plays out time and again. Other parts of the business are often optimizing for different things: different goals and different customers. I know that product managers are often told to work closely with their immediate team, but in some ways, it's even more important to get to know people in other parts of the business. With your team, you still have the same set of goals and day-to-day concerns. But you may be totally at odds with another part of the business and not even know it. You may be thinking about the needs of your end user, but unaware of relationships with vendors and partners that are actually critical for keeping the business running.

And here's the thing: as a product manager, it is your job to figure this all out. Your role is cross-functional by definition, but everybody else's role isn't. You were hired to be a communicator, while somebody else may have been hired because they're really good at math or have great relationships with vendors. **Communication is your job, and you can't expect everyone else to be good at it.** My two favorite questions are "What are your goals?" and "What are you optimizing for?" I use them often and with great sincerity, and my product manager life (and non–product manager life!) is much better off because of it.

Egregious Overcommunication in Practice: Three Common Communication Scenarios for Product Managers

Though product managers might find themselves communicating with a lot of different people in a lot of different contexts, there are a few scenarios that tend to present themselves time and time again. In this section, we look at three common communication scenarios for product managers and how you might approach each of them. After reading the setup for each scenario, take a moment to think about how you would be inclined to handle it. This will help you square these suggestions with the rhythms, personalities, and issues at play in your specific organizational context.

SCENARIO ONE

Account Manager: We have to build this feature in two weeks, or we will lose our biggest client.

Developer: That feature will take at least six months to build if we want to do something that's even remotely stable and performant. (Figure 4-1)

Figure 4-1. An "emergency" request meets technical pushback

What's really going on

This is a classic and common case of misaligned incentives. The account manager's job is to retain customers. The developer's job is to create software that is not embarrassing, buggy, and held together with tape and string. The account manager is not directly incentivized to care about things like whether the software is performant. The developer, on the other hand, is not (usually) directly incentivized to care whether the customer is retained—if anything, one less unreasonable customer is one less set of last-minute demands. Both the account manager and the developer are advocating for their own respective short-term goals.

What you might do

There are multiple assumptions at play in both the account manager's and the developer's positions here. Does this customer really need this *exact* feature? Will we *really* lose the customer if we don't build it? Does the developer fully understand the customer need, or is she using the six-month timeline as a more defensible way to say no? Rather than debating the specific feature that your account manager is asking for, dig deeper into the fundamental problem the customer is having. Enlist the account manager as a partner in better understanding the customer's needs and the developer as a partner in exploring possible solutions. You might discover that no new feature is required at all, just a quick conversation with the customer to help them better understand an existing feature.

Patterns and traps to avoid

OK, well, let's decide whether we're looking at two weeks or six months.

Both two weeks and six months might be totally arbitrary time frames. The account manager might have said, "two weeks" as shorthand for "really soon," and the developer might have countered with "six months" as a way of saying, "Hell no, I do not want to work on that." Avoid the false choice and get to the heart of the issue.

Yes, I agree that we need to solve this in two weeks. And I agree that the software needs to be performant and stable.

Don't try to play both sides! This will simply not work. There are likely opportunities to level up to a more goals-oriented conversation, and it is your job as a product manager to facilitate that conversation. Best-case scenario: you will discover a solution that takes less than two weeks and incurs minimal concerns about performance and stability. Keep the conversation open and exploratory, but don't try to score quick points by telling people what they want to hear.

Our planning process happens every two weeks, and we're all full up. Come back to me later.

If you are working in a world of truly fixed iterations, last-minute additions like this are often avoided at all costs, and there are good reasons to keep these guardrails in place. But good reasons often won't stop these requests from coming in, and I've generally found it more helpful to have a process for evaluating and prioritizing them, rather than shooing them away entirely. (We'll discuss this more in Chapter 12, "Prioritization: Where It All Comes Together".)

SCENARIO TWO

Designer: I made four different versions of this design—which one do you like most? (Figure 4-2)

Figure 4-2. A designer presenting multiple options

What's really going on

The designer might have created four versions that he feels are equally well suited to the goals of the project, but with subjective differences (such as color choice) where he doesn't have a strong point of view. Or, the designer might not be clear about the goals of the project and is trying to defer responsibility by forcing you to make a choice. Or, the designer might have one approach he's really hoping you'll pick and has made a few "dummy" options to create the illusion of choice.

What you might do

This is an opportunity for you to demonstrate your trust in the designer by asking him which option he feels best aligns with the goals of the project. If he feels that one choice is clearly superior, this prompts him to think about that choice in the context of goals rather than preferences. And, if he doesn't have a strong preference, it might compel you both to have a conversation about whether the goals of the project are sufficiently clear. If multiple options seem equally viable, you might discuss with your designer how you could test these options to see which one best meets the goals of the project. After all, your team can have different opinions—but you should always have the same goals.

Patterns and traps to avoid

I like choice B—let's go with that!
> This is an easy and tempting response. After all, the designer asked you what you think. In some cases, the question really is that simple: the designer doesn't care and just wants you to choose among a few subjective variations. But you're better off digging a little deeper than you are rushing to a decision without a clear set of reasons beyond your personal preference.

Let's bring all four of them to the whole group and see what they think!
> For a long time, this was my strategy, until a thoughtful UX designer informed me that I was driving our visual designer to the point of quitting with "design by committee." Nothing is worse than having a whole bunch of people spout their opinions at you about the job you were hired to do.

I don't care. Whichever one you want is fine.
> It's very rare that somebody puts in the work of doing something four different times unless there's a reason. Don't dismiss that effort—and the deeper issues that might be underlying it—by refusing to engage.

...And a bonus question

What if the designer only gave me one option?

Avoid the temptation to launch immediately into a critique, even if it feels like a generous critique. Instead, ask the designer to walk you through how he arrived at the design. This will give you an opportunity to learn more about how the designer understands the project's overall goals, and it might reveal a subtle miscommunication or two that you can work to resolve.

SCENARIO THREE

Developer: Sorry, I just don't understand why you're trying to force us to follow all this unnecessary process. Can you just let me do my job? (Figure 4-3)

Figure 4-3. A developer protesting "unnecessary process"

What's really going on

Although phrases like "This process is just way too heavy for us," or "I don't want to follow all of these unnecessary steps," or "This is big-company corporate bulls***," might seem like generic grumblings of the process averse (we'll discuss this more in Chapter 7), they are important and valuable signals that you have some work to do. If your team does not feel invested in your development process, and/or if they see that process as an impediment to getting their work done, you might have fundamentally failed in your role as a communicator and facilitator, even if you have succeeded in getting your team to formally adopt a certain development framework or process.

What you might do

First and foremost, take your developer's feedback seriously. Thank him for his candor and make it clear that your team can succeed *only* if people are up-front about sharing their concerns. Rather than trying to resolve his concerns in an offline one-on-one conversation, ask if he can repeat this feedback during the next team meeting. This will help establish that you are not looking to be the brutal enforcer of your team's processes, but rather a facilitator who helps the team identify and adopt the processes that will best meet their goals.

Patterns and traps to avoid

Just try it for a while—I promise it will make your life easier!
> There is a subtle but critical distinction between "I promise this will work" and "Let's collaborate to make this work." Asking anybody on your team to uncritically accept process changes is a fundamentally dismissive gesture, not a connective and supportive gesture. If your team does not feel invested in its process, that process is likely to fail.

You're right. Forget this process stuff—what do you want to work on?
> Although giving engineers free rein to work on whatever they want might feel like an empowering or at least suitably deferential gesture, it ultimately leaves them deeply disconnected from the user- and business-facing impact of their work. Eventually, somebody is going to hold your team accountable for the actual results of what they build. And the longer your team goes without any kind of process to connect the work they're doing with the goals of your organization, the worse that day of reckoning is going to be.

I know, I know, I'm the worst, but my boss said we should put some more process in place. I promise I'll try to make this as painless as possible!
> As we've discussed, self-deprecation is a common coping mechanism for product managers. But if you cast yourself as an unwitting pawn in some-body else's quest to instill meaningless processes, you are guaranteeing that the process will be meaningless. If you don't believe that the process you're using is the right one, but, hey, your boss asked for some process, it is time for you to have an uncomfortable conversation with your boss.

Summary: When in Doubt, Communicate!

The day-to-day work of communication requires attentiveness, adaptability, and nuance. But the most important decisions you make as a product manager will often come down to this simple question: are you willing to bring up something that might seem obvious, uncomfortable, or both? The more fearless you are about starting these conversations—and the more space you create within your team and organization for these conversations to play out—the more successful you and your team will be.

Your Checklist

- Err on the side of overcommunication. When you aren't sure whether something is worth mentioning, mention it.

- Don't be afraid to ask "the obvious." In fact, the more obvious something seems, the more insistent you should be about making sure everybody is on the same page.

- Create a document like "Good Product Manager/Bad Product Manager" that clearly lays out the behavioral expectations for product managers in your organization.

- Avoid starting sentences with phrases like "It would be great if..." or "Do you think it might be possible to..." that deflect responsibility. If you are asking for something, ask for it—and be clear about why you are asking for it.

- Try to refocus conversations about emotions and intentions around outcomes by asking questions like "Did this situation deliver the desired outcome?"

- Never forget that "Looks fine" often means "I'm not paying attention," and always aim for engaged, affirmative, and specific feedback and buy-in.

- Make sure that people are given a chance to voice their opinions in meetings by using "disagree and commit" or any other approach that achieves similar goals within your organization.

- Remember that people have different communication styles. Don't write somebody off as a "bad communicator" or assume that they have bad intentions if their style is different from yours.

- Avoid the temptation of being a "meeting hater" or "email hater." Don't apologize when you're asking for somebody's time, but make sure that their time is well spent.

- Ask your teammates about the most valuable and well-run meetings they've attended. Then work with them to set a clear vision for what a "good" meeting looks like for you.

- Level up tactical conversations about things like design choices or development timelines to strategic conversations about business goals and user needs.

5

Working with Senior Stakeholders (or, Throwing the Poker Game)

The first time my dad met his future father-in-law, he was invited to join in for a friendly game of after-dinner poker. My dad, much like myself, is not somebody who has generally excelled at competitive rituals associated with male bonding. He also, much like myself, is not very good at cards. However, in this particular situation, he wasn't too concerned about his skill level. My dad's goal was not to win the poker game, but rather to make sure that his potential future father-in-law won the poker game. From what both of my parents have told me, this worked quite well.

I've thought about this story many times during my career as a product manager, especially when I've found myself sitting in meetings with people who have much more organizational authority than I do. In most high-stakes meetings—as in some high-stakes poker games—"winning" doesn't necessarily mean the same thing to everybody at the table. And when you are working with senior stakeholders, the best way to "win" is often to help somebody else win.

For better or worse, senior stakeholders often have access to important high-level information about the business that you simply do not. Based on this information, they might override your priorities or shift those priorities when you're midway through a project. They might even wield the bludgeon of "because I said so" if they can't reveal the sensitive details of conversations that are playing out between themselves and other senior stakeholders. In short, senior stakeholders will always win the poker game. Your mission, should you choose to accept it, is to ensure that your business and your users win along with them.

In this chapter, we look at some real-world strategies for working with senior stakeholders (a challenge often referred to in business parlance as "managing up"). Note that, for our purposes, *senior stakeholders* refers to anybody who has direct decision-making authority within your organization. At a small startup, that might be a founder or investor. At a large company, that might be an executive from your own department or another department.

From "Influence" to Information

The idea of "leading through influence" is ubiquitous in the literature around product management, including the first edition of this book. And sure enough, most product managers must find ways to get things done without wielding direct organizational authority. But I've cooled on the word *influence* in the past several years, largely because I have seen too many product managers attempt to "influence" senior stakeholders toward a predetermined path by cherry-picking information, omitting risks and assumptions, or overpromising around both timelines and outcomes. In many of these cases, successfully "influencing" senior stakeholders is seen as a win, even if that "win" yields dubious results for the business and its users.

There will be times when senior stakeholders make decisions that seem wrong or illogical to you. Sometimes, these are simply bad decisions. Sometimes, this is because senior stakeholders have access to high-level information (such as a pending acquisition or forthcoming change in company strategy) that you do not. And sometimes, this is because you failed to make senior stakeholders aware of the tactical trade-offs that should have been considered when making these decisions.

For these reasons, I've found it more productive to think of a product manager's job as to *inform* stakeholders, not to *influence* them. If you have successfully informed stakeholders about the decision at hand, the goals of that decision as you understand them, and the real-world trade-offs that go into making that decision, then you have successfully done your job—even if you don't get the decision you thought you wanted.

Many times, I've seen challenges around "influence" play out around issues of head count and staffing, where product managers may feel *highly* accountable but have very little direct control. At least once in your product career, you will likely find yourself staring down an ambitious roadmap and worrying that you simply don't have enough resources to deliver against the commitments you've made. "When we made our roadmap, I thought we'd have ten engineers," I often hear from product managers I coach, "and now we only have two. Leadership has told us many times that our work is mission critical. How are we supposed to deliver against this?"

For product managers—many of whom, as we have discussed, are overachievers by nature—this situation suggests a clear mission: *convince your leaders to give you more resources.* But when I actually speak with those leaders, I usually hear a very different story. I have never heard a senior stakeholder say, "I expect a team with two engineers to deliver the work of a team with ten engineers." What I *have* often heard is "Yeah, that work was really important to us a few months ago, but we're reevaluating a few things at the company level, and for the time being we're not sure if that's the best place for us to put our resources."

The best product managers help leadership make informed decisions—and, as we discussed in Chapter 3, provide options, not arguments, to make sure that leadership actively understands the trade-offs involved in those decisions. Rather than arguing for more resources, try presenting multiple options with a solid recommendation: "If we have ten engineers, we can probably deliver roughly against our original roadmap. If we have two engineers, we can probably deliver roughly against this descoped roadmap. And if we have five engineers, we can expand the descoped roadmap based on company priorities. We believe that we can provide the highest ROI for the business with ten engineers, as evidenced by the data provided. The choice is yours—good day!"

Having the Courage to Challenge Executive Decisions

Ashley S.
Product Manager, enterprise electronics company

I was working on a product for a large electronics company, and my team was responsible for building a workflow and asset management tool. At the project's outset, we got word from a senior executive that we were to build our product around a specific piece of workflow management software that was being used in one of our European offices—the idea being that as long as one team was already using this particular software, we could just build around it and expand upon the core functionality.

As soon as we started talking to the company that had built this software, it became clear that the path forward would not be so easy. We kept hearing, "Our software doesn't do that." They couldn't even meet some of our basic functional requirements. At every roadblock, we kept moving forward with a series of ever-more-complicated workarounds. We often found ourselves asking, "Why was this technology even selected?" The answer usually amounted to "We've already invested in this, so keep going." The longer the project went on, the harder it was to revisit that decision, in part because we had spent so much time developing workarounds specifically for the software we were instructed to use. We didn't show the product to users until it was "finished," and by that point, we had gotten so wrapped up in technical workarounds that we had failed to really understand our users' needs. Our users told us, "This sucks," and we said, "Yup." At the end of the day, we had to decide not to launch the product at all. So, all of that concern about sunk cost actually led us down a path where everything we invested in the product was just a straight-up loss.

If I could do it over again, I would have pushed back on the top-down decision around technology. **One of the things that I feel has contributed the most to my career as a product manager is having the courage to push back and to have challenging conversations.** We are trained to follow the chain of command, so this can be very difficult when you're in a room full of executives. You have to first understand that their questions and criticisms are not personal. I've seen that in some junior product managers—they interpret questions and criticisms from senior leaders as personal attacks. You need to remove yourself emotionally. You need to have the courage to say, "Can I push back on this? Can we talk about why you're making this assumption?"

As a product manager, you're always being asked, "Why does this take so long?" You have to be able to unpack that question without getting defensive about it. Help senior leaders understand that the decisions they make aren't made in isolation—help them see the "invisible" work that they don't think about when they decide that they want a new feature. Give them options and make them aware of the trade-offs of each approach. Always make sure that the decision is in their hands—that they have ownership. That way, it's not an us-versus-them situation—it's just us.

An Answer You Don't Like Is Still an Answer

A few years ago, I was training a group of product managers on the importance of getting clarity around the "why" behind company-level plans and initiatives. One product manager in the room quickly raised their hand and interjected, "I'm sorry, but I've tried that a bunch, and it doesn't seem to get me anywhere." I asked for an example, and they continued: "Well, the last time I kept hearing from my manager that there was a specific feature we needed to build, I asked 'why' until everyone was sick of hearing it, and eventually I was told, 'Look, the CEO promised someone we'd build it, so we have to build it.' So why bother?"

Frustrating though it may have been, this product manager *did their job*; they found out "why," even if they didn't get the answer they wanted. In the real-world practice of product management, there will be times when you find yourself and your team working on something that seems ill-advised or arbitrary. But knowing the reasons behind those ill-advised or arbitrary-seeming directives can work to your advantage.

For example, I have worked with many product managers who go about seeking the "why" behind a feature only to discover that it "came from marketing." For some product managers, this discovery is met with frustrated grumbling about how the organization is "marketing led" and not "product led." For other product managers, this discovery empowers them to better understand the constraints and opportunities that they might need to consider as they move forward. A few open and curious conversations with folks on the marketing team might reveal that some specific promises were made to executives: promises like "We can say that the feature is AI powered" or "We have something to show off at our next big event." A better understanding of these constraints means being able to work within them, while still delivering something that will prove valuable to the business and its users; a *lot* of things could be described as "AI powered," and needing to deliver *something* by a specific date still gives your team a whole lot of room to figure out what that something might be.

"Our Boss Is an Idiot," or, Congratulations—You've Ruined Your Team

When product managers don't get the answers or decisions they want from senior stakeholders, they tend to retreat into building cohesion within their own team at the expense of those very stakeholders. Early on in my career as a product manager, when a request came in from senior leadership that felt unreasonable, my first thought was always, "Oh no, my team is going to blame me for this."

In an attempt to emerge blameless, I would end the conversation with senior leaders as quickly as possible, go back to my team, and say something to the effect of, "Can you believe how those idiots are jerking us around? WELP, I guess this is what we've got to work on now. *Cough* NOT MY FAULT."

In the moment, this can feel like the only way to keep the trust and respect of your team while also placating senior stakeholders. But in the long term, it never works out. The second you go to your team and say something like "Our boss is an idiot," you have effectively ruined your team. They will begin to see any and all requests that come down from senior stakeholders as arbitrary and unreasonable. The time and energy they spend working on projects that align with organizational goals will feel like grudging concessions to the powers that be. And the time and energy they spend working on projects that do *not* align with organizational goals will feel like "sticking it to the man." They will see your role as protecting them from senior stakeholders, rather than connecting them with senior stakeholders. And you will have backed yourself into a corner where the trust and support of your team hinges on you dutifully performing this role. In the interest of protecting and defending your team, you will have set them up to fail on the organization's terms.

So, how do you communicate effectively with your team when you disagree with a decision or directive from senior leadership? Stay calm, explain the goals and constraints of the work at hand as you understand them, and engage your team in finding ways to make the work as impactful as you can. I've been surprised at how quickly a team can be turned around with a simple and transparent acknowledgment to the tune of "Yes, I don't necessarily agree with this decision—but we work for a company with a lot of moving parts, and we won't always agree with every decision that gets made. I *do* think that we have some great opportunities here to make sure that this work solves a real problem for our users, and I'm excited for us to explore those opportunities together."

Here's a funny story: the first draft of this section was written five years ago in a fit of self-recrimination after having a conversation with a product manager who was, at the time, feeling embattled in their role in a way that rang all too familiar to me. I recently had the pleasure of catching up with that very product manager, Abigail Pereira, who is now thriving as a product leader and managing two phenomenal product managers herself. She shared the following reflection on that moment in her career:

> Earlier on in my product career, I was ill-equipped to handle the emotional side of the job. So much of product management is leading without

authority, which means repeating yourself a million times over—something that requires an inordinate amount of patience and confidence. Lacking both patience and confidence, I'd take refuge in product and engineering team meetings—"product therapy," as we'd call it. During these meetings, I found myself commiserating with my team over difficult stakeholders, not being appreciated enough, and everything else that was/is part of the job. At first, these meetings seemed like a safe space to say what I needed to say and to get things off my mind. The us-against-them, David-versus-Goliath mentality felt invigorating. It gave me a sense of purpose, like if I couldn't succeed in moving a product idea forward, at least I had the support of the people.

In the end, none of this worked out well. The safety of the moment was fleeting, but the frustrations were kindling for a longer-burning fire of emotions. It's easier to say this looking back, but I fueled a lot of these fires out of a need to soothe my own ego, rather than accepting what I could control and moving on. The in-the-moment trauma bonding was addictive, and gave me the sense of a higher mission. While I have remained friends with some of my coworkers, I see in some instances that apart from the negativity we shared, we really didn't have much in common. Being a product person requires extreme ownership and at times unwavering faith in your ideas. What I realize now is that, holding onto those ideas shouldn't come at the cost of losing sight of the playing field. Now when I need to vent, I reach out strategically to the right people. I view myself not only as an owner, but as a leader, and have come to recognize that the delicate balance of moving people forward requires developing relationships, but not at the expense of others.

Keeping this kind of us-against-them trauma bonding in check can be an ongoing struggle for product managers looking to build camaraderie and cohesion with their teams. But, as Pereira notes in the above passage, the "patience and confidence" required to be a great product manager and product leader can only be found on the other side of that struggle.

The Dangers of "Protecting" Your Team from Business Goals
Shaun R.
Product Manager, growth-stage ecommerce startup

I was working as a product manager at an ecommerce startup in London, and my team was responsible for creating a Black Friday sales page. Black Friday is a big deal for ecommerce companies, and the business had a very clear idea of what success would look like. We had an idea for a product that felt very closely aligned with our user needs, but relatively high risk from a business perspective. I wanted my team to feel emboldened toward this more user-centric approach, so I didn't worry them with the specific goals the business had in mind.

Everything went along smoothly—until we actually launched the product. Even though the product we built did meet the underlying user needs as we understood them, it did not level up to the success metrics that the business had in mind. Had I been more up-front with my team about how the business was looking to define success, we could have built a solution that better aligned the needs of our users with the concerns and constraints of our business. Instead, we wound up having to defensively rethink the product after it had already launched, on a tighter timeline and with a significant drop in morale.

In hindsight, this is a moment when I insulated the team rather than trying to surface the underlying conflict. I created a situation in which I saw myself as the filter for any problems between my team and the business at large, which can help you feel like you're protecting the tech folks from the nontech folks and can seem manageable in the short term. **But when there's a fundamental mismatch between what the business wants and what your team wants, you can't resolve it by ignoring the business in the name of "protecting" your team.**

No Alarms and No Surprises

Several years ago, I was tasked with putting together a new roadmap for a company where I worked as a product manager. I spent countless hours slowly getting buy-in from all parts of the organization, hearing people's concerns, making adjustments, and putting something together that seemed both impactful and achievable.

After the meeting where our leadership team collectively agreed to this roadmap, one senior stakeholder pulled me aside. "You're such a creative person," he said, "I'd love for you to present a more creative option the next time we all meet." Oh, *heck* yes! I put my "creative person" cap on and spent the better part of the next week putting together something *truly awesome*—the plan that I had really wanted all along.

The day before the next week's roadmap meeting, I sent that senior stakeholder an email, which, to the best of my recollection, was approximately 10,000 pages long. It detailed my plans for a brave new direction and thanked him for unleashing my creativity. I slept very well that night, confident that I had the blessing of one of the most senior and important people in the organization.

The next day's meeting was, in short, a bloodbath. No sooner did I begin to present my great new idea than another senior stakeholder jumped in with, "Wait, I thought we had already agreed to a roadmap last week? What the hell is this?" To my great shock and indignation, the very senior stakeholder who had asked me for a more "creative solution" then began berating me for taking the project so thoroughly off course. I threw my arms up in exasperation and did my best to fight back tears. *How could he do this to me?*

I was very angry about this for a long time. But in retrospect, I made no less than two huge mistakes in the way I approached that fateful meeting. First: I essentially betrayed the trust of every other person who had bought into the original roadmap I worked so hard to synthesize and socialize. Second: though I had laid out my "creative" product vision to this senior stakeholder in an inexcusably long email, I had no idea if he was actually supportive of it or not. These two huge mistakes added up to one colossal mistake: I surprised senior stakeholders with something completely new to them in an important, high-stakes meeting. And, to make matters worse, I did this at an important, high-stakes meeting full of senior stakeholders whom I knew were wrestling with different visions for the future of the company. However much blame there was to go around, a lot of it fell on me.

The solution here is pretty simple: nothing that you are telling a senior stakeholder in a "big" meeting should ever be a surprise, ever. There are many reasons why it is always a good idea to individually walk senior stakeholders through a new idea *before* you present it in a group setting. But, to return to the heavy-handed metaphor at the heart of this chapter, a senior stakeholder is always going to win the poker game. And if you've taken the time to ensure that every senior stakeholder in the room is invested in an idea that is truly beneficial for the business and its users, then the odds are very good that, whichever senior stakeholder wins this particular hand, the business and its users will win along with them.

Note that getting time on the calendar with senior stakeholders is often easier said than done, especially in the era of remote work when you can't just "stop by" somebody's office. In situations where you simply *cannot* get time with senior stakeholders before a big meeting, I recommend breaking down any "big ideas" you plan to present into smaller pieces—and, again, presenting multiple options rather than arguing for a single path forward. For example, rather than rolling out a whole new roadmap at my fateful meeting, I could have taken a moment to refocus the group on our high-level company goals, then presented the original roadmap and the new roadmap as two different options that might help us achieve those goals. This would have opened up more space for the senior stakeholders in the room to *choose* the original roadmap, rather than reflexively attacking the new roadmap.

Getting Incremental Buy-In and Avoiding the "Big Reveal"

Ellen C.
Product Management Intern, enterprise software company

When I was working as an intern at a large software company, my first project was building a closed-captioning system for a popular office product suite. I was provided a good amount of guidance going into the project: there was a clear business case, a set of well-understood regulations around implementation, and a pretty well-defined sense of what success would look like. I was able to manually test out a bunch of different approaches to execution and run them by stakeholders. It went really well.

The second project I was given to work on was a system for commenting in that same office suite. I was really excited about this one. Although closed captioning had not been something that I personally needed, I had a lot of ideas about what I could use from a commenting system. I had grand plans for making something really, really cool. I worked really hard on a specification that covered everything from the "why" to specific design and execution details. This was going to be my Big Win.

When it came time to review the spec I had put together, it did not go so well. It was terrible, actually. I was expecting everybody to be, like, "This is the greatest thing ever, why haven't we done this yet?" Instead, everybody told me all the reasons why it wouldn't work. A lot of things that seemed really obvious to me had contexts behind them that I just didn't understand. And because I was so emotionally invested, I didn't want to accept the feedback.

In retrospect, I made a mistake that I've seen a lot of new product managers make: trying to sell in everything at once with a "big reveal." I hadn't done the work of getting people to agree on the core user need or presenting different possible paths to addressing that need. Instead, I just laid out, "This is exactly what we should do and why." People don't know where to give you feedback when you present everything all at once in a big meeting that way. If you go to people individually, they might say, "This is terrible—and here's how to fix it." But when you try to do "the big reveal," there's really no way forward.

Staying User Centric in a World of Company Politics

Navigating company politics can seem like a lot of work—and in most cases, it is a lot of work. However, it is critical for you to remember that your success ultimately hinges not on your ability to make stakeholders happy but rather on your ability to make users happy. If you build something that your boss and your boss's boss like but falls short of delivering any real value to your users, then you are failing to follow one of our guiding principles of product management: "live in your user's reality."

Here are a few tips for staying user centric even as you navigate company politics:

Let your users make the case for you.

Remember that you are ultimately building a product not for your stakeholders but for your users. If you are doing the work of regularly talking with and getting feedback from your users—which you absolutely should be—you should have plenty of information at your disposal to bring your users' needs to life as you present options to senior stakeholders. If you find that you don't have a clear sense of why your users might need a thing you are proposing to build, you probably shouldn't be proposing it in the first place.

Connect user needs and business goals.

It is not uncommon for product managers to find themselves feeling like they are advocating for "what's good for the user" against executive mandates to build "what's good for the business." But the biggest problem in this scenario is not an imbalance between user needs and business goals, but that these two things are perceived as being at odds with each other in the first place. If you feel like you are caught in a tug-of-war between business goals and user needs, the solution is not to pull harder, but rather to make sure that a clear and positively correlated relationship has been established between the needs of the user and the goals of the business.

When proposing a specific feature or product, be very exact and precise in explaining how you see the relationship between user needs and business goals. For example: "If we can make our onboarding experience faster and less burdensome, we believe that we can increase new user registrations by about twenty percent. Given that each new user is worth about one dollar in advertising revenue, we see this as a critical step toward meeting our revenue goals for the quarter."

Flip the script and ask senior leaders about users.

If you're looking to encourage user centricity throughout the organization, ask your senior leaders what they know about the needs of your users. Make it clear that your goal is to help them deliver value to users and meet the goals of your business. Invite them into a conversation in which you are collaboratively exploring multiple solutions to a well-understood user need, rather than debating a single, predetermined solution.

Unlike your stakeholders, your users can rarely be found standing over your shoulder forcefully advocating for their goals. But understanding and advocating for those goals can bring alignment and purpose to even the most contentious stakeholder conversations.

The Not-So-Mysterious Case of the Disappearing Search Bar

M.P.

Product Manager, nonprofit

When I was working as the product manager at a medium-sized nonprofit, I was tasked with overseeing a major site redesign. I knew that this would be a difficult task; the organization had a lot of senior stakeholders with very strong opinions about how their particular corner of the organization should be represented.

I put together a steering committee with the people whose direct sign-off I needed for the final design. I showed incremental work every week and was able to keep up momentum on the project. Sure enough, there were a few times when people fought hard for their particular department to be featured more prominently, but we were always able to find a compromise that was amenable to the group. Miraculously, we were able to launch on time and on budget.

The project seemed like a huge success, until a few weeks later, when I actually had to use the website to find some information about an event we were hosting. From a product manager's perspective, the site felt like a success, but from a user's perspective, it was a confusing mess. The top-level navigation mapped out perfectly to the departments whose leaders I had to wrangle, but these categories made little sense from a user's perspective. And, worst of all, the search bar—which had no senior stakeholder advocating for it—was completely buried.

I realized in retrospect that I had become so wrapped up in keeping senior stakeholders happy that I had completely forgotten to advocate for the user's needs. Now, whenever I'm working with senior stakeholders, I make a point of starting with the user's needs before trying to reach any kind of conclusion so that we're making the decision that's best for the user, not best for the egos of the people in the room.

Senior Stakeholders Are People Too

Last but not least, remember that senior stakeholders are people too. They have their own concerns keeping them awake at night, their own battles to fight, their own hopes and ambitions and frustrations. Your interactions with them may seem very important and significant to you, but they are likely preoccupied with *lots of other things.*

Keep this in mind when you feel like you aren't getting the recognition or validation that you want from senior stakeholders, or when you are convinced that senior stakeholders are purposefully withholding information from you. Odds are they're just really busy, and the information you think they're withholding may very well be information that they themselves simply don't have.

Throwing the Poker Game in Practice: Three Common Scenarios for Senior Stakeholder Management

Let's look at three common scenarios you are likely to encounter as you work with senior stakeholders. These are all variations of the dreaded "swoop-and-poop," in which a senior stakeholder swoops in on work in progress and delivers some kind of criticism, out-of-nowhere demand, or insistence to stay the course no matter what. Every product manager I know has experienced at least one swoop-and-poop. As with the example scenarios from Chapter 4, take a moment to reflect on how you might handle this situation before reading on.

SCENARIO ONE

Executive: I just saw the work your designer is doing. I don't like the colors, and it doesn't look anything like the product I signed off on! (Figure 5-1)

Figure 5-1. A classic swoop-and-poop

What's really going on

The executive in this case feels like he's out of the loop. Something is moving forward that he doesn't recognize, and it implicitly threatens his sense of authority and control. Returning to our CORE skills, an organization-minded product manager might recognize this as a sign that something is fundamentally broken in the way that her team is communicating with senior stakeholders, and she would look for scalable ways to fix that disconnect.

What you might do

First, you might want to straight-up apologize. If the executive is seeing something that feels new to him, then something about the way you are getting product ideas and designs approved is not working as well as it could. Explain to the executive that you never want anything to feel like a surprise or catch him off guard. Ask what you can do to make sure that he can see works in progress on a timeline that makes sense for him. Does he want to carve out a standing weekly meeting? Where in the process does he feel that he lost touch with the direction of the product? Look for ways in which you can address the fundamental problem, rather than trying to wriggle out of this uncomfortable moment.

Patterns and traps to avoid

This is the exact thing you signed off on. The only differences are purely cosmetic!
> Because you are speaking with somebody whose power and authority greatly exceed your own, you likely do not want to go into litigation mode. What is the real issue here? Is it the changes themselves, or the fact that this executive is seeing something that seems new to him?

I sent you the updated mock-ups last week and asked if you had any feedback, and you never responded!
> Anything short of affirmative and specific buy-in is not really buy-in. If your updated mock-ups were one of 10,000 messages to hit somebody's inbox and you received no response—or even a generic "looks fine" response—you might as well have not sent those mock-ups at all. Trying to win on a technicality won't help you.

OK, we'll change the colors to whatever you want.
> If you read the executive's comment carefully, you might notice that he is not actually asking you to change anything about the product. He is

essentially describing a communication problem, not a product problem, and looking to change the latter won't fix the former.

Yeah, well, that's just, like, your opinion, man.

Even if "the colors are all wrong" is just an opinion, you're better off not going down this road. Getting into a battle of opinions with anybody—let alone a senior stakeholder—is a bad move in the best of circumstances, and doing it in this context will rarely result in a positive outcome.

SCENARIO TWO

Executive: I know that your team is already working on something this week, but I'm really excited about that other feature we discussed a few days ago. Do you think you could find a little time to work on this as well? (Figure 5-2)

Figure 5-2. An executive swooping in with a new feature request

What's really going on

On the surface, this might seem like an executive trying to sneak her own pet projects into your team's tightly scoped work plan. But if you take this executive at her word, her motivation is *excitement*, not sabotage. If an executive is taking the time to come to you and express her excitement about a specific feature—

even if it's one that you are not currently planning to build—this is a great opportunity for you to better understand her priorities and how they align with your team's priorities.

What you might do

Have an open and transparent conversation about what makes this specific feature so exciting to the executive *and* why it was not prioritized by your team as part of the current week's work. Maybe this executive was part of a high-level conversation that potentially shifted your organizational goals and you simply are not aware of that conversation. Or maybe this executive is really just super excited about this idea and is not aware of the specific goals against which your team is executing. Be open to the possibility that the feature that this executive is suggesting might actually be more important to the organization than what your team is building. But, rather than manually overriding the work your team has currently prioritized, talk with this executive about how you might change your overall approach to prioritization to make sure that the most important work is prioritized moving forward.

Patterns and traps to avoid

Yes!

Immediately agreeing to a request like this not only undermines the existing processes your team uses to prioritize work, it also sets up the executive for disappointment when the actual thing you deliver doesn't live up to the abstract idea in her head. Unless you have taken the time to fully understand why this feature is being requested, you are in no position to promise anything.

No!

If an executive has taken the time to come to you and share their excitement about a specific feature, there is almost certainly an important reason. Even if you ultimately plan to stand firm on your team's original priorities, take the opportunity to understand why this executive is so excited about this feature.

Maybe. We'll see how much time we have.

The fundamental question here is not whether your team will have time to work on the new feature, but rather why this executive is so excited about the new feature in the first place. If you make this merely a matter of capacity, you are missing out on a critical opportunity to better understand the goals and motivations of a senior stakeholder in your organization.

SCENARIO THREE

Executive: Listen—I've been doing this for a long time, and I just need you to trust me when I say that I know that this feature is going to be a big success. OK? (Figure 5-3)

Figure 5-3. An executive insisting that a feature is going to succeed

What's really going on

Executives are people too, and there are times when they get just as defensive and exasperated as you do. The difference is, they are able to trot out a more dressed-up version of "because I told you so," whereas you almost certainly are not. There will be times in your career when you find yourself talking to an executive who would rather give you opaque marching orders than slog through the work of finding common ground—especially when you're dealing with an executive from outside your immediate team who may not be familiar with your day-to-day work or experience.

What you might do

By the time somebody reaches an executive position, they likely have many perceived wins under their belt, and those perceived wins have shaped their experience and expectations in ways that are always good for you to understand. One approach I've found particularly helpful is to say something to the effect of,

"I'm super excited that you think this feature is going to be a win for us—help me understand your thinking here so that I can make sure I execute against this in a way that will continue to build on the success we've had so far." Ask open, curious follow-up questions and stay interested and engaged. And if you get the sense that the conversation isn't going anywhere and you're just catching this executive on a bad day (which is entirely possible), see if you can get some time on their calendar to ask those questions at a later date.

Patterns and traps to avoid

Whatever you say, boss!
> If the feature you build fails, it is very unlikely that this executive will say, "I was the one who insisted that this feature would be a success, so its failure is totally my fault." It is much more likely that this executive will find some minor flaw in the execution and insist that "this whole thing would have been a huge success if they had just done it the way I told them to!"

Well, I think that this feature is going to fail.
> Unless you have built a very strong relationship with this particular executive, you are very unlikely to get much out of an opinion versus opinion battle. Even if you do think that this feature is going to fail, both you and the executive are almost certainly working with an incomplete set of information. Your job is to get as much of that information as possible on the table so that everybody involved can make better decisions.

Sorry, but I'm not going to build something just because you tell me to.
> From the executive's position, they are likely not telling you to build something "just because they tell you to." They almost certainly have their own reasoning, and it is your job to understand that reasoning as best as you can, even if you don't fully agree with it. As always, openness will get you much further than defensiveness.

Summary: This Is Part of Your Job, Not an Impediment to Your Job

Working with senior stakeholders is a particularly challenging and high-stakes part of a product manager's job. There can be times when these stakeholders— especially founders and executives—seem to have an incredible amount of control over your fate and destiny. But remember, executives are people too, and they can fall into the same traps of self-doubt and defensiveness that you do. Help them make the best decisions they can, learn from their experiences, and stay patient and curious.

Your Checklist

- When working with senior stakeholders, don't set out to "win." Help empower them to make great decisions and demonstrate that you can be a valuable and supportive thought partner.

- Come to terms with the fact that you won't always get the answer you want from senior stakeholders and that this is not a reflection on you personally.

- Don't try to "protect" your team from senior stakeholders by talking about how ignorant, arrogant, or out of touch these senior stakeholders are. Instead, openly acknowledge the constraints within which you are working and maximize the impact you can have within those constraints.

- Never surprise a senior stakeholder with a big idea in an important meeting. Socialize ideas slowly and deliberately in one-on-one meetings if at all possible.

- Don't let company politics drown out the needs of your user. Let user needs guide your decision-making, and bring the user's perspective to life in meetings with senior leaders.

- Take every opportunity to connect business goals with user needs to reinforce the business value of user centricity.

- When senior stakeholders ask you questions like "Can this be done by Tuesday?" take their questions as actual questions, not as implicit demands.

- When confronted with a swoop-and-poop, don't try to litigate the details of past conversations. Look for opportunities to diagnose and address the underlying issues so that the swooper-pooper does not feel out of the loop moving forward.

- If a senior stakeholder suddenly wants your team to work on something different, find out why. There might have been an important high-level conversation of which you are not aware.

- Remember that senior stakeholders can get defensive and exhausted, too. Stay open, curious, and patient.

6

Talking to Users (or, "What's a Poker Game?")

Now imagine that you are at a very different poker game. You are working for an online gaming startup, and you've asked a group of poker players if you can sit in on their game to better understand their fundamental needs and behaviors around card games. After a round of introductions, your host asks, quite generously, "I'm not sure how familiar you are with poker. Do you want me to walk you through the rules?"

You might not realize it, but in this moment, you could be opening yourself up to some breakthrough insights about your users—or you could be completely shutting them out.

You pause for a second. You want these people to trust you, and if they think you're a total rube, why will they volunteer anything particularly interesting or insightful? With an air of knowing confidence, you offer, "Oh yeah, I love to play poker! Are we doing Texas Hold 'em or Omaha?" You get a cordial response of "Hold 'em!" and the game begins. *Whew.* They bought it. That time you spent on Wikipedia last night really paid off. As the first hand begins, you get right down to business: "Thanks so much for inviting me to your game tonight. As you know, I'm here doing some research about online card games. What would y'all want from your ideal online poker app?"

The people around the table are slow to answer. Nobody seems all that excited about the question. After a bit of a lull, the person next to you chimes in with, "I installed a poker app once, I think, on my phone, a few years ago. Didn't wind up using it much, though."

Yes. You're getting somewhere. "What didn't you like about it?"

"Well, I don't really remember, to be honest. I guess it just didn't hold my interest."

So close. "Why do you think it didn't hold your interest?"

"Uhh, I don't know. I guess they just didn't make the game very exciting."

You nod vigorously. *Nailed it.*

On the way home, you pull out your notebook and write down the following sentence:

People need an online poker app to be exciting.

You can see it all now: high-res graphics, loud music, explosions...the most action-packed online poker game ever made. That tag line is pretty good, actually. And, hey, when you ran that "What do you want from a poker app?" survey a few months ago, "graphics" and "sound" both showed up as relatively high priorities. You are going to build the most successful online poker app ever.

Now, let's imagine you choose to take the other path.

After a round of introductions, your host asks, quite generously, "I'm not sure how familiar you are with poker. Do you want me to walk you through the rules?"

You pause for a second. You don't want these people to think that you're a total rube, but you also don't want your own assumptions about the game to get in the way of learning what the game means to *them*. Timidly, you respond, "You know, I'm actually pretty rusty. Would you mind walking me through it?"

A few people roll their eyes. You begin to feel flush (no pun intended) with embarrassment. But your host is up for it and begins explaining the rules to you as if you know absolutely nothing about poker. As your host continues walking you through the game, some of the people at the table begin exchanging knowing glances with one another and chuckling. "I'm sorry," you say, "am I missing something?" "No, no," says the person next to you, "it's just that we've been playing this game together for so long, I guess we've made up some of our own little rules along the way. If you tried to play this game the way we do with anybody else, they'd probably throw you out!" Everybody laughs.

On the way home, you pull out your notebook and write down the following sentence:

Players changed the rules of the game to meet the particular needs and expectations of their social group.

You furrow your brow for a moment. This is really different from what you heard when you ran that "What do you want from a poker app?" survey. You've uncovered something genuinely surprising—and something that might have major implications for the product you're building. You are left with a lot of questions you hadn't thought to ask previously. What role do informal rules play in card games? How is playing cards with strangers different from playing cards with friends? You aren't quite sure where these questions will lead you, but you sure are glad that you know to ask them.

Stakeholders and Users Are Different

In many ways, talking to users seems like it should be the easiest part of a product manager's job. I mean, how difficult can it be? Find some users, talk to them, and before you know it, you've got the whole "user centricity" thing in the bag. But talking to users can actually be the most difficult thing for a product manager to learn. Why? Because many of the behaviors that can help a product manager successfully work with stakeholders are exactly the wrong behaviors for learning from users.

When working with your stakeholders, you want to draw compelling connections between high-level strategy and executional details. You want to present options, explain trade-offs, and empower your stakeholders to make the best possible decisions they can. And when it comes time to make those decisions, you want specific and affirmative commitment to a path forward.

When talking to users, your goals are very, very different. Your job is not to explain, to align, or even to inform. Instead, your job is to learn as much as you can about *their* goals, their needs, and their world. Returning to our third guiding principle, this means immersing yourself in your users' reality, rather than dragging them into your company's reality. Putting this idea into practice involves less "sounding smart" than it does "playing dumb."

For many product managers, this can be a jarring transition. Product managers are often expected to have extensive knowledge about their product, their business, *and* their users. Successfully talking to and learning from users requires product managers to actively resist the temptation to provide concrete answers and specific solutions. As one product manager candidly told me after doing their first-ever round of user interviews, "That made me feel really stupid, and I understand why so many product managers don't want to do it."

The Danger of "Pitching" Your Idea in a User Feedback Session

T.R.

Product Manager, early-stage entertainment startup

Earlier in my career, I worked as the first product manager at an early-stage entertainment startup that was building a tool to help podcasters streamline the process of collaboration and publishing. It was a really cool idea with a really specific and engaged audience, and I was excited to be a part of it.

Once I got into the early product prototype, though, I was pretty confused. I had a fair amount of experience with podcasting, and the workflows that were being presented to me just didn't make a lot of sense. They felt, frankly, more like software development workflows than like podcast creation workflows. Curious as to how the product had taken this particular shape, I asked the company's founders if I could attend the next user feedback session.

Within minutes, I understood exactly what was going on. Before our user even had a chance to introduce herself, our founder was already explaining how this product was going to *revolutionize* the podcasting space. Rather than letting the user walk through the prototype herself, our founder guided her through every step, explaining exactly what was going to happen and finishing each step with a beaming "Pretty cool, right?" Needless to say, this user feedback session was deemed a grand success.

Knowing that I was not going to get very far bursting our founder's bubble—and truly believing in the core idea of the company—I asked if I could do one of my own user feedback sessions and video it for the team to review. During this session, I provided very little guidance to the user at all; I just sat him down in front of the prototype and asked him to walk me through his expectations and actions. From the outset, he really had no idea how to interact with the product—in fact, it took him a few minutes to understand what the product was even supposed to *do*.

Watching the video of this session with our founder was *not* easy. At first, he was quick to suggest that I hadn't done enough to explain the product or help the user understand its value. But at the end of the day, **you can't watch someone stare at your product in bewildered silence for nearly an hour without it having some kind of effect on you.** That moment opened up our founder to reevaluating fundamental

things about the product that he *never* would have considered if they had
come from a product manager and not an actual user.

Yes, You Need to Learn How to Talk to Users

The extent to which a product manager is explicitly tasked with doing user
research can vary enormously from organization to organization and team to
team. But informal user research happens everywhere, from friendly chats at
product conferences to "tech support" calls with family members. For that reason, it's helpful for every product manager to spend some time learning about
user research. This will set you up to get the most out of every interaction you
have with current and prospective users, whether or not those interactions are
formally considered "user research."

Over the past handful of years, I have been extraordinarily lucky to work
with some fantastic user researchers and ethnographers. My business partner,
Tricia Wang (*http://triciawang.com*), has been generous enough to mentor me
in my journey from doing bad user research ("MY AWESOME TEAM MADE
THIS SUPER COOL PRODUCT—DO YOU LIKE IT?") to doing *less bad* user
research. Her guidance has shown me, time and time again, that the only way to
improve at user research is through frequent practice and candid reflection. In
other words, I never would have gotten better at user research if I hadn't done a
whole lot of *bad* user research first.

This book is not intended to be a comprehensive guide to user research,
though I have recommended a few such guides in the "Your Checklist" section
at the end of this chapter. But in the interest of candid reflection, I'm happy to
share some of the most notable takeaways from my own experience conducting
user research:

Ask about specific instances, not generalizations.

> This one comes up a lot in books and courses about user research, and
> it remains the single most helpful on-the-ground tactic I've absorbed. In
> practice, this means that rather than asking, "What do you usually eat
> for lunch?" or "What is your favorite food?" you might use a prompt like
> "Walk me through the last meal you ate." The idea here is that a single
> concrete example will more accurately reflect your user's *reality* than a
> synthesized, abstract answer. I've found this tactic particularly useful when
> speaking to users about things like music and food, for which there might

be significant value judgments associated with certain tastes and preferences. For example, people are generally pretty quick to talk about specific instances of listening to music ("I put on the new Dua Lipa album on my last run") but freeze up instantly when you ask them about their "taste in music" or "favorite artists."

Don't get too excited if you hear what you thought you wanted to hear.

Sometimes, a user will outright volunteer the exact thing you were hoping they would say fairly early in a conversation. When I began talking to users, I would often jump in with "Wow, you know, that's exactly what we've been talking about doing! AWESOME! Thank you SO much!" It took me time—and some gentle redirection by my mentor—to see how this was in fact stopping me from getting a deeper understanding of the user's real needs. It is entirely possible that a user will describe the very solution you've been planning to build, but for entirely different reasons. If you fail to understand those reasons, you may very well build a product that fails to deliver value.

Don't ask users to do your job for you.

The story of OXO's "read from above" measuring cup is often trotted out in design-thinking workshops, and it is featured in Mark Hurst's phenomenal book *Customers Included* (*https://oreil.ly/aD7Ic*) (Creative Good). When OXO's researchers asked customers, "What do you want from a measuring cup?" they rattled off a list of reasonable-sounding features: "I want it to be sturdy! I want it to have a comfortable handle! I want it to have a smooth pour!" When those researchers asked users to actually interact with a measuring cup, they saw a consistent pattern: after filling up the measuring cup, the user would squat down next to it so that their eye was level with the reading on the side. And so, the "read from above" measuring cup was born (Figure 6-1).

This story illustrates the pitfalls of asking your users to do your job for you. If you ask users to rattle off a list of features, you might feel emboldened going back to your team and saying, "I know this is a good idea—our users specifically asked for it!" But your users are not responsible for connecting their own goals and needs with your company's unique opportunities to address those goals and needs. That is your job, not theirs.

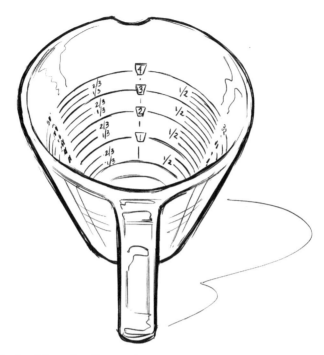

Figure 6-1. The "read from above" measuring cup

Long story short, you can always learn more about how to talk to your users. You should read books and articles about user research. You should seek out the user researchers in your organization and ask if they can mentor and guide you. Continue practicing user research, even if it doesn't come easy to you. Remain open and curious not just about learning from your users, but also about learning how to learn from your users.

Personae Non Grata

As you set about learning from your users, you will almost certainly find yourself asking, "Which users should we be thinking about in the first place?" In navigating this question, you are likely to find yourself working with "user personas": generalized profiles of different user types that are often given their own unique names and backstories. For example, interviews with 10 different small business owners might yield 2 named user personas (let's call them "Bert" and "Ernie") who represent 2 different clusters of needs and behaviors that emerged from the research.

Early on in my career as a product manager, I straight-up threw a fit when a UX designer I worked with suggested that we create some user personas: *Yeah, um, I don't have to make up a bunch of fake users because I understand our real users, thank you very much.* For all of my attempts to sabotage and undermine the efforts of my persona-peddling colleague, I actually wound up finding this tool quite helpful. Yes, we were building for "fake" people (composited from interviews with real people). But having anybody other than ourselves in mind, and having the ability to distinguish broadly between different sets of user needs, helped us make better decisions and ultimately deliver better products.

Of course, that does not mean that personas cannot be used *very badly*. Perhaps more than any other tool or technique in the product world, user personas can become a way to codify our assumptions and biases into truly harmful fictions that carry the unchecked authority of a "best practice." Here are some tips to make sure that you are not falling into these traps:

Make sure your personas are grounded in actual research.

I have a friend who is a practicing dermatologist in a midsized American city. I found out, recently, that he is also a cosmic jazz musician who once wore Sun Ra's cape on stage. Real people are complicated and surprising like that. If you are making your personas without talking to any real people, then you are likely making stereotypes, not personas. Nearly every product manager has a story of the most egregiously misogynistic, racist, or otherwise deeply problematic persona they have encountered in their work. And indeed, when your personas are grounded only in demographic-based assumptions—not in actual insights into user goals, needs, and behaviors—stereotypes are all you've got.

Refresh your personas on a regular cadence.

Products change, markets change, and people change. In my experience, teams that don't commit to refreshing their personas on a regular cadence are unlikely to refresh their personas at all. There is very little downside to frequent, planned persona refreshes; even if a robust round of research convinces you to leave your personas unchanged, you can move forward confident that those personas are up-to-date. As an added bonus, the new research you conducted will almost certainly offer up other valuable (and fresh!) insights.

Use anti-personas to be clear about who you're not building for.
It is usually more defensible to make broad personas than to make specific ones—which means you may very well wind up with a set of personas that, when taken as a whole, are little more than a stand-in for "everybody." For teams and organizations truly looking to focus their efforts, "anti-personas" —composite profiles of the people we are *not* building for—can be a powerful forcing function to get to a more productive level of specificity in day-to-day decision making. For example, if you are building a feature for "Ernie, the ambitious small-business owner investing in his dreams," you might decide to explicitly *not* build that feature for "Bert, the risk-averse small-business owner who studiously avoids overhead costs."

Given the pitfalls of user personas, there are many who now advocate for alternate approaches like Jobs to Be Done, which you can read more about in Jim Kalbach's book *The Jobs to Be Done Playbook* (Two Waves). But the same pitfalls described above—codifying assumptions, letting your work stagnate, and being too broad—can compromise any such approach.

The Siren Song of "Power Users"

Jonathan Bertfield
Product Manager, early-stage publishing startup

When I was working on an audience development tool for authors, we were very excited to get early prototypes and mock-ups in front of some real users. It seemed like we were in a great position to do so: we had great contacts in the publishing world, a well-respected leadership team, and a product that was solving a real problem for a small and well-defined user base.

We started reaching out to folks through our professional networks and were very encouraged by the response we got from some pretty high-profile authors. This was the early days of social media, and these were the folks at the forefront of using platforms like Twitter and Facebook to reach fans directly. They usually had their own employees or teams of employees managing their online presence, and they were eager for new tools. We had a clear signal that this product was destined for success.

At the same time, however, we started to hear some pretty clear dissenting voices coming from lower-profile authors and from professionals in the publishing industry. A lot of authors told us flat out, "I won't do that," and many professionals in the publishing industry were telling us, "Authors won't do the things that you are expecting them to do." But we didn't want to hear that; after all, we had more successful authors who were excited to use our product. We believed that the authors who did not think they wanted the product would change their behavior when they saw what we were offering.

This story does not have a happy ending: the startup failed. We just didn't get enough customers. **We had listened only to the people who were already successful, and those were not the actual target customers we were going after.** Those users were telling us very clearly that they did not have the time, the resources, or the understanding to do what we wanted them to do. But we chose to listen only to the people who were telling us what we wanted to hear—and when the product hit the market, we paid the price.

Product and Research: From Frenemies to BFFs

In some organizations, a product manager might be the sole designated "voice of the user." In other organizations, a product manager might be working with an extensive team of designers and researchers who are tasked with conducting exploratory interviews, developing user personas, and overseeing usability tests. In theory, product managers and researchers should be closely aligned; after all, any successful product must provide value to users, and user research is a critical tool for discovering what exactly that value might be. In practice, the relationship between product managers and researchers is often much more fraught and contentious.

Much of this tension comes from the simple fact that product managers must balance user insights with business goals, executive whims, delivery timelines, and all the other things that make "user centricity" so challenging in practice. From a researcher's point of view, this can leave product managers looking like deadline-obsessed, customer-ignoring corporate toadies.

Indeed, product managers don't always react well when presented with user insights that don't align well with their existing plans and commitments. Here are a few tips for keeping research and product better aligned.

Explain constraints calmly and fearlessly.

Researchers will often present valuable user insights to product managers, only for those product managers to dismiss them as "off-strategy," "impossible," or simply "too late" to drive any meaningful action. These dismissals are often grounded in defensiveness; when a product manager has committed to a plan, any insight that calls into question the soundness of that plan can be taken as a threat.

Rather than dismissing potentially disruptive insights out of hand, the best product managers calmly and fearlessly explain the constraints within which they are working and collaborate with researchers to explore opportunities within those constraints. Try taking a direct and open approach by saying, for example, "Thank you so much for sharing this with me. I see how this insight could shift our direction, but we've committed to delivering this feature in the next month. What opportunities do you see to incorporate what you've learned from our users into our release plan?"

Don't bury critical insights in massive slide decks.

Decks are where insights go to die. When researchers *and* product managers complain to me about insights going unheeded by executives, those insights are usually buried in massive slide decks. If an insight is truly critical, bring it up directly and do your best to explain to stakeholders how it might help them meet their goals. One research team I worked with held a monthly open-door "insights share-out" over Zoom to facilitate direct collaboration with a far-reaching group of stakeholders. This meeting involved a quick read-out of the last month's research, followed by an open conversation about how to activate that research and what new research to prioritize moving forward. Over time, these monthly meetings became a place not only for product managers and researchers to work together, but also for product managers to better understand the priorities and goals of *other product managers* by aligning around common user needs and insights.

Involve the whole team.

Researchers are often hesitant to invite product managers into their work, for fear that those product managers will ask leading questions, push predetermined solutions, or do any number of the other annoying things that *I totally did* when I was less experienced. Similarly, product managers are often hesitant to invite engineers and designers into *their* user research, for fear that those engineers and designers will speak in technical jargon, defend their existing work, or do any number of the other annoying things that engineers and designers *may very well do* as they build up their own experience. Doing research with your team can be frustrating and patience trying, but it has the twofold benefit of leveling up the research skills of everybody involved and shortening the distance between your users and the people who are actually building solutions for them. People who actively participate in user research are much more likely to actually *do* something with that research.

Product managers and researchers can often find themselves on opposite ends of the tension between user needs and business goals. But the more closely you work together, the more likely you are to navigate that tension effectively. As always, stay open, be honest, and don't take it personally.

Summary: No, Seriously, You Need to Learn How to Talk to Users

As all of these examples illustrate, talking to users is not something that comes easily or naturally to every product manager. Developing the skills needed to "live in your user's reality" often means unlearning specific behaviors that have helped you to successfully manage internal stakeholders. And it *always* means taking an open and curious approach to anyone and anything that might help you to better see the world from your users' perspective.

Your Checklist

- Talk to your users!
- Accept and acknowledge that talking to users is a real skill that takes time to develop.
- Remember that talking to users and working with stakeholders are different and require different approaches.
- Read Teresa Torres's book *Continuous Discovery Habits* (Product Talk), Mark Hurst's book *Customers Included* (Creative Good), Steve Portigal's book *Interviewing Users* (Rosenfeld), Erika Hall's book *Just Enough Research* (A Book Apart), Tomer Sharon's book *It's Our Research* (Morgan Kaufmann), and anything else that might help you improve your research skills.

- Don't try to impress users with your knowledge or expertise. Create as much space as you can for them to explain their reality to you, even if it feels like "playing dumb."

- If there are user researchers in your organization, reach out to them and ask for their help walking you through the tools and approaches that they use.

- When talking to users about their experiences, ask about specific instances rather than broad generalizations.

- Don't ask users to do your job for you! Do everything you can to understand their needs and *then* think about the specific products and features that might best address those needs.

- Make sure that any user personas (or "jobs to be done") that your team uses are grounded in actual research, and refresh them regularly.

- Don't hide critical insights in massive slide decks where they are sure to perish!

- When working with researchers, calmly and specifically describe the constraints you are working with (such as budgets, deadlines, and feature commitments) rather than shooing away insights that might threaten to derail your existing plans.

7

The Worst Thing About "Best Practices"

When I train product managers at large and small organizations alike, the first thing they usually ask for is "best practices." "How does Netflix do product management?" "How does Google define the difference between a product manager and a program manager?" "What are the things we can do to make sure we're running product like a best-in-class organization?"

These are great questions to ask, and the answers to these questions are great to know. But implicit in these questions is often an unspoken and counterproductive addendum: "How does Netflix do product management...because if we do the same thing, then surely we will become a massively successful company."

The appeal of this thinking is not difficult to understand. Given the ambiguity around the work of product management, it makes perfect sense to look for guidance from the companies that in many ways defined the discipline in its current form.

But the dangers of this thinking are a bit more insidious. Here are three particular ways in which a focus on best practices can actually make it more difficult for working product managers to succeed:

Focusing on best practices leads to an incurious mindset.
> Reducing product management to a set of repeatable best practices means wishing away all of the messy, unpredictable, and truly unavoidable human complexity that must be navigated in the role. Product managers who rely too much on best practices become deeply incurious about the people they work with—and sometimes even the product they're working on. Anyone

and anything that does not conform to the best practice becomes a threat to the one-size-fits-all approach that they are hoping will lead them to success.

Best practices bring the false promise of fairy-tale endings.
Nearly every published case study about "best practices" concludes with a business equivalent of "and they lived happily ever after," "and the business sold for a bazillion dollars," "and the company exceeded its Q4 revenue goal by $700k," or "and the team achieved 100% adoption of a scaled Agile framework." But in real-world organizations, there is no "happily ever after." The business that was sold for a bazillion dollars might be completely dismantled by its new owners, the company that exceeded its revenue goal might go out of business in a year, and the team that achieved 100% adoption of a scaled Agile framework might be using that framework to deliver completely worthless features. Life goes on, change is inevitable, and no "best practice" is ever a permanent fix.

Magical thinking around best practices inevitably leads to sadness and disappointment.
Initial conversations about best practices are often full of optimism and hope. But as these best practices inevitably run up against an organization's existing habits and rhythms, this quickly gives way to fatalism and frustration. Why aren't these best practices working for us? Whose fault is this? Who doesn't *get it*? These questions usually end with a grim and decidedly unhelpful conclusion such as "Our organization is just too hierarchical to be good at product management" or "The rest of the organization just didn't give us the support we needed to make these changes." The very things that make an organization unique wind up being seen as unstoppable impediments to change, rather than guiding the ways in which change is implemented.

None of this is to say that conversations about best practices should be avoided altogether—after all, this book is full of them! But it's important to remember that many factors go into any company's enviable success stories, including but not limited to its processes, its people, and a huge amount of good luck and good timing. Let's look at a few important things to keep in mind when learning and communicating about best practices to make sure that they become valuable resources—not broken promises.

Don't Believe the Hype

Sometimes, when I'm fielding a volley of questions about how Company X manages to be so good at product management, I'll ask people to do a simple exercise:

> *Spend five minutes using Company X's product and write down all the product issues and problems that seem obvious to you—the ones you would want to fix on day one if you wound up working there.*

The next words I hear are usually "Can I have five more minutes?" or, if I am running this exercise in person, "Do you have any more paper?" The goal here is not to leave people feeling disillusioned and defeated, or even to suggest that "best in class" companies are missing obvious flaws in their products, but rather to remind people that *every* company has its own political struggles, resource constraints, and logistical challenges. No matter how many stories you've heard about how product managers at Google are locked in a constant free-snack-driven high-five with their developer counterparts, or how product managers at Facebook are given free rein to *literally push any code change to a billion users whenever they feel like it because startups, maaaaaaan*, the day-to-day challenges that product managers at these organizations face probably look a lot like the day-to-day challenges that product managers in your organization face.

Most case studies about "best-in-class" companies are, to put it bluntly, recruiting propaganda. Companies that are competing for product and engineering talent have very little reason to paint an accurate picture of their workplace situations, let alone an even remotely negative-leaning one. If you want a more nuanced and realistic understanding of how people are navigating "best practices," talk to the working product managers in your network. Their stories will likely align much more closely with the challenges you are facing in your organization and will certainly provide more insight into the potential drawbacks and limitations of their chosen tools and techniques.

Prioritizing Product, Team, and Mental Health When Your Company Is "Doing It Wrong"

Rachel Dixon
Product Director, media company

Early in my career, I had the pleasure of joining a distributed product team that was very high trust and high collaboration. We shared responsibilities, we worked together to solve problems, and we were able to communicate openly with each other and say things like "This requirement is still a little bit unclear" without any blame or recrimination. We were empowered and autonomous, and I felt like I was a real product manager.

When I moved on to a similar role at a different company, I was a little bit horrified to find a very different situation. Even though we were all sharing a physical workspace, there was very little collaboration taking place. Engineers were treated like ticket takers, not strategic partners. We were using different tools—which, based on my previous experience, I strongly believed to be "the wrong tools." Long story short, it seemed very clear to me that this company simply did not know how to do product development, or product management, the "right" way.

I spent a lot of time stressing out about this, and that stress took a serious toll on me. I found myself in a lot of frustrating, circular conversations with company leadership about how they needed to make big changes to the way they thought about product development. But, in retrospect, none of it made our product any better or our team any stronger. I was spending a lot of time railing against the organization at large and not nearly as much time as I could have working within that organization to do right by my team and our users.

If I could go back in time and give myself any single piece of advice, it would be "Focus on the product, the team, and your mental health—and don't worry so much about whether your organization is doing product management 'the right way.'" There might be times in your career where you go from a more empowering environment to a more constrained environment. There might be times in your career where you need to completely rebuild a team's trust. There might even be times in your career where what looks like a "promotion" on paper actually feels like a step backward in terms of your responsibilities. It's natural to get lost in the downside from time to time, but this often is where the sneaky, fun part of product management happens. Long after these imperfect moments in your career, you will see how you made an impact even when you didn't feel like you were empowered to operate at your full capabilities.

Falling in Love with Reality

Whether I'm talking to the first product hire at a new startup or a senior product manager at a gigantic multinational corporation, it rarely takes long for the conversation to turn to the myriad ways in which their company isn't really doing product management the right way—or in many cases, isn't *really* doing "product management" at all. This kind of communal venting can help product managers recognize that every company has its own struggles, but it can also veer into aggrieved and paralyzing self-righteousness. After all, if your company doesn't even know what product management *is*, why bother trying to do it at all? It is very rare that "best practices" will win out over best excuses, and there is no better excuse than "My company *just doesn't get it.*"

The truth is that all organizations have some fixed constraints to work within. Those constraints might be a function of their business model, their scale, or the attitudes and experiences of their leaders. And the sooner you acknowledge and understand those constraints, the sooner you can do your best work within them. Recognizing that your particular organization's fixed constraints are unlikely to change—or at least that *you* are unlikely to change them—allows you to refocus your attention on all the things you and your team *can* do to deliver value to your users. I've come to think of this process as "falling in love with reality."

Here's a visual metaphor I've found helpful (Figure 7-1): imagine your organization as having a floor and a ceiling. The ceiling may not be as high as you'd like for it to be. It may leave you feeling claustrophobic and uncomfortable. At times, you may feel like you are contorting yourself to do things that should be easy. So you decide to focus your efforts on raising that ceiling so you have a little more room to stretch your legs and do your best work. You begin pushing *hard* for your organization to do product the "right way," until your arms are sore and you are deeply exhausted.

So, what's wrong with this picture? All that energy you're putting into raising the ceiling is energy that you are *not* putting into delivering value to your users. And while that low ceiling may very well mean that you can't deliver as much value as quickly or efficiently as you'd like, there is likely room to deliver a whole lot *more* value before you find yourself completely boxed in.

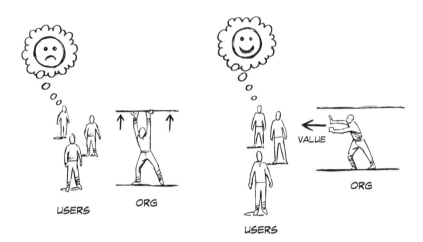

Figure 7-1. Pushing up on the organization's proverbial ceiling versus working within that ceiling to deliver value to your users. Which is more likely to deliver positive outcomes?

None of this is to say that it is never worth challenging the limits of your organization—or that constraints and limitations should be accepted uncritically. But, in my experience, the best path to expanding constraints and limitations starts by doing *the very best work you can* within them. When you have consistently run up against the limits of what you are able to accomplish on behalf of your business and its users, you will be in a much better position to help others understand and interrogate those limits.

Here's the best part: once you fall in love with reality, the work of product management gets *so much easier.* When you give up on the idea that there is such a thing as doing product management "perfectly," or even doing product management "right," you can begin to focus on how *you* do product management effectively within your own unique context and constraints. (And yes, there are always constraints.)

Frameworks and Models as Useful Fictions

Earlier in my product career (including a few times in the first edition of this very book), I found myself outright dismissing some of the fundamental tools, frameworks, and concepts of product management as too abstract, theoretical, and ill-suited to the realities of the role. The more I fell in love with the reality of product management, the less patience I had for anything that felt like an oversimplification of that reality. When folks asked me about common product management tools like business model canvases, I would respond with a snappy,

"Yeah, when was the last time a working product manager actually used a business model canvas to come up with a new business model from scratch?" Then I'd high-five myself and get on with my day.

In retrospect, this was its own kind of defensiveness and in no way helped me to become a better product manager, coach, or leader. Sure, no working product manager I know has ever used a business model canvas to fully invent a new product from scratch in a real-world organization. But many product managers I know *have* used the ideas from a business model canvas to focus and sharpen their thinking in advance of a product ideation session. Similarly, no working product manager I know has ever told me that their organization is taking a perfectly by-the-book approach to "minimum viable product," a core concept from Eric Ries's book *The Lean Startup* (Currency) that has become ubiquitous in the world of product development. But many *have* told me that the conversation around "minimum viable product" helped their organization ask some really important questions about how often they are learning from their customers and how they are defining "done enough."

Recently, I've found it helpful to think about most product management frameworks and models as *useful fictions*—with an equally generous emphasis on both words. The concept of "useful fictions" comes from the philosophical school of fictionalism, defined by Wikipedia (*https://oreil.ly/JpDZ8*) as the belief that "statements that appear to be descriptions of the world should not be construed as such, but should instead be understood as cases of 'make believe,' of pretending to treat something as literally true (a 'useful fiction')." You can read more about the concept of fictionalism at the Stanford Encyclopedia of Philosophy (*https://oreil.ly/mazeG*).

With this framing in mind, you can save yourself the trouble of asking, "Is this framework or model an accurate representation of the day-to-day work of product management?" (Spoiler alert: the answer will always be some version of "Maybe, sorta.") Instead, you can start with the understanding that *any* model or framework is necessarily a work of fiction and then ask, "What about this fiction can be useful to *me*?" This question has helped me cultivate a more open and productive relationship with some of the product management frameworks and models that I once reflexively pooh-poohed. For example, I've found the fiction of "product lifecycle frameworks" tremendously useful for facilitating an often-difficult conversation about which product and features are no longer accomplishing their goals and should be fundamentally reevaluated.

Useful fictions can help move us forward when the ambiguity and complexity of product management become overwhelming. And recognizing that they are in fact *fictions* helps us adapt "best practices" to meet the particular needs of our teams and organizations.

Scaling and Systematizing Small Steps to Make a Big Impact

Jared Yee
Product Manager, government agency

One of the most important things I've learned doing product management in both private-sector and government roles is that there's always wiggle room to improve the way you're working, even if you work at an organization that isn't doing product management "by the book." And when you patiently and generously bring your colleagues along with you, they begin to understand that there is always a step forward, and a safe step backward if unforeseen challenges emerge.

In a government context, you can't have a situation where one person leaves and the whole thing falls down. It's not about being the visionary hero who brings innovation to government, but rather about finding ways to scale and systematize every opportunity for government to better serve its constituents. **In that sense, small and obvious-seeming steps can actually have a tremendous impact.** Sometimes it's as simple as making a templatized content management system that multiple government agencies can use. Sometimes it's as straightforward as working with contractors to apply a simple set of design principles. There's always a trade-off between speed and scale, and while government work can compel you to slow down and move in baby steps, those baby steps can have an appreciable impact on lots of people's lives.

Some product people will look at a government agency and say, "They're doing it wrong! They're not empowering teams! They're still doing Waterfall!" But if your grander goal is to build technology that truly helps people, then these operational challenges are well worth navigating. You might not always be able to do things exactly the way you want, but the things you *are* able to do can have a meaningful and lasting impact on people's lives.

You Are Here

Depending on your team and organization, you might be working within a very well-understood and well-documented product development process full of "best practices," or you might be starting from scratch. Or, rather, you might *think* that you are starting from scratch. In many ways, the lack of formal process is very much a process in and of itself. Teams with zero formal structure often resist change for the same reason as teams with a *lot* of formal structure: because they've gotten used to doing things a certain way and they don't want something to upset the status quo.

Regardless of whether you are working in an organization that has a formal product development process in place or one that is using an ad hoc system, I always find it helpful to take the time to sit down and map out how products are developed at your organization right now. How do you decide what to work on next? How do you estimate how long something will take? How do you break down something on a roadmap into actual tasks that can be completed? And how do you know when something is *done?*

I've often asked folks I'm working with to grab a pen and paper and literally *draw* how their product development process currently works. These drawings (Figure 7-2) can reveal profound and unfiltered observations that would be harder to express in words, such as an angry face representing an executive, a massive gap between an engineer and a designer, or the conspicuous absence of any users or customers. If you, like me, are terrified of picking up a pen to do anything other than scrawl some borderline-incomprehensible words on a page, I highly recommend Christina Wodtke's excellent book *Pencil Me In* (Boxes & Arrows).

Even if your organization has no formal process in place, creating some visual or textual representation of the way you work together will help you communicate to your team that there *is* in fact a way that things are currently done, which will make it easier for you to evaluate how your current approach is and is not helping you achieve your goals. You should never make any changes to your process without having a clear sense of where you are and where you're going.

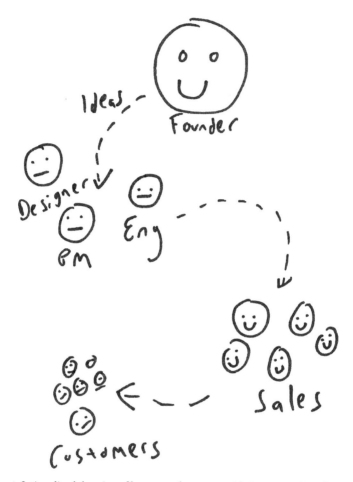

Figure 7-2. A fictionalized drawing of how a product team with "no process" works together, drawn by the author's decidedly amateur hand. What can you deduce from this visual masterpiece?

What Are You Solving For?

If you want "best practices" to deliver real-world results, you are always better off starting with the specific needs and goals of your organization and *then* thinking about practices that might help you achieve these goals. In the absence of this approach, you run the significant risk of implementing a change that is poorly understood, met with skepticism and resistance, and ultimately destined to fail.

Of course, understanding a complex set of human problems takes time— and when product managers feel pressure to "demonstrate results" quickly, there is an unfortunate tendency to rush the adoption and deployment of tools and frameworks. In an excellent essay called "The Tools Don't Matter (*https://oreil.ly/ PUblu*)," which I have often joked would make a perfect full-length tattoo sleeve, Ken Norton recommends a set of questions for shifting the conversation away from tools and frameworks and toward the underlying human issues:

- "What tools do you recommend for roadmaps?" → "How do you communicate what's coming in the future to internal and external audiences?"

- "What tool do you use for product visions?" → "How do you motivate your team around a shared future vision?"

- "What's the best tool for tracking OKRs?" → "How do you decide and communicate what's important to the company and what's not?"

- "Which do you recommend, Scrum or Kanban?" → "How do you decide what to build and what not to build?"

- "Can you recommend a wireframing tool for sharing concepts?" → "How do you communicate early product ideas?"

When working with teams and organizations to better understand their unique challenges and opportunities, I've found it helpful to start with specific examples of how these questions have been answered in the recent past. For example, everybody on a particular team might have strong opinions about how they *should* be deciding what to build and what not to build. But when you ask, "How did you decide what to build and what not to build *during your last planning meeting*," you are more likely to uncover the real issues that are affecting a team's ability to deliver against their goals.

"But This Worked at the Last Place!"

As product managers move between different organizations, they tend to amass their own set of "best practices" from past companies. These best practices are often the stories that product managers tell in job interviews: "We implemented this new Agile process and were able to hit all of our release targets for the next year" or "We started setting rigorous quarterly goals and were able to increase revenue faster than projections." When a product manager starts at a new organization, they often bring with them the expectation that whatever worked at the last place will also work at the new place.

This expectation glosses over the reality that any and all "best practices" succeed or fail for reasons that are unique to the organization in which they are implemented. Odds are, a lot of trial and error went into getting those best practices to a place where they could even be described as "best practices" in the first place. And, like it or not, that same process of trial and error, testing and learning, failing and adjusting needs to take place at *every* organization.

One of the biggest mistakes I've seen product managers make is showing up and immediately trying to make their new organization work exactly like their last organization. They implement so many changes all at once that it becomes impossible to observe and measure the effect of each individual change. And, taken as a whole, all those big new changes create big new problems.

Suppose, for example, that you have just been hired as VP of product for a distributed team that is struggling to build trust and alignment (a challenge you will read more about in Chapter 13.) In your first conversation with the CEO at your new gig, she asks if you have any ideas for how to build a healthier and more collaborative distributed product team. Thinking back to your last organization, you remember how a yearly in-person "product summit" helped build alignment and camaraderie among folks who were accustomed to communicating through video calls and chat windows. Eager to demonstrate your extensive experience and to make an impact as quickly as possible, you suggest scheduling a similar "product summit" for the following quarter. Your CEO, who always preferred doing product planning in person and hired you in no small part for your experience leading distributed teams, agrees.

A month later, you send out an email announcing COMPANYCO'S BIG PRODUCT SUMMIT, to be held for a week at a swanky hotel in an exciting locale. You expect a hero's welcome from your colleagues, who have been grumbling to you about misalignment and burnout since your first round of interviews. To your great surprise, the responses you receive range from muted to outright furious. "Thanks for scheduling this, but I think the next quarter is going to be pretty busy for me and I'd rather sit this out if I can." "Is this the best use of our budget? I was asked to let one of my best developers go last year." "Is this mandatory? No offense, but I took this job specifically so that I wouldn't have to travel." Some people seem vaguely excited, some people seem frustrated, and most people seem confused and wary. An executive from another part of the organization writes a furious email to the CEO asking why "product" is trying to further consolidate its power and influence at the expense of marketing and sales, both of which are already frozen out of critical roadmap decisions. You begin to hear rumblings that this whole thing is just a pretext for your CEO—who has often shared her nostalgia for "the days when we all just figured things out in a room together"—to roll back the product team's "work from anywhere" policy. The situation is, simply put, a big mess.

So, what went wrong? You recognized a problem, and you suggested a solution that you have seen work at another organization—and you offered an overworked team a week of free travel too! But between two organizations, the same symptom can be caused by a very different disease—and the cure for one disease might make the other much worse. Maybe the reason that this particular distributed team is struggling has nothing to do with the lack of face-to-face time but rather stems from a fundamental misalignment of goals and incentives. Maybe the "work from home" culture is newer and more tenuous here than it was at your last organization. Maybe you now have to be very careful about even using the word *product* without some people at this organization hearing it as, pointedly, "not marketing or sales."

If you don't take the time to truly understand the problem you are trying to solve, then any best practice you implement is effectively a shot in the dark. The best product managers always take time to learn about what makes an organization unique *before* they start implementing—or even suggesting—specific best practices. And when they do start implementing those best practices, they start small and build incrementally. By contrast, the worst product managers usually wind up blaming their colleagues when a fast and furious deluge of "best practices" fails to deliver the promised results. Here's a fun fact: the product managers who wind up getting frustrated because "The idiots at this company just don't understand how to do things the right way" are often the same product managers who complained about the idiots at their *last* company when they were being interviewed. Product managers who put abstract best practices above the people with whom they work tend to repeat this pattern over and over again.

A Slow and Steady Approach to Building Team Process
Ashley S.
Director of Product Management, ad tech company

When I started my job at a growing ad tech company, I was eager to apply the best practices I had used at my previous job. I showed up full of enthusiasm, ready to hit the ground running and to transform a disorganized group of high-performing individual contributors into a true software product team. And yet the team didn't seem to share my excitement. They acknowledged that they had a lot of room to improve, but they seemed deeply skeptical of the changes I was suggesting—changes that I had just seen work at another company. What was going on?

I was very lucky to have somebody on my team sit me down and say, "Think about it this way: maybe we want to start small, see what works, and then go from there." It stopped me in my tracks, and I realized, "Wow, I know better than this." I was so full of genuine enthusiasm and wanting to make things better that I was ready to roll out everything I had seen work at my last company. But everything was different now; the team was different, the needs were different, company communication was different.

So instead of trying to rebuild the approach I used at my last job, I stepped back and tried to learn where the communication problems were at my new company. I worked with my team to figure out what needed fixing and what steps we could take to make things better. We introduced changes slowly and steadily, constantly refining our approach based on what worked and what didn't work. One sprint, we would introduce daily standups. The next sprint, we would tweak the way we did our release notes. Slowly but surely, we built up a process that helped the product team collaborate and deliver better products.

So much of being a product manager is about going through the pieces that you think will work and then feeling the pain when they don't work as intended. Once you know where the pain points are, you can start making adjustments. It's not about changing everything all at once, and it's not about forcing a team to work in a certain framework or adopt a certain set of rituals. **It's about really just iterating on your process constantly. When it doesn't work, you figure out why it doesn't work, and you try something else. It's always a process to get to your process.**

Working with the "Process Averse"

As we discussed earlier in this chapter, there is really no such thing as "no process"—but there certainly *are* people who self-identify as "process averse" or, to be more specific and generous, "not terribly excited about process that might seem unduly heavy or arbitrary." The colloquial wisdom among product managers is that these people tend to be engineers, but I've encountered the same general degree of self-professed process aversion from designers, marketers, and even other product managers.

In practice, navigating a general aversion to process or "too much process" often goes like this: you identify a change you think would be worth making, you propose that change to a group of people, and one or more members of that group rattle off a compelling list of all the reasons why your proposed change will lead to *terrible, horrible things*. (I once proposed to my team a minor change in the way we handled incoming requests from account managers, only to be told that this change would surely result in *nothing less than the complete destruction of our autonomy and self-determination*.) After a few minutes of litigating these things, you find it easier to just give up altogether and walk away with some good will from your team (hopefully) left intact. You may even find yourself thinking, "Well, I *tried*, and if the people on my team don't want to make things better, that's now officially *their* problem."

This is yet another situation where staying off the defensive can lead you to much better outcomes. If you set about to "defend" your proposed process changes from those who would "attack" them, you are setting up an intrinsically adversarial situation—and one in which "let's just keep doing what we've always done" usually feels like the safer and easier conclusion.

Here are a few approaches I've used in my work to more successfully navigate working with folks who might reflexively resist or attack any changes to the way a team works together:

Enlist the most process averse as your early advisors and let them shape your ideas.

> If you are proposing process changes to a group that involves one or more process-averse individuals, you are setting yourself up for a world of hurt— *unless* you've already talked to those process-averse individuals and invited them to review and shape your ideas. I like to schedule time with these folks before I've written down anything definitive or even committed to any particular language or terminology. As trivial as it may seem, giving somebody the opportunity to shape the naming and framing of a "best practice" can go a long way toward helping them feel valued and recognized.

Openly acknowledge and document all those terrible, horrible things that might happen.

> When you're operating from a defensive position, your impulse might be to dismiss your colleagues' fears and concerns as alarmist nonsense. But when you engage openly with those fears and concerns, you may discover

that you have a lot to learn from them. After all, your colleagues' specific experiences are always going to be different from yours. It's entirely possible that somebody you work with has seen your favorite "best practice" backfire for a reason you have yet to experience, and understanding that reason will be hugely helpful to you and your team. Through these conversations with process-averse early advisors, I often compile a collaborative FAQ where the team's concerns can be documented and addressed openly.

Frame everything as an experiment, not a certainty.

One of the most powerful ways to redirect your team's fears around changes to your shared process is to acknowledge that nobody really has *any idea* what will happen until it happens. Simply stating, "Yeah, that may very well happen! Let's treat this as an experiment and see how it's going in a few weeks," can help people feel safe to try new things. If your team is working in an Agile environment and retrospecting on a regular cadence (we'll discuss this more in the next chapter), you may very well already have the time and space set aside to evaluate the results of these experiments together.

Focus on things you can do "next time" rather than trying to make changes "this time."

There are rarely times in the world of product development when people aren't stressing about a deadline, an impending product launch, or something else coming up on the short-term horizon. As tempting as it may be to propose process changes for in-flight work—after all, what could be more relevant and impactful than improving the way your team approaches *the work it is doing right now*—you are not going to get very far when people are scrambling to get something out the door. I've generally found it more fruitful to expand your horizon and start thinking about how you can bring some new ideas to the *next* sprint, launch, or project.

When you give up your defensive posture and enlist the process averse as partners in addressing your team's challenges, you may be surprised at how helpful their insights and experiences can be. The very concerns and hypotheticals that once seemed like challenges to your best-laid plans may very well help your team avoid missteps that you had never even thought to consider.

The Best Thing About Best Practices

There is one particularly great thing about best practices that can serve as a crucial first step toward making positive change in an organization: because best practices often come with the halo of authority from a well-respected organization, it is much easier to get people to give them a try. Saying, "Let's try this weird thing where we write out three to five goals for the quarter and then also measure some things and call the things we measure 'results' even though they're actually more like 'indicators,'" will probably not get you far. But saying, "Let's try out the Objectives and Key Results framework, which they've used with great success at Google" sounds pretty reasonable.

Summary: A Place to Start, Not a Guarantee

Just remember: best practices are a place to start, not a guarantee of success. Keep a close eye on what is working for you and what can be improved and refined. And, above all else, keep the goals of any best practice you use in mind so that you have a clear sense of what "working" means in the first place.

Your Checklist

- Approach best practices as a place to start, not a prescriptive one-size-fits-all solution.
- Ask yourself how a particular best practice might help your team deliver value to your business and its users, instead of just how it will change the way you work.
- If you're curious about how a particular company approaches product management, try to find some people who have actually worked there and ask them.
- Take the time to truly understand the goals and needs of your organization before rushing to implement any particular best practices.
- When you encounter an abstract framework or best practice, treat it as a "useful fiction" and ask: "What about this fiction could be useful to my particular team at this particular moment?"
- Reframe tool-related and framework-related questions as broader, outcome-oriented questions. Then start with specific examples of how those questions have been answered in the recent past.

- Use a "slow and steady" approach to implementing best practices so that you can test and measure the impact of every incremental change.
- Avoid the temptation to solve the problems that seem the most familiar to you, as opposed to the problems that are having the most impact on your team and your users.
- Enlist the "process-averse" folks on your team early, working with them to openly address and document fears and concerns.
- Approach any new best practices as time-bound experiments rather than permanent changes.
- Expand the horizon to focus on future-facing change rather than trying to adjust in-flight work.
- Utilize the "organizational halo" effect of best practices to get buy-in to trying new things, but be prepared to continuously adjust course based on what is working and what is not working.

8

The Wonderful, Horrible Truth About Agile

First: a hearty and heartfelt hello to those of you who picked up this book and skipped immediately to this chapter. For many product managers—especially those whose job description skews more toward scrum master or Agile product owner, navigating the finer points of Agile processes can seem like the sum total of one's job. There are countless books, manuals, and step-by-step guides out there to implementing the Agile framework of your choice, whether it is Scrum or XP or a scaled framework like SAFe or LeSS.

This book is not one of them. Regardless of how orthodox, prescriptive, and by-the-book you are in your implementation of Agile, you can't process-ize out the human complexity of product management. Regardless of which Agile (or non-Agile) processes and practices you choose to implement, you still need to connect, communicate, and collaborate. The wonderful truth about Agile is that it revolves around a set of values that reinforce and strengthen the connective work of product management. The horrible truth about Agile is that the work of implementing these values is never truly done, requiring constant reflection and refinement.

This chapter focuses on strategies and approaches that will help guide you through the successful implementation of *any* practices, processes, and frameworks that could fall under the broad banner of Agile. And if you are not working for a team or organization that has chosen to operate under that banner, it just might help you bring some of the best ideas from the Agile movement into your ostensibly non-Agile environment.

Debunking Three Common Myths About Agile

Over the past two decades, the word *Agile* has gone from a tactical distinction among software developers to an inescapable nugget of business jargon. Before we talk about the specific history of Agile and how we can use its core values and principles in our work, let's look at a few common myths and misconceptions about Agile that I've encountered many, many times:

Agile is a rigid and prescriptive methodology.

Fun fact: Agile is not really a methodology at all. As we will discuss, Agile is a *movement* that began when people who had worked on multiple software development frameworks and methodologies came together to discuss the common values expressed in their respective approaches. Many practices that are implemented under the guise of "doing Agile" actually run fundamentally counter to these values.

Agile is a way to do more work, faster.

On numerous occasions, I have stood in meetings while executives describe Agile as a way to "increase our output" or "get things done quicker." If I could capture the looks on the faces of experienced engineers during these meetings, I would be happy to simply present them as the entirety of this chapter and call it a day. Agile is not a matter of working more or of working faster, but rather of working differently. In fact, following the core values of Agile often means slowing down, at least momentarily, to reflect on how we currently work and how we could work better.

The Agile framework/approach used by your organization determines the shape (and often impact) of your work as a product manager.

Different Agile methodologies and frameworks often carry different titles, team structures, and day-to-day practices. But, as we discussed in Chapter 1, no title or job description can definitively resolve the intrinsic ambiguity of product work. While the particular framework we use might change *how* we do our day-to-day work, it does not in any way relieve us of the responsibility to deliver value to our business and our users— even when, as we will soon discuss, our company seems more focused on "doing Agile the right way" than on actually doing the right thing.

Turning to the Agile Manifesto

The Agile movement kicked off in earnest in 2001, when a group of 17 software developers gathered at a ski resort in Utah to discuss alternatives to the "documentation driven, heavyweight software development processes" of the day. The resulting Agile Manifesto (*https://oreil.ly/hsYOO*) reads, in its entirety, as follows:

> *We are uncovering better ways of developing software by doing it and helping others do it. Through this work we have come to value:*
>
> *Individuals and interactions over processes and tools*
>
> *Working software over comprehensive documentation*
>
> *Customer collaboration over contract negotiation*
>
> *Responding to change over following a plan*
>
> *That is, while there is value in the items on the right, we value the items on the left more.*

It is worth taking the time to read this over thoroughly. More than once, I've had it taped up over my desk as a team with which I'm working begins to explore Agile principles and practices. Fundamentally, Agile is not about following a single prescriptive set of rules; rather, it is about designing and implementing practices that align with a set of values. Core to these values is the embrace of human uniqueness and complexity. Truly valuing individuals means looking beyond titles and org charts to understand the actual people with whom you're working. Processes and tools can help facilitate our connection with those people, but they cannot *replace* that connection.

It is also worth noting that the Agile Manifesto's preamble pointedly states that its authors *are uncovering* better ways of developing software—not that they have *already uncovered* these ways and are just now thinking to share it with us less enlightened souls. In a very real sense, all of us developing software and helping others do it (the latter being a fairly solid definition of *product management*) are active participants in the process of uncovering new and better ways of working, not passive recipients of some sacred text dreamed up on a ski weekend two decades ago.

From Manifesto to Monster

Those who have spent a good deal of time navigating the world of Agile soft-ware development and "Agile business transformation" might note the irony of the Agile Manifesto's explicit call to value "individuals and interactions over processes and tools." In the years since the Agile Manifesto's signing, the Agile ecosystem has become a dizzying Lovecraftian swirl of frameworks, practices, tools, and certifications. This irony is not lost on many of the people who actually wrote the Agile Manifesto. Back in 2015, Manifesto signer Andy Hunt wrote a blog post called "The Failure of Agile (*https://oreil.ly/HuwWb*)" that lays out his perspective on how a set of inspiring ideas got turned into a prescriptive ideology that fundamentally violates its own core values:

> In the 14 years since [the Agile Manifesto], we've lost our way. The word "agile" has become sloganized; meaningless at best, jingoist at worst. We have large swaths of people doing "flaccid agile," a half-hearted attempt at following a few select software development practices, poorly. We have scads of vocal agile zealots—as per the definition that a zealot is one who redoubles their effort after they've forgotten their aim. And worst of all, agile methods themselves have not been agile. Now there's an irony for you.

Hunt goes on to describe why he feels that the Agile methodology has been so badly misinterpreted:

> Agile methods ask practitioners to think, and frankly, that's a hard sell. It is far more comfortable to simply follow what rules are given and claim you're "doing it by the book." It's easy, it's safe from ridicule or recrimina-tion; you won't get fired for it. While we might publicly decry the narrow confines of a set of rules, there is safety and comfort there. But of course, to be agile—or effective—isn't about comfort.

My intent in sharing this is not to insist that "I liked Agile's first album bet-ter" but rather to note that even the people who came up with this stuff are well aware that simply "doing Agile" is in no way a guarantee of success. Again, we return to our first guiding principle: clarity over comfort. It is always worth keep-ing in mind that clarity does not mean absolute unflinching certainty. Achieving and maintaining clarity is ongoing, difficult, and at times deeply uncomfortable work. At its best, Agile provides us with a way to value and protect that work. But

Agile won't get us very far if we turn to it only for certainty, for absolutism, for "the right way to do things" regardless of the specific individuals involved.

Rediscovering Alistair Cockburn's "Heart of Agile"

The tragedy of Agile's "sloganization" is that many of the practices used in Agile software development really can help us enact its stated values. Alistair Cockburn, another signer of the Agile Manifesto, responded to what he called the "overly decorated" state of modern Agile by distilling the entirety of Agile practices and processes into four actions at the "Heart of Agile" (*https://oreil.ly/sUyhQ*):

- Collaborate
- Deliver
- Reflect
- Improve

Cockburn explains how the simplicity of these four actions provides a needed counterpoint to the jargon-heavy discourse around modern Agile practices:

> *The nice thing about these four words is that they don't need much explanation. They don't need much teaching. With the exception of "Reflect," which is done all too little in our times, the other three are known by most people. You know if you're doing them or not. So simply saying, "Collaborate. Deliver. Reflect. Improve." already says most of what you need to say and do.*

These four actions provide a bridge between the values of the Agile Manifesto and the practices that come with specific Agile frameworks and methods. They get to the very, well, heart of what makes a truly Agile approach different from other ways of working—whether those ways of working are ostensibly called "Agile" or "Waterfall" or some portmanteau-riffic hybrid of the two. And, most importantly, they provide a simple and plainspoken prompt for teams to evaluate whether they are truly living up to the Agile movement's underlying principles.

One of my very favorite things about Agile—and about Cockburn's "Heart of Agile" in particular—is that it contains within it the blueprint for its own success. If you are taking time to truly reflect and improve, then wherever you start, you will wind up somewhere better. The single biggest mistake I've seen organizations make when implementing any kind of Agile process is to take an all-or-nothing approach in which a framework or set of practices is implemented and then declared an outright failure when it does not work perfectly right away. If, per Cockburn's actions, you don't take the time to reflect on the way you're working and improve the things that don't work, then *any* Agile practices will stagnate, fall into disrepair, and ultimately fail.

Agile and the "Proprietization of Common Sense"

The most eye-opening thing I've ever read about Agile wasn't actually about Agile at all; rather, it was in a book about the history of medical quackery. In his book *Bad Science* (Farrar, Straus, and Giroux), journalist Ben Goldacre describes a concept he calls the "proprietization of common sense":

> *You can take a perfectly sensible intervention, like, a glass of water and an exercise break, but add nonsense, make it sound more technical, and make yourself sound clever. This will enhance the placebo effect, but you might also wonder whether the primary goal is something more cynical and lucrative: to make common sense copyrightable, unique, and owned.*

In other words, it's hard to sell a lot of books telling people to drink enough water and exercise regularly—and it's hard to sell a lot of consulting hours telling product teams to adjust course more frequently and work together more closely.

The bottom line about Agile—and the reason why I'm so consistently drawn to simple and plainspoken approaches like Cockburn's—is that most of what it tells us to do is pretty much common sense. If you want to change the way your team works? Reflect and make the change together. If you want to get more value into the hands of your users? Deliver working software more frequently.

Similarly, the reasons why Agile *doesn't* work often have more to do with common sense than with fiddly distinctions between frameworks. For executives who are used to control and predictability, the notion of "responding to change over following a plan" can be scary. For teams who have historically enjoyed working on large projects with minimal day-to-day scrutiny, frequent releases can seem like a terrible idea. These are human issues, and talking candidly and nondogmatically about them will always be more fruitful than chiding others for not "getting it."

Setting Expectations When Transitioning from Waterfall to Agile

Noah Harlan
Founder and partner, Two Bulls (*https://www.twobulls.com*)

Before we adopted Agile, we were working in a very "Waterfall" way, starting each project with these huge spreadsheets that listed out every feature we intended to build. When we were working this way, our clients tended to feel great on day one of a project. Everything felt very certain and very finite: "In four months, we'll have our product, and we know exactly what it will be!" For some bigger products, this could even be a year or two years. But a lot can change in a year or two years, or even a month. Competitors change, technology changes, regulatory environments change. Apple might release a new version of iOS that breaks a finished product right after you launch it. That feeling of comfort and certainty naturally starts to decline when you go about building products in the real world.

Adopting Agile practices meant that those initial conversations with clients had to change pretty dramatically. Rather than haggling over how many features we could build within a client's budget, we explained to them that we would start down a certain path, track our velocity, show them the work every two weeks, and allow them to work *with* us on changing, adding, or subtracting features as the product took shape. We got a lot of responses like "Yeah, but how much does it cost, and when will I get it?" At first, we struggled to answer those questions. But now that we've been working in Agile for a number of years, we have a much clearer sense of what can be accomplished in a given timebox, and we can provide some fence posts along the way. With Agile, you constantly refine and explore the delta between your estimated velocity and the reality of your work, which is actually much more powerful than trying to predict it all at the beginning (Figure 8-1).

Working in Agile, our team feels more like *your* team. As the project goes on, it becomes clearer and clearer that our interests are truly aligned. With Agile, our profit is maximized by you being successful and continuing to develop the product, whereas the end of a Waterfall project is us trying to maintain our profitability by limiting the number of things you can squeeze in and limiting the warranty. **Though Waterfall projects may provide your clients with a seductive sense of certainty at the beginning of a project, they set you down an**

inherently adversarial path. Working in Agile, we've been able to collaborate much more closely with our clients and deliver better products.

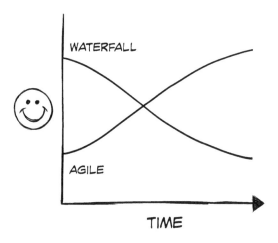

Figure 8-1. Happiness over time in Agile and Waterfall projects

When Doing Agile "Right" Makes Things Worse

Depending on the specifics of their role, a product manager might have more or less direct authority over the Agile frameworks, methods, and practices used by their team and organization. But it is critical to remember that reflecting upon and improving Agile practices is, itself, an Agile practice. Even if you see yourself as simply being a passive practitioner of Agile, making sure your team works well together is always part of your job.

Thankfully, most Agile methodologies and frameworks include a ceremony intended to help you do this very thing: a "retrospective" in which the team reflects on how it is working together and commits to changes moving forward. Several books have been written solely on the topic of running effective retrospectives, and I highly recommend Esther Derby and Diana Larsen's *Agile Retrospectives: Making Good Teams Great* (Pragmatic Bookshelf) as a place to start.

In theory, having a conversation with your team about what's working well and what's not working well should be pretty straightforward. In practice, I've been surprised at how many teams—including my own teams—never bothered to discuss what constitutes "working well" in the first place, beyond "we're doing the Agile thing the way we think you're supposed to do the Agile thing." Whether or not you incorporate them into a formal retrospective, I've found that the following two questions are a great place to start any conversation about a particular Agile ceremony or ritual:

- What are the goals of this particular Agile ceremony or ritual?
- On a scale of 1–10, to what extent do we think that this ceremony or ritual is achieving its goals?

I've often deployed that second question "scrum poker" style, asking everybody on my team to privately write down their answer and then share their answer with the group at the count of 10. This approach minimizes groupthink and often reveals a fairly alarming range of answers, especially around rituals like the daily standup that can be much more valuable to those receiving information than to those reporting information.

Unsurprisingly, asking "why" about a given Agile ritual can feel like opening a can of slippery and disruptive worms. I once worked with a product manager at a financial services company who had been told that his primary responsibility was to maintain and "groom" a backlog of user stories (short descriptions of things that the product team could build to deliver value to its users). But over time, this product manager began to suspect that this backlog was becoming a dumping ground for stale, company-centric, and completely untested ideas. Sure, his team was technically writing out user stories, but these stories were starting to feel less like descriptions of actual user problems and more like the executive-mandated, years-long project plans that the team was trying to move away from.

After months of creeping discomfort, this product manager asked his team, "Do we think that the backlog is actually helping us stay user centric?" The designers and engineers on his team froze. Were they allowed to say what they were all thinking? Could they question the orthodoxies of the scaled Agile framework they were using? Was this product manager actually a cop? (He has to tell them if he's a cop!) Sensing that the team needed to see some swift and decisive action, this product manager *physically destroyed* his team's backlog and declared, "If we're not hearing about it from our users, I don't want us to waste another second thinking about it here."

I recognize that such extreme actions are not always possible, or advisable. But creating and protecting time to retrospect and ask these occasionally scandalous-seeming questions is critical if you want your team to feel any sense of real accountability and control over the way you work together. I've seen many product managers either half-ass the retrospective or omit it altogether because it does not involve actually producing software. Often, this is because the team has been given a mandate to "do more work in less time," so anything that does not involve cranking out code is seen as inefficient. This might feel like a defensible short-term optimization, but it has serious ramifications in the longer term. Without making time to reflect and refine your process, you may wind up depleting your team's morale in deference to made-up ceremonies and rituals that are ultimately delivering zero value to your business or your users.

When Doing Agile "Wrong" Makes Things Better

So you've realized that doing Agile "by the book" is potentially leading your team astray, or at least failing to fully deliver on your shared goals. Congratulations! Any time you've found a specific, identifiable disconnect between what you're *trying* to do and what's *actually happening*, you've found an opportunity to improve the way that your team works together.

For example, many teams I've worked with have come to the realization—as did the product manager in our last story—that the "user stories" they are writing are not compelling them to actually *speak with* or *learn from* their users. Different teams have chosen to address this disconnect in different ways. Some have started formally requiring a link to a user interview or research report in every user story. Some have decided that user stories should be written by the entire team together, and only immediately after conducting user interviews. (Again, I highly recommend Teresa Torres's *Continuous Discovery Habits* for further reading on how product teams can conduct discovery interviews together.) Some teams have come to the difficult conclusion that the user-story format is not a great fit for the work they're currently doing and have chosen to capture planned work in a different way.

When changing your team's Agile practices and ceremonies, I've found it very helpful to document the reason behind the change, the nature of the change itself, and the intended purpose of the change. I recommend creating a simple template for capturing such changes, which might include the following prompts:

- We've been doing the following Agile practice or ceremony:

- ...because we thought it would help us achieve the following goals:

- Here's what actually happened:

- So, for the next iteration of work, we are changing it in this way:

- We hope that making this change will help us achieve our goals in the following ways:

This template provides an opportunity for you to tie back any changes you make to the goals you've aligned on with your team. It also lets you explicitly track the difference between what you think a new practice or ceremony will accomplish and what happens when you implement that practice or ceremony. This template accounts for the fact that *no* Agile practice or ceremony will ever go exactly according to plan and creates room for you to continuously reevaluate your approach.

As you embark upon this journey of continuous improvement, you might find yourself changing some things that feel like immovable orthodoxies of Agile software development. That is totally fine. Nearly every product manager I've worked with has at some point made a major change to Agile sacraments like the daily standup meeting or the writing of user stories. In keeping with the guiding principle of living in our user's reality, our users don't know or care how well we are adhering to the rules of an Agile methodology or how well-groomed our backlog might be. If our ways of working do not help us deliver better outcomes for our users, then we should not be beholden to those ways of working.

Killing the Daily Standup
A.J.
Product Manager, enterprise analytics startup

When I started working as a product manager, I didn't know all that much about Agile processes. But as the company grew, it became clear that the ad hoc system we were using to build products wasn't working very well. I picked up a few books about Agile and Scrum, and I turned to a few developers in the organization who had experience with Agile development.

One thing that every book and person seemed to agree on was that we needed to have something called a "daily standup meeting." For anyone who has not worked in Agile software development, this is a meeting, usually at the beginning of the day, where everybody on the product development team stands up and says what they've completed since the last standup, what they're working on, and what is currently blocking them. So, as a very first step toward building out an Agile process, I started holding daily standup meetings with my team.

These meetings were...not great. They felt kind of like elementary school book reports, with everybody grudgingly standing up and reading off a list of what they had done. One of the developers I worked with started referring to the daily standup as the "What have you done for the company lately?" meeting. I knew that the meetings weren't working well, but I had no idea what to do about it. Everybody agreed that you needed a daily standup to "do Agile." And as a relatively junior product manager, I was certainly in no position to assume that I knew better.

There was one developer on my team who always seemed particularly averse to the daily standup meeting. He would show up late, roll his eyes, and just generally be a pain about it. Ironically, it was this very developer who wound up giving me the courage to reevaluate whether the standup was working for our team. During one particularly drab Monday morning standup, he remarked that he had been blocked on something "since Friday afternoon." The developer who had been blocking him offered, sincerely, "Why didn't you tell me?" He responded, "Because that's what this meeting is for."

That exchange helped me understand that the daily standup meeting was actually doing the exact opposite of what it was supposed to do. And furthermore, it helped me understand that I had never taken the time to talk with my team about what it was supposed to do in the first place. **The meeting that was supposed to help people get unblocked had actually been giving people an excuse to stay blocked.** After talking it over with the team, we decided to kill the daily standup; if anybody was blocked, it was their job to jump on our team chat and say what was blocking them immediately. It wasn't "by the book" Agile, but it wound up doing what the "by the book" practice hadn't done for our specific team.

Seven Conversations About Agile I Never Want to Have Ever Again

Over the last decade, I have wasted untold hours of my life having maddening debates about Agile with sad-eyed people in windowless conference rooms. I cannot get this time back, but I can share these conversations with you in the hope that you can cut these conversations short and get on with your life:

"Product managers working in [Agile framework] aren't real product managers!"

As more enterprises have adopted scaled Agile frameworks, I've heard more dismissals of product managers working within those frameworks as "glorified project managers" or "not doing strategic work" or even "not *real* product managers." I hate this, not only because it gives these product managers an excuse to do shoddy work and blame it on a framework, but also because I've seen project managers, program managers, and other people in supposedly "nonstrategic" roles do *incredibly* valuable, important, and strategic work.

"We can't really do Agile because we're [a regulated industry/an enterprise/a startup/too big/too small]."

One reason I keep returning to the Heart of Agile is that it (hopefully) short-circuits some of these often-pointless conversations. Even if we can't do Agile-that-looks-like-a-diagram-of-Agile-you-found-on-the-internet-Agile, what opportunities do we have to collaborate, deliver, reflect, and improve? If you believe in the underlying principles of the Agile movement, there's always a path forward. (For what it's worth, I've found it's sometimes easier to introduce these principles without dropping the A-word at all, to minimize the amount of historical baggage carried into these conversations.)

"Even if [some part of an Agile ritual that is part of an Agile framework] isn't working for you, you can't change it or you're not really doing [Agile framework] anymore."

If a unicorn loses its horn, is it just a horse? If a pegacorn becomes incapable of flight, is it still a pegacorn? These are all made-up things, and I'm not particularly sympathetic toward any suggestion that a team should continue doing a made-up thing that is causing real-world harm.

"Agile is outdated! We need a new Agile Manifesto. Or we have to reframe it as the [Your Word Here] Manifesto!"

Believe me, I've gotten pretty deep into this one before. (My sincere apologies if I talked your ear off about how "What we really need is *elastic* organizations" circa 2018.) But here's the thing: any set of ideas that grows popular enough to challenge the status quo will ultimately be co-opted by the status quo. If the "next thing" catches on like Agile, we'll be right back to saying that we need *another* "next thing." That said, I am fully supportive of any team or organization choosing to rewrite the Agile Manifesto to meet their own specific needs or to reflect their own unique perspectives.

Since you are "developing software...and helping others do it," it's *your* Manifesto too.

"Agile certifications are silly and ridiculous."

I have observed (and been unfortunately complicit in) a tendency among long-time tech workers to dismiss certifications and those who seek them out. Does the idea of being "certified" in a movement rooted in 68 words about the inevitability of change seem a little ridiculous? Sure. But people who seek out certification have taken a genuine interest and made a serious commitment to learning something—and it's very hard to see that as a negative.

"Agile is the worst! Let's talk about how terrible Agile is!"

Assuming that Agile will make everything worse is no more nuanced or helpful than assuming that Agile will make everything better. Though the text of this chapter may not show it, even "fake Agile" bashing has lost some of its luster for me in the last several years. The less we ascribe intrinsic positivity or negativity to the almost absurdly broad set of things called "Agile," the more room (and responsibility) we give ourselves to actually make all this stuff work.

Yes, the wide world of Agile can be overwhelming, and it can lead to some truly infuriating, circular, pointless debates. At the very least, I hope you can acknowledge that these debates are likely not going to have any appreciable impact on the quality of the work your team delivers. (Or, at the very, very least, I hope you can drop a solid question about pegacorns into your next debate about the finer points of Agile methods and practices.)

Summary: Ambiguity Lives Here Too

With all of its frameworks, methods, and "best practices," Agile might seem like a way to bring standardization to a role riddled with ambiguity. But at its heart, Agile is *all about* learning to respect and embrace uniqueness—of individuals, of interactions, and of the inevitable curveballs that will lead you away from your best-laid plans and into the great unknown.

Your Checklist

- Avoid vague and misleading jargon around Agile—say exactly what you intend to do and why you intend to do it.

- Spend some time digesting (and socializing) the core values and principles of the Agile movement and remember that you are an active participant in carrying this movement forward.

- Create and protect time and space to retrospect with your team, even—especially!—when time and space are hard to come by.

- Make sure your team has explicitly discussed the purpose behind any Agile practice or ceremony that it has adopted and that it is regularly reflecting on how well that practice or ceremony is achieving its purpose.

- Document process changes along with their intended goals so that there is clarity around what people are doing and why.

- Don't let user-centric Agile rituals serve as a stand-in for actually talking to your users.

- Remember that following the rules of an Agile framework is no guarantee that you are delivering value to your business or your customers.

- Resist the temptation to seek absolute role clarity and definition from any Agile framework; remember that product work always involves navigating some ambiguity.

- Be wary of any declaration that a particular framework or practice is "always good" or "always bad."

- If you feel that your organization is becoming too zealous about Agile, feel free to print out a whole bunch of blog posts by people who actually wrote the Agile Manifesto, describing how Agile zealotry has derailed the movement they started.

9

The Infinite Time Suck of Documentation (and Yes, Roadmaps Are Documentation)

Many of the most impactful things we do as product managers are also the least tangible. The most meaningful contributions we make to our team are often manifest in the miscommunications that we resolve, the conversations that we redirect toward our high-level goals, and the tactical trade-offs that we explain to company leadership. But none of these things provide a quick, easy, and material answer to that anxiety-provoking question we considered toward the beginning of this book: "What exactly did *you* do, anyway?"

It is for this very reason that I spent so much of my product management career crafting comprehensive and (hopefully) impressive product specs, road-maps, and many, many PowerPoint decks. Every fancy document I created was something I could point to and say, "Look—I did *this thing*!" But very few of these fancy documents were actually helping my team achieve its goals.

None of which is to say that documentation is intrinsically bad. Quite the opposite: writing good documentation is a critical part of a product manager's job. The day-to-day challenge is to understand what exactly makes documentation "good" in the first place and to recognize that "good" and "impressive" are not always the same thing. In this chapter, we will look at how we can make documentation more useful by spending *less* time on it. And we'll start with the final boss of documentation: the roadmap.

"The Product Manager Owns the Roadmap!"

I recently had coffee with a friend of mine who had just started working as a product manager at a large education company. A few weeks prior, he had attended a training for new product managers that was intended to provide him with more clarity on what would be expected of him in his new role. In walking through the high-level responsibilities that participants could expect to fall on their shoulders, the trainer stated, "The product manager owns the roadmap." My friend—whose willingness to ask an uncomfortable question speaks to his skill as a product manager—interjected, "What about product manager roles where you don't own the roadmap?" The trainer, genuinely confused by this question, responded, "No. The product manager *owns* the roadmap." My friend did not press further.

Yes, in theory, the product manager often "owns" the roadmap. But in practice, that ownership is never easy, absolute, or uncontested. In fact, the product managers who seek absolute and unilateral "ownership" of the roadmap *as a document* are the very ones who prove least effective at helping their teams deliver the actual *software* described in that roadmap.

Here's an example of how this might play out. You recently started as a product manager at a medium-sized software company, and you're eager to step up to all the big responsibilities that were listed in the job description. So you begin putting together a new roadmap for your team. You know that this is a make-or-break moment for you, and you are genuinely worried that if you let too many people contribute to the roadmap, you won't be demonstrating the level of absolute accountability that is expected of you. So you are *very* careful about who has access to the roadmap as a work in progress slowly and selectively incorporating suggestions and ideas until you've crafted something that seems... well, perfect.

Finally, the time comes to present your masterpiece. You gather your team together and unveil the beautifully formatted, impeccably researched roadmap that you've been meticulously crafting for the last month. As you finish your presentation, you are absolutely beaming. "I'm very confident that this roadmap will help us achieve, or even exceed, our team's goals for the next quarter. Any questions?"

To your surprise, you're met with a kind of tense, frustrated silence. One of the engineers on your team chimes in, with an exhausted tone in her voice: "Um, yeah, there are few things on that roadmap that would probably take us way more than a quarter to build. How do we plan to approach that?" You pause. "Oh, um, yes, well, um, I'm sure we'll be able to figure that out!" More tense silence. Another engineer chimes in, "Have you talked to any other product managers about this? I can already see a number of dependencies that we'd need to address in order to deliver against any of this." Again, you pause. "Uhhhh...not yet but, again, I'm sure we'll be able to figure it out!!!" More tense silence and a few raised eyebrows. Uh-oh.

In the weeks that follow, you do your best to adjust the roadmap based on feedback from your team, but much of the damage is already done. You've lost credibility with the engineers who need to *build* the things you were quick to put into your beautiful document. And, to make matters even worse, you now find yourself in the position of constantly redelivering your roadmap to an increasingly skeptical team. You start to fall into a circuitous and exhausting pattern: you present the newest version of the roadmap, your team tells you why it won't work, and you go back to the drawing board. This cycle sure is keeping you busy, but, in the meantime, your team isn't actually delivering much of anything.

The best product managers treat roadmaps the same way they treat all documentation: as a helpful conversation starter for their team rather than a sacred monument to their own hard work and importance.

It's Not the Roadmap, It's How You Use the Roadmap

One of the best pieces of advice I ever received as a working product manager was to think of roadmaps as a strategic communication document, not as a hard-and-fast plan for what will be executed and when. Unfortunately, I immediately misinterpreted this advice to mean that *everybody already understood* that the roadmap was not a hard-and-fast plan for what will be executed and when. This got me into hot water more than once, as I had to explain to various stakeholders (ranging from engineers to [clears throat] board members) that the roadmap I had provided did not actually reflect what my product team was planning to build but was just, you know, a helpful conversation starter for the team. After all, somebody really smart told me that a roadmap isn't a promise but rather a strategic communication document. Didn't everyone get the memo?

If my misstep illustrates one key lesson, it is this: your team and your organization need to have an explicit and shared understanding of what a roadmap means and how it is to be used. Is it a hard-and-fast promise? A set of high-level "maybe" ideas? Are the next four years of your product roadmap as set in stone as the next six months? Unless you have taken the time and effort to address these questions, roadmaps can create more miscommunications than they resolve.

Here are a few guiding questions to help you get started with creating a clear sense of how your organization intends to use its roadmap:

- How far into the future should our roadmap go?
- Does our roadmap make a distinction between "short-term" and "long-term" plans?
- Who has access to the roadmap? Is it customer facing? Public facing?
- How often is the roadmap reviewed and by whom?
- How are changes to the roadmap communicated and how often?
- What could somebody within the organization reasonably expect if they see a feature on the roadmap three months from now?
- What could somebody within the organization reasonably expect if they see a feature on the roadmap one year from now?

The answers to these questions will vary based on your product, your organization, and your stakeholders. What is most important is not how you answer these questions but rather that you ask and answer them at all.

One helpful step I've seen many teams take is to write a "roadmap readme" that serves as the first page of any roadmap document that travels throughout the organization. This "roadmap readme" speaks to the questions listed above, and it helps stakeholders better understand what they can expect from the roadmap and how the roadmap is to be used. Often, I will ask teams to craft this "readme" *before* they begin working on the roadmap itself so that the format and content of the roadmap can be tailored to its intended use.

Going from 0 to 1 with Organizational Roadmaps
Josh W.
Product Executive, ad tech startup

When I started working as a product leader at an ad tech company, we didn't have a roadmap at all. I knew that we needed one, but I also knew that a roadmap can be a very dangerous document. I had worked in sales previously, and I knew that when junior salespeople have access to a roadmap, they will use it to sell. That's not a bad thing by any means

—they *should* be using everything they can to sell. But at an organization that had never used a roadmap before, there was significant danger associated with salespeople seeing a roadmap as a set of promises when we were still figuring out what that document should even look like.

So, the first thing I did was ask if I could do a presentation about "thinking like a product person" at the sales team's offsite. I know that a sales offsite can sound like a nightmare to a lot of product folks, but it's situations like these that really give you an opportunity to bond with people outside of your role or function. Rather than trying to tell them that the way they approach things is wrong, I wanted to help them understand why product people might seem frustrated when requests come in from sales. I wanted to make sure that they knew where the product team was and why the roadmap we were working on was a work in progress and not a series of promises.

When we finally did create a roadmap—and our first roadmap was, of course, a mess—I was very sure to label it "VERSION 0." I always use highly visible versioning to communicate when something is a work in progress, and nearly everything is a work in progress. When I shared this document with the head of sales, I communicated with him very clearly that this document was not to be used by sales folks as a set of promises. I made him accountable for managing how the document was communicated with his team and for any problems that would arise if it was used incorrectly. This helped ensure that salespeople knew they were accountable to their direct manager if they used the roadmap the wrong way. As a person on the product side, I had no direct authority, but the head of sales certainly did.

Every quarter, I would sit down with the leadership team and run a retrospective on both the roadmap itself and how we were using it. By the third quarter, everybody could clearly see the value of having a roadmap, and we had gotten much better at understanding what information we needed on the roadmap and what information was extraneous or misleading. **I don't think we could have gotten there if we hadn't taken the time to truly retrospect on not just the roadmap itself but also on how and why we were using the roadmap.**

You Gantt Always Get What You Want

A Gantt chart is a form of data visualization that uses horizontal lines to represent the amount of work delivered (or to be delivered) over a period of time. At some point in your career, you will almost certainly read an article that tells you exactly why a Gantt chart is the *worst possible way* to deliver a product roadmap. You will study up on much better options, including outcome-based roadmaps and problem space–based roadmaps. You will make an impassioned case for why Gantt charts create a false sense of certainty and limit your team's ability to adjust course and prioritize outcomes over output (something we will discuss more in the next chapter).

And yet, you will still almost certainly wind up delivering a roadmap that looks an awful lot like a Gantt chart.

I say this not to discredit those much better options, nor to discourage product managers from making those impassioned cases. But most people in most organizations are accustomed to seeing information laid out on a Gantt chart, and you will likely have more success trying to make those Gantt charts *better* than you will trying to convince people to abandon them altogether. There may be some perfectly valid reasons—like ad buys that require months of advance planning—why your particular stakeholders need a general sense of what exact features will be delivered by what exact dates. Do your best to understand those reasons and be direct and fearless in communicating things that might be uncertain or subject to change.

For a comprehensive and visually compelling guide to making roadmaps work for you and your team, I highly recommend the book *Product Roadmaps Relaunched* by C. Todd Lombardo, Bruce McCarthy, Evan Ryan, and Michael Connors (O'Reilly).

Your Product Spec Is Not Your Product

Each of the products and features on your roadmap will likely be captured in one or more documents called product specifications, or "product specs" for short. These documents help structure, facilitate, and prioritize the creation of your product. But *they are not your product*. Until your team actually builds something, your product spec delivers absolutely zero value to your users.

Bad product managers think of product specs as opportunities to show off their individual strengths and expertise. Their product specs attempt to answer every possible question and address every possible implementation detail, *all* without input from their team. These product managers expect the people building the product to just go ahead and *execute* their perfectly crafted product spec without asking too many questions or putting up too much of a fuss. And, without fail, their products—and, ultimately, their users—are worse off for it.

Good product managers think of product specs as a way to capture and synthesize the shared strengths and expertise of their team. Their product specs are often messy works in progress full of unanswered questions that they can work through in close collaboration with their colleagues. They make sure that the people building the product are engaged and invested in how and why the product is built. If somebody questions their product spec, they see it as an opportunity to make the product better, not as a personal attack.

Once product managers realize that their product specs don't need to be perfect, they are able to better focus on making them useful—and in some cases, even *playful*. Jenny Gibson, a phenomenal product leader I've had the pleasure of working with for the last several years, asks her team to describe the "Yugo," "Toyota," and "Lamborghini" versions of each proposed product or feature. I've read a lot of product specs, and I can say with confidence that these are both more illuminating than most (you can learn a whole lot from comparing and contrasting multiple solutions to the same problem) *and* more enjoyable than most.

Just as your product spec is not your product, remember that your "user stories" are not your users. As we discussed in Chapter 8, simply writing out the things you plan to build in an ostensibly user-centric format does not mean that you are building anything that your users want or need. If you aren't sure about your users' goals—or what your users want to *do* in order to achieve those goals—bring those questions to your team and talk through them together.

The Unanticipated Ramifications of Complex Product Specs
Jonathan Bertfield
Executive Producer, large publishing company

About 15 years ago, I stepped into a big job at a publishing company in New York. My title was executive producer, which was kind of like head of product management in those days. I was working on a really high profile project within the company—it had launched an early beta that was in pilots, but it wasn't scalable. The job was "Come in and turn this into a real business." I took that directive as "Rewrite the specifications for this project in excruciating detail." The documents we had were kind of all over the map and haphazard, and I assumed that *this* was why the product was not scalable. How could the product team possibly execute against this vision if there was no blow-by-blow for them to follow?

So, I said, "Let's sit in my office with one subject matter expert and spend four months hacking together a detailed product spec." As a result of this approach, two disastrous things happened. First, we didn't speak to a customer for that entire time. What we ended up producing was way more complex than it needed to be, because we effectively stopped learning what it needed to be from our customers. Second, because we wound up writing such a complex product spec, we decided that we must need a really sophisticated development team. So, we got a fancy product agency to sign on and threw the spec over the wall to them. And from there, I largely excused myself from dealing with the day-to-day work of building the product—after all, I had written everything out in the spec.

We finished the product, and it was a train wreck. It took 18 months longer than it should have, and it was a total disaster. But the lessons I learned informed everything I've done since then. Writing stuff down is very much a double-edged sword. The more you write down, the more time it takes, and the further removed you can become from the actual work that needs to happen. **Writing a long and detailed spec might help you feel like you're doing a lot of work toward building a product, but it isn't always the right work.** As a product manager, you can never think that just because you did a brain dump, you are excused from the work of translating that brain dump into an actual product.

The Best Documentation Is Incomplete

One way to make sure that your product specs and other documentation will serve as a conversation starter is to leave it intentionally incomplete. Over the last several years, I have grudgingly become more comfortable presenting documentation that is messy, unpolished, and riddled with unanswered questions. I am a perfectionist by nature, and I *still* worry that incomplete documentation I share will be seen by my colleagues as lazy or half-assed. But, as I keep reminding myself, *impressing* my colleagues is ultimately far less important than *engaging* them.

I am by no means the first person to notice that purposefully incomplete documents can align and accelerate a team's collaboration. In a 2008 paper entitled "Incomplete by Design and Designing for Incompleteness (*https://oreil.ly/ JKMoH*)," Raghu Garud, Sanjay Jain, and Philipp Tuertscher argue: "Rather than pose a threat, incompleteness acts as a trigger for action. Even as actors try to complete what has been left incomplete, they generate new problems as well as new possibilities that continually drive the design." In other words, bringing incomplete things to your team doesn't just mean that you are working together to solve a problem—it means that you are continually and collaboratively reshaping the problem as you work together to solve it. How cool is that?

There have been many moments in my product career when I've spent weeks crafting a complete and "perfect" document, only to have my team ask some (fair, thoughtful, constructive) questions that leave me spending weeks *reworking* that very document. By contrast, when I've shared an "incomplete by design" document, questions and contributions from my team are *literally a necessity to move us forward.* The level and quality of participation you get from "I need your help to make this unfinished thing awesome," is exponentially higher than the level and quality of participation you get from "I made this thing and it is finished and perfect. Any questions?"

So, my challenge to you is to bring something incomplete to your next team meeting. Rather than bringing a fancy PowerPoint deck, bring a messy one-pager. And when your team suggests helpful changes to that one-pager, make those changes on the spot, together. You'll be amazed at how much easier it is to work through a document together than to go through multiple cycles of presenting, critiquing, and editing.

No First Draft Should Ever Be More Than One Page and One Hour of Effort

A few years ago, my business partners pointed out to me that, even as I coached teams on reducing the amount of time and effort spent on documentation, I was still creating elaborate, impressive, polished documents and deliverables for our internal meetings. "Of course I am," I told them, "y'all are the best, and I want to make sure you think I'm doing my job well." We all paused for a moment. "Oh."

In an effort to curb my perfectionist tendencies, we agreed that I would only work in one-pagers for the foreseeable future. Much has been written about the value of one-pagers for product teams (this talk (*https://oreil.ly/FFzbq*) from John Cutler is a classic and well worth a watch). But for those of us who are incorrigible overachievers, crafting the *perfect* one-pager can still take hours, or days, or weeks. Even after I committed to creating shorter documents, I was still spending a *long time* on those documents and, in turn, presenting them to my business partners as if they were impeccably carved marble word-sculptures worthy of praise and adoration.

In a fit of well-earned self-recrimination, I wrote up and shared a simple pledge with my business partners: "I will spend no more than one page and one hour working on *any* document or deliverable before sharing it with my team." I printed it out, taped it to my laptop, and told my business partners to hold me accountable to it *no matter what.*

Needless to say, this has not been easy for me. There have been innumerable times when I've been so sure that my business partners and I are aligned that I've skipped ahead to the final project plan, the final training deck, or the final draft of a chapter (oops) without sharing a time-bound one-pager first. And every single time, I have come to regret it—both because it has inevitably resulted in my having to rework those "final" documents *and* because it has prompted my business partners to ask me, quite fairly, why I broke my pledge to them.

At the urging of those very business partners, I published the One Page/One Hour Pledge at *onepageonehour.com*, where it has now been signed by scores of people from organizations like Disney, Amazon, American Express, and IBM. If the idea resonates with you, I hope you'll sign the pledge as well!

Using a "One Page/One Hour" Approach to Create Alignment Across a Large Organization

B.E.
Product Manager, large marketing software company

I work at a large marketing software company with lots of product teams working on lots of loosely interconnected bits. Staying coordinated with other product managers is a major challenge, one that often feels insurmountable.

Several months ago, a product manager from another team came to me asking if I had any documents I could share to help him understand what my team was working on. While I certainly had plenty of lengthy product specs and piles of Jira tickets, I didn't have anything that would really give him an overview of what we were doing and why. But I knew how important it would be for our teams to stay coordinated, so I offered to spend an hour putting together a one-pager.

The one-pager itself turned out pretty straightforward: our team goals at the top, then a list of the things we were considering building to achieve those goals, and finally some of the open questions and unknowns toward the bottom of the page. To be honest, I had no idea if this is what that other product manager was expecting, and I was worried that he'd see the slapdash document I gave him as proof that I was a slapdash product manager. Instead, he told me it was exactly what he needed—and it actually inspired him to put together a similar document capturing his team's work.

That's it. That's the story. **I spent an uncomfortably short amount of time putting together documentation for my team, and it wound up being much more useful than I thought it would be.**

If You've Got It, Template

I am a big believer in lightweight and flexible templates, for everything ranging from product specs to quarterly roadmaps to team process changes. Templates can help get people and teams started when a blank page is too intimidating, and they can help ensure that the most important information is consistently prioritized.

And yet, templates can also be *really frustrating* if they are heavyweight, inflexible, and difficult to complete—which, unfortunately, they often are. Here are a few tips for making templates useful and valuable for your team:

Keep the structure of the template "in play" as well as its content.
Templates can be a great way to structure your thinking, but they shouldn't limit or dictate your thinking. Always be willing to change around the structure of the template if it does not seem to be helping your team achieve its goals. For bonus points, change the structure of the template *with your team*, to model for them that documentation can always be changed in the service of delivering better outcomes.

Refresh and revisit your templates regularly.
I once worked with a team that needed to complete a hated 10-page template every time they wanted data from their colleagues in analytics. Nobody on this team could remember how the template started or where it

came from, but they assumed that their manager had deemed it necessary and would not budge from this position. When I asked their manager about this template, she rolled her eyes and said, "Ugh, I hate the template. But the team keeps using it, so I guess they think we need it."

As with any other team processes, templates can become stagnant and frustrating if you aren't making a point of revisiting them regularly to make them more useful. One great activity to run during a team retrospective is to ask, "Knowing what we now know, how would we change the templates that we used for our last sprint or iteration?" This affords your team an opportunity to modify your templates together, while staying focused on the specific lessons you learned from using those templates the last time around.

Always fill out a template at least three times yourself before you ask anyone else to fill it out.

Here's the thing about templates: they are sometimes really easy to make and really hard to fill out. An innocuous-seeming question that you throw into a template "just in case" might be something that a team spends weeks chasing down—weeks that they could have spent doing something much more important and impactful. As a rule, I now try to fill out any template I'm sharing with my team *at least three times* before it leaves my desk—and to share those three examples along with the template itself.

Of course, what exactly a "good" template looks like will vary enormously from team to team and from organization to organization. If you aren't sure where to start, a quick Google search will turn up hundreds of templates for nearly any document you can imagine. So long as your team is learning and retrospecting together, *any* template can provide a good place to start.

A Quick Note on Proprietary Roadmapping and Knowledge Management Tools

If you will allow me an "old man yells at cloud" moment...back in my day, the only tools we had to make documentation were plain ol' spreadsheets, slides, and Word documents. Today, there is an ever-expanding universe of proprietary roadmapping and knowledge management tools, each promising to help teams find all the information they need in a single, accessible place. Many of these tools integrate with platforms like Jira that teams use to manage their day-to-day tasks. Many of them charge some kind of fee *per user*, which often creates a perverse incentive for organizations looking to use documentation as an instrument of transparency and visibility. All of them involve some kind of learning curve for less experienced users. And, in my experience, the time and effort that goes into deploying them does not always justify the benefits they offer over simpler tools.

Yes, if you are trying to do information management at a massive enterprise with tons of interconnected pieces, it is probably a good idea to put substantial time and energy into evaluating potential tools. (If you are doing information management at a massive enterprise, there are also likely folks at your organization *whose job* is to evaluate such tools.) But for too many product teams I've worked with, "Which roadmapping tool should we use?" is an easier and lower-stakes conversation to have than "What should go on our roadmap?" or even "What does a roadmap mean to us?"

Years ago, I worked with an organization that was investing heavily in a new knowledge management platform. Seats had been purchased, trainings had been booked, and emails had been sent out notifying teams that they would soon need to transfer their existing mess of documentation into this simple, new, all-in-one platform. But rather than consolidating this company's information ecosystem, the new platform only fragmented it further. Some teams dutifully re-created their roadmaps in the new platform but kept their "real" roadmaps in separate documents. Some executives who had neither the time nor the inclination to learn the new platform continued asking for documents in other, more familiar formats. Eventually, this company had to go through a similarly thorough and costly process to formally *stop* using their new knowledge management platform, not even a year after rolling it out.

Just as fancy proprietary tools don't guarantee success, they also don't guarantee failure. Here's one area where I wish I could have taken my own advice a few years ago: if you're working with a team that is already using a proprietary roadmapping or knowledge management tool, stay focused on *how* the tool is being used rather than raging against the tool itself. Knowledge management is, first and foremost, a communication challenge. People will generally seek out the information they need regardless of whether it's stored in a fancy roadmapping platform or a hacked-together Google doc. The challenge is to get people communicating openly and directly enough for them to understand and identify the information they need—and why they need that information in the first place.

These days, I generally advise teams to start with the simplest tools available to them, then graduate to more complicated tools if and when they run up against *specific* limitations. If you're still learning how to ride a bike, you probably don't need to invest in a motorcycle that shoots lasers.

Summary: The Menu Is Not the Meal

Alan Wilson Watts, author of the life-changing *The Wisdom of Insecurity* (Vintage), once said that "The menu is not the meal." This quote is worth keeping on a sticky note above your desk. Your roadmap is not your road, your product spec is not your product, your user stories are not your users. Stay focused on making a delicious meal rather than crafting the world's most impressive and comprehensive menu.

Your Checklist

- Understand that the most impactful parts of your job might also be the least tangible. Don't stress out if you can't point to something and say, "I did that all by myself!"

- Remember that "The menu is not the meal." The documents you create are not your actual products, and they do not necessarily offer any value to your users.

- Don't set out to be the sole "owner" of the roadmap, no matter what it says in your job description.

- Avoid making assumptions about what roadmaps mean to your team or your organization. Have an open and explicit conversation about how roadmaps are to be used, and document that conversation along with the roadmap itself.

- Accept the reality that, yes, you will probably need to make some Gantt charts—and do whatever you can to make those Gantt charts useful and valuable to your stakeholders.

- Make your product specs and other documents "incomplete by design" to encourage team engagement and collaboration.

- Spend no more than one page and one hour on the first draft of *any* document you are creating before sharing it with your team.

- Use lightweight, flexible templates to structure and standardize your thinking, and reevaluate these templates regularly.

- Before sharing a template with your team, make sure you've filled it out yourself at least three times.

- Think carefully about the real costs (including costs to people's time and energy) that go into deploying proprietary roadmapping and knowledge-management tools.

Vision, Mission, Objectives, Strategy, and Other Fancy Words

No fewer than three of the fancy words in this chapter's title appear in nearly every product job listing, whether it is for an associate product manager or a chief product officer. And yet, these job listings are rarely quite so generous in stating plainly what exactly they mean.

The good news is, there is no shortage of well-written magazine articles, elegant cascading diagrams, and aggressively worded Medium posts offering the definitive take on what these terms mean and how they should all fit together into a neat little cascade of clarity and purpose.

The bad news is, none of these equally authoritative-seeming sources actually seem to agree with each other. Some insist that strategy and objectives are wholly distinct concepts, while others use the word "strategy" to encompass both. Some declare that a compelling mission is far and away the most important thing for a product team to have in place; others dismiss mission statements as meaningless fluff. What is a product manager to do?

This chorus of decisive-but-conflicting opinions created a lot of anxiety for me early in my product career. Whenever company leadership asked me to deliver a product strategy, I froze in terror. Did I even know what a good product strategy looked like? What if I turned in something embarrassingly off-base? For fear of revealing myself as a complete impostor, I would often rattle off a list of righteous and defensible-sounding reasons why the company had left me in no position to deliver a workable strategy: "Our company goals simply aren't clear enough!" or "Given the arbitrary deadlines that have been simply handed to us by leadership, what's the point of putting a strategy together?" Or, I would just say, "OK sure, yeah, sounds good," and then slink away and hope that everybody forgot about it.

I have seen many product managers deploy similar evasive maneuvers when pressed to develop a product strategy, or vision, or objectives, or any other of these important-sounding things. I have also seen many of these product managers react with wide-eyed incredulity when I suggest that they start by simply jotting down what they hope their teams will achieve in the next year and how they broadly intend to achieve it. Their eyes only get wider when I suggest that they spend no more than one page and one hour working on this oh-so-important document before bringing it to their team for feedback.

Many of the big, fancy words of product management simply come down to those two questions: what are you trying to achieve, and how do you intend to achieve it? In this chapter, we'll take a look at those two broad categories (the former generally encompassing "mission," "vision," "objectives," and "goals" and the latter generally described as "strategy"). The more simply, directly, and collaboratively you can answer these questions, the better equipped your team will be to make decisions. And it is the quality of those decisions that will ultimately determine your team's success or failure.

This is a short chapter, with good reason: the less time you spend searching for the "right" way to set goals and strategy, and the sooner you start working with your team to articulate where you're going and how you'll get there, the better.

The Outcomes and Output Seesaw

At a high level, the words in this chapter's title exist to keep us focused on the actual *outcomes* we are working toward: the results we deliver for our business, the problems we solve for our customers, and the (hopefully) positive impact we want to make on the world at large.

These outcomes are, presumably, the reason that our businesses and teams exist. But they are not always front and center as we set about shipping features and hitting deadlines. For this very reason, "outcomes over output" has become a ubiquitous corrective slogan for product people. It is also the name of a great book by Josh Seiden (Sense & Respond Press).

As with many ideas turned into slogans, "outcomes over output" can also be easily misinterpreted and weaponized. I've seen many product managers cite this phrase to righteously defend their teams against any inquiries as to what exactly they intend to deliver and when they intend to deliver it. As we discussed in the last chapter, there are legitimate reasons why our stakeholders might be asking us annoyingly specific questions about our delivery and release timelines. Understanding those reasons will always get us further than throwing up our hands and saying, "See, this company is a total feature factory that only cares about output and will never be truly outcome focused!"

As with many "this over that" statements, I've found it helpful to reframe "outcomes over output" as "output *in service of* outcomes." (This approach also works well for the Agile Manifesto's "working software over comprehensive documentation" and "responding to change over following a plan.") Once we start thinking about outcomes and output as a connected system, not an either/or choice, we can start thinking about how we want to design and maintain that system to make sure that the output we deliver helps us achieve the outcomes we desire.

As I've worked with teams and organizations to better understand how they connect output and outcomes, an interesting pattern has emerged: the teams that seem the most hyperfocused on output are often the very same teams working toward the broadest and least specific outcomes. After running many retrospectives with teams and their leaders, I've come to see this as a function of our very human desire for certainty and predictability. Specificity around targets and deadlines needs to come from *somewhere*, and if it is not articulated on the order of outcomes, it will be demanded on the order of output. In other words, if teams truly desire flexibility and leeway around output, they need to get *really, really specific* about the outcomes they are seeking to drive. In this way, you can picture outcomes and output as a kind of seesaw (Figure 10-1), where pushing down on one side with specific dates and targets raises up the other side to the order of open-ended themes and opportunities.

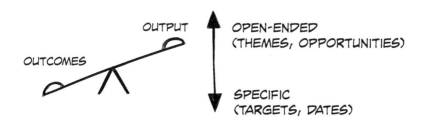

Figure 10-1. The outcomes and output "seesaw." To get more open-ended with one, you must get more specific with the other.

This has been a jarring realization for folks who, like me, have sought to avoid micromanagement by setting open-ended goals for their teams. But it has also helped me understand why every single time I've tried to set a broad goal like "increase conversions" or "delight customers," my team has inevitably wound up scrambling to ship specific features by specific deadlines.

For this reason, I now advise product managers to work with their teams to be as specific as possible—uncomfortably specific, in fact—about the outcomes they seek to achieve and when exactly they seek to achieve them. As counterintuitive as it may seem, "Increase new user conversion rate by ten percent in the next three months" is *more* likely to give your team the freedom to explore multiple approaches and solutions. When your stakeholders can get a clear picture of the specific goals you are seeking to achieve and the specific time frame in which you seek to achieve them, they are far less likely to demand specific features by specific dates. And, best of all, your team will be motivated to explore all the different ways they might achieve those specific and time-bound goals, even the ones that don't look much like new "features" at all. (We'll discuss this more in Chapter 12.)

How a Lack of Specific Goals Can Create a Team of Product Martyrs
M.G.
Product Leader, nonprofit

I recently joined a nonprofit product shop that primarily builds products for other nonprofits. Like many nonprofits, we face some pretty major resource constraints. When I first sat down to talk with the product owners who report to me directly, each was working on at least three products and seemed stressed out and spread thin. Thankfully, I was able to get some more resources allocated our way to hire a few more product owners. This, I thought, was the answer to our problems: more product owners meant each product owner could devote more time and attention to one thing at a time.

To my surprise, my direct reports did not seem all that excited about this news. In fact, their initial reactions ranged from skeptical to outright defensive. What seemed to me like an opportunity to focus and streamline our efforts as a company was instead being interpreted as a personal attack: "Why are you taking some of my products away from me?" This reaction was particularly confusing to me because it was coming from some of the same people who had been complaining about how over-worked they were just a few weeks prior.

It took me a while to realize it, but those initial complaints about being overworked weren't just a reflection of our lack of organizational resources. They were symptomatic of a much deeper and more complex problem: our product owners had no way of measuring their own suc-cess other than how hard they were working and how many products they owned. Why? **Because there was no common sense of the goals we were working toward as an organization. In the absence of these goals, each individual product owner was left to their own assump-tions and ad hoc success metrics.**

The funny thing is, if I had simply gone ahead and hired more prod-uct owners without addressing this underlying issue, it just would have made things worse. In the absence of clear, organization-wide goals, more product owners would have just meant more competing assump-tions about what success looks like. As soon as I started bringing all of our product owners together to talk about shared goals, a lot of the competition and defensiveness I had seen naturally started to melt away. Product owners started looking for ways to share resources and knowl-edge, knowing that their success would be measured against how well we were able to deliver value to our customers, not how many products they "owned" or how late they were willing to stay in the office on a Friday evening.

SMART Goals, CLEAR Goals, OKRs, and So On

There is no shortage of information out there about different ways to bring specificity to the goals you choose to set for your product, your team, and your organization. You've got your SMART goals (Specific, Measurable, Achievable, Relevant, Time-bound); you've got your CLEAR goals (Collaborative, Limited, Emotional, Appreciable, Refinable); and you've got your Objectives and Key Results, or OKR framework. Which of these works best for you will depend enor-mously on your specific product, team, and organization, as well as your own preference for more numbers-based approaches versus story-based approaches. Even a cursory scan of SMART versus CLEAR can help you think through whether your particular team would be more receptive to "measurable" goals or "emotional" goals, for example.

In my own work, I have come to favor the OKR framework, primarily because it allows for both a qualitative rallying cry (objective) and quantitative measures that indicate that you are moving in the right direction (key results). To provide a quick example, a fintech startup might have "Democratize access to complex financial instruments" as a qualitative objective and "Onboard 1,000 new users by the end of the quarter" as a measurable key result that indicates they are on track toward achieving that objective.

There are a number of great resources out there for learning more about the OKR framework, but I am particularly fond of Christina Wodtke's book *Radical Focus* (Cucina Media). Wodtke writes in vivid narrative detail about the common pitfalls that teams encounter when implementing OKRs, making an incredibly strong case for the subtractive and focusing power of having clear and well-understood goals.

Of course, simply articulating your goals as OKRs is no guarantee that they will be any more useful to you or your team. The ultimate test of your team's goals is not whether they fit a predetermined format or framework, but rather whether they—along with your team's strategy—help you make better decisions.

Good Strategy Is Inexorably Tied to Execution

If we think of our goals and objectives as a way of capturing the outcomes we seek to achieve, then we can think of our strategy as *how* we intend to achieve those outcomes. (That's about as specific a definition of strategy as you're going to get from me, and even that is subject to debate!)

My favorite take on strategy comes from product leader Adam Thomas, who describes the purpose of strategy as improving a team's decision fitness. I love this description, because it makes room for the fact that every team and organization's strategy can and should look different—but at the end of the day, if it isn't helping folks on the ground make better decisions, it isn't really a "strategy" at all.

Indeed, the single biggest mistake a product manager can make around strategy is to approach it as something separate and disconnected from their team's day-to-day execution. I have seen many product managers fall into this trap when they are finally offered the shiny prize of stepping up into "strategic" conversations. They go off to their desk, cobble together everything they can possibly find from every google result for "good product strategy," and try to put together the World's Most Comprehensive Strategy Presentation. They work on this presentation for days, sometimes weeks, sometimes months. By the time it's finished, it feels like a highlight reel for all the things a "strategic" product manager is supposed to do well. It's got frameworks! And financial models! And user personas! And even a few nods to "Jobs to Be Done" for the *true heads* in the crowd. Surely, nobody could accuse this presentation—or this presenter—of missing anything important.

And, sure enough, the presentation is well received by executives, who nod seriously and toss around a lot of questions about "product-market fit" and "innovation." Each executive's feedback is thoughtfully incorporated, and the initial 10-slide strategy deck quickly becomes a 20-slide strategy deck. When the updated deck is presented at the next super-important strategy meeting, everybody seems pleased.

The real problem occurs when our executive-approved strategy deck makes its way from the rarified air of a super-important meeting into the calloused proletarian hands of the product team. After all, it is ultimately that product team—the same one that our hypothetical product manager has likely been "too busy working on the strategy deck" to interact with—that brings products to the market and, in turn, outcomes to the business. And in the cold light of "What are we actually supposed to do with this thing?" the World's Most Comprehensive Strategy Presentation can start to look an awful lot like an incoherent, designed-by-committee patchwork of business jargon, confusing diagrams, and wishful thinking.

As a product manager, the visibility and importance that come with strategic work can threaten to pull you away from your team. But it is your job to keep strategy and execution connected at all times. The best product managers recognize that strategy and execution are two inexorably linked sides of the same coin. They value strategy as a particularly high-leverage way to guide their team's day-to-day decisions. But they also understand that strategy, no matter how comprehensive and formally impressive, is utterly useless if it is disconnected from those day-to-day decisions.

In practice, this often means bringing incomplete and unfinished strategy documents to your team and "test driving" those documents together to see if they can actually help guide your day-to-day decision-making. You may find that the fancy strategy framework you read about on Medium is actually too abstract and complicated to help your team answer its most pressing real-world questions. In fact, you may find that the strategy your team needs is simpler and more straightforward than you had thought or feared.

Establishing a "Hierarchy of Needs" to Prioritize Layers of Strategy and Execution

J.W.
Product Manager, 1,000-person SAAS company

A few months ago, I found myself juggling a whole bunch of distinct-but-related conversations with my counterparts in engineering and design about what we should build and how we should build it. Our team leadership meetings oscillated between high-level questions around goals and strategy and more tactical questions around staffing and team processes. These topics seemed to blend and swirl together until it was difficult for us to move things forward without getting stuck.

In the hopes of bringing some clarity to our conversation, I reached out to the project manager on our team who has a lot of experience navigating complex challenges within organizations. Working together, we walked through the most important decisions we had to make as a team, which unsurprisingly boiled down to "What goals should we be working toward, and what should we be doing to achieve those goals?" From there, we created a visual "hierarchy of needs" (Figure 10-2) showing the specific information that was *most* important for us to figure out to answer those critical prioritization questions.

Figure 10-2. A "hierarchy of needs" for product decision-making

Having this hierarchy of needs visualized helped us focus on seeking out and synthesizing the information that was most important to get our team unblocked and moving forward. With our visual hierarchy in place, we were able to put a hold on conversations about roadmaps, staffing, and process while we focused on better understanding company-wide goals and building out our team's product strategy. **Visualizing and prioritizing the different levels of information we needed to make important decisions helped us better manage our own time and efforts, ultimately putting us in a position where we could get unblocked and build momentum.**

Good Strategy Is Simple and Obvious

At the very beginning of his classic book *Good Strategy/Bad Strategy* (Profile Books), Richard Rumelt sets forth perhaps my favorite statement about strategy: "Good strategy is almost always...simple and obvious and does not take a thick deck of PowerPoint slides to explain."

To that end, I recently ran an exercise with a product team that was nearly a month into trying to define their product strategy. They had put together about 20 slides of impressive-looking diagrams and frameworks, but they were still not sure if they were "doing product strategy the right way." So I asked them to take their strategy as it was written and try using it to individually prioritize a backlog of work that they were considering building in the coming weeks and months. If the strategy was effective, I explained, each of them would wind up prioritizing more or less the same things in more or less the same order.

Instead, two wildly different patterns emerged among the 10 or so product managers, engineers, and designers on the team. "I'm sorry," offered one engineer, "but I think it's pretty clear which of these things is going to be most valuable for new users." A moment of silence. Sheepishly, a product manager responded, "I thought we were building primarily for existing users?"

You'd be surprised how often product managers get so wrapped up in worrying about whether or not they are doing product strategy "right" that they forget to ask and answer such fundamental questions with their team. In my experience, the most actionable product strategies tend to focus on answering simple questions: "Who is our user?" "What problem are we helping them solve?" and "Why are we the right company to help them solve that problem?"

Simply answering these questions together can help provide a good starting point for many product teams. For example, imagine that you are working on the algorithmic playlist team for a music-streaming company. Your team's job is to provide users with automated playlists leveraging the company's extensive data. But that doesn't necessarily tell you *which users* you are making those playlists for—or why they might want those playlists in the first place. In the absence of a more specific product strategy, your team would likely struggle to make day-to-day decisions about what to build, how to build it, and—perhaps most importantly—what *not* to build.

A more specific strategy doesn't need to be—and often should not be—a long and complicated strategy. Your team would likely be empowered to make better decisions with a simple and straightforward strategy like "Help casual users discover their next favorite artist by analyzing data from users with similar taste profiles." Here, it's clear who you're focusing on: casual users, not power users. (Remember "The Siren Song of 'Power Users'" from Chapter 6!) It's clear what you're helping them do: discover their next favorite artist. And it's clear why you're the right company and team to do it: you have enough data from similar listeners to make really good recommendations. Depending on your team and company goals (and your monetization model), you could likely make a good case for why and how you believe this strategy will help your team impact key metrics such as revenue and retention.

Now, imagine that you are working for the *editorial* playlist team at the same music-streaming company. Your team's job is to manually curate high-quality playlists that will be prominently featured across the product. Here, again, your team might benefit from a simple strategy such as "Provide power users with high-quality shareable playlists by leveraging our editorial expertise." Here, again, it's clear who you're focusing on: power users (likely defined in this case as users we believe are likely to share playlists with their networks). It's clear what you're helping them do: share high-quality playlists. (The extent to which they *want* or *need* to do this is debatable and hopefully backed up by solid user research.) And it's clear why you're the right company and team to do it: you have extensive editorial expertise to call upon. Again, depending on your team and company goals, you could likely make a strong case for how and why this strategy will help you impact key metrics such as new user sign-ups.

Of course, these are just theoretical examples. Here are a few signs that your own strategy is actually helping your team make better decisions:

Everybody on your team can recite your strategy in a sentence or two.

My least-favorite answer to the oft-asked question, "What is your team's strategy?" is "I'll forward you the deck!" If your strategy is so complicated that it can't be summarized in a sentence or two, then the odds are very slim that your team is actually thinking about it when they make important executional decisions.

Your strategy helps you decide what not to build.

In many cases, overstuffed and overcomplicated strategy is symptomatic of a broader reluctance to commit to any specific user personas or problems. If your strategy can effectively justify building *anything* for *anybody*, then it is probably not a very good strategy.

Your strategy starts to feel outdated after a while.

If your strategy is truly driven by an understanding of customers and markets, and you are truly doing the hard work of staying close to those customers and markets as they change, then there will come a time when your strategy clearly needs to be updated. This is by no means a bad thing! In fact, if your strategy has remained unchanged for a suspiciously long period of time, odds are it is too disconnected from the broader world to help your team or company succeed. As with your user personas, consider refreshing your strategy on a regular cadence to make sure it does not become stale.

As you progress through your product career, you may very well find that committing to a smaller set of user personas and problems is much more challenging than adding another page or another framework. But the shorter, sharper, and more focused your strategy is, the more likely it is to help your team deliver meaningful outcomes for the business and its users.

If You're Not Sure, Ask for an Example

Without a doubt, there will be times in your career when somebody asks you for a strategy, a vision, a mission, or a set of objectives and you will be genuinely unsure as to what they want from you. In my experience, the most productive way to handle these scenarios is to simply ask for an example or two. Rather than rushing off to provide what you think constitutes an impressive answer to an ambiguous question, consider saying something like "Thank you. Yes indeed, I am happy to work with my team and put together a product strategy for the next quarter. I've seen strategy approached a lot of different ways by a lot of different organizations—do you have any examples you've found particularly helpful that you could share with me?" Having a few specific examples to work from can help you build upon approaches that have already proven successful within your organization. And, if the person asking you for a strategy or a vision doesn't have any examples to share, they may very well be just as unsure about what they're asking for as you are—in which case you are likely doing them a big favor by providing something specific and tangible.

Summary: Keep It Simple, Make It Useful

In order for your team to succeed, you must have a clear sense of where you are going and a plan for how to get there. But if your destination is too vague and your plan is too complicated, you might not get anywhere at all. Keep your goals specific and your strategy simple, and—above all else—work closely with your team to make sure that your goals and your strategy are *useful* for the folks actually building stuff for your users. Remember that a big fancy strategy deck might make you feel important, but it won't necessarily help your team make better decisions.

Your Checklist

- Give up on trying to find the single correct canonical definition of terms like *vision*, *mission*, *strategy*, and *objectives*.

- Remember that the purpose of all these big fancy words is to help your team understand what goals you are working toward and how you intend to achieve those goals. Stay focused and keep it simple.

- Think of outcomes and output as a connected system, not an either-or choice.

- If you want your team to have more leeway and freedom around output, get specific about the outcomes you want to achieve and the timeline in which you want to achieve them.

- Experiment with different goal-setting formats and frameworks like SMART goals, CLEAR goals, and OKRs to see what works best for your team.

- Resist the urge to approach strategy as something separate from—and more important than—execution. Keep strategy and execution closely connected at all times.

- Take your goals and strategy for a "test drive" with your team as quickly as you can, to see if they can actually help the team make better decisions.

- Keep your strategy so simple and straightforward that anyone on your team can quickly and easily recite it without having to refer to a deck or document.

- If somebody asks you for a "vision" or a "strategy" and you aren't sure what they mean, ask them to provide a few examples.

- Stop reading this chapter and go jot down a quick and dirty draft of your team's goals and strategy, then workshop it together. Seriously!

"Data, Take the Wheel!"

These days, it seems like everybody wants to be—or hire—a "data-driven" (or at least "data-informed") product manager. And why wouldn't they? For a product manager, "data-driven" can be handy shorthand for "in this ambiguously defined role full of squishy human complexity, I know how to do *serious data business things*." And for a hiring manager, "data-driven" can be handy shorthand for "Don't make any mistakes, ever." What could possibly go wrong?

In all seriousness, there is a lot to be gained from looking at user, product, and market data. If our goals help us see where we are going and our strategy helps us decide how we will get there, then data can help us understand whether or not we are actually on the right track. Of course, this requires knowing what the "right track" means for your particular product and team. In your product career, there will likely be times when you don't have access to the data you think you need and times when you have access to so much data that it feels impossible to make a decision. Navigating both these situations requires cultivating a strong point of view about what data matters to you, why it matters, and what *specific* decisions it will inform.

In this chapter, we focus on the high-level, tool set–agnostic approaches that will help you use data to your advantage without handing over the wheel.

The Trouble with the "D" Word

Let's begin with the word *data* itself. This word can be used to describe a *lot* of things. In theory, data describes objective information, whether it is qualitative or quantitative. In practice, I have often seen the word *data* thrown around to describe conclusions drawn from information, filtered and structured representations or visualizations of data, or "anything that kinda looks like a number or a chart." In its common and colloquial use, the word *data* does little to clarify what it's actually describing, while handily imparting an air of certainty and rigor. The word *data* is dangerous for the very reason it is useful: it wields authority without specificity.

To that end, I've often advised product managers to implement a counterintuitive-seeming rule if they want to take a truly data-driven approach: don't use the word *data* at all. If you're discussing a particular set of information, describe that specific set of information. If you're discussing conclusions that you've made based on that information, describe those specific conclusions and how you reached them.

Take, for example, this somewhat hypothetical sentence: "Our data shows that millennials are highly receptive to our value proposition." Now imagine rephrasing this as "The email survey we conducted shows that millennials are highly receptive to our value proposition." There are still many points here that need clarification. (What is the value proposition? How does the email survey show this?) But at the very least, this rephrasing opens up a more meaningful conversation about what information was gathered, how it was gathered, and how it is being interpreted.

To use a more general example, imagine replacing the overused and often misapplied phrase "social data" with something more specific and descriptive, like "sentiment analysis conducted on our customers' tweets." The latter phrasing seems to invite more questions, but these are the very questions that make information both accessible and actionable. The absence of the d-word makes it easier to distinguish information from assumption and to set clear and reasonable expectations.

Start with the Decision, Then Find the Data

As we discussed in Chapter 10, our goals and strategy are only as good as the decisions they empower us to make. The same holds true when we get into the wide world of data and metrics. A 2012 *Harvard Business Review* article (*https://oreil.ly/RpgVO*) by Dominic Barton and David Court asks a question that I've used in many workshops and coaching conversations: "What decisions could we make if we had all the information we need?"

Answering this question often proves surprisingly difficult. (The best answer a whole room of product managers and data analysts were able to come up with in a workshop I delivered a few years ago was "Buy a lottery ticket," which is *not how any of this works*.) You'd be surprised how often a product manager has told me, "Our single biggest problem is that we don't have enough data to make decisions," and then struggled to name a single decision that they are actually trying to make. Lack of access to important data is certainly a real problem for many working product managers. But when you *start* with the decision you are trying to make, you are much more likely to find alternate data sources, rough-but-acceptable proxies, and other ways to move yourself and your team forward.

Imagine, for example, that you've been tasked with improving the checkout experience for an ecommerce application. The team's last product manager was so focused on shipping new features that they didn't prioritize the instrumentation tools that would allow you to see where your users are getting stuck. What are you supposed to do? How can you prioritize improvements to the checkout experience if you don't know what your users are experiencing?

For starters, you could spend some time diving deeper into the actual decision(s) you are setting about to make. Do you have a sense of the specific improvements to the checkout experience that your team is considering? If not, could you walk through the experience yourself and document the moments that seem the most confusing or discouraging? Maybe there are some user researchers in your organization who have walked through the checkout flow with actual users and could share their findings with you?

Once you've taken the time to better understand the current checkout experience, you might realize that the missing instrumentation data is more of a "nice to have" than a "need to have." One or two parts of the experience might be so obviously in need of an overhaul that your team can prioritize them with a high degree of confidence. Or, you might realize that the most meaningful opportunity for your team is not to fix any individual parts of the checkout experience but rather to reimagine how *all* those parts flow together—in which case an overreliance on granular instrumentation data may have actually led you down the wrong path.

In your product management career, there will likely be many times when you can't get the data you want. But there is always a path forward, and you can often find that path by taking the time to better understand the decision you are trying to make and seeking out any and all information (quantitative and qualitative) that might help you make that decision.

Trusting Your Instincts to Find "Invisible" Evidence

Shaun R.
Product Manager, B2B advertising software startup

When I started at my first product manager job, there were a lot of different things I could work on but not a lot of guidance as to where I should start. But the business itself was asking me to demonstrate that we should go down this route or that route. I got the sense that they were looking for hard data to support any particular product direction or prioritization decision.

At the time, we had a user interface that was clunky, but serviceable. If you spent time learning how to use it, it made sense. But, out of the box, it was very confusing. I had a strong suspicion that making a very simple, modern, usable interface would effectively cut down training time and create more affinity for the product. But there was no specific data that proved that this was the right approach. I was hesitant in suggesting that we work on this because I felt like I was missing some kind of incontrovertible signal that this was the right thing to do.

After about three months, the business reluctantly accepted my suggestion to work on the dashboard: "OK, there aren't any other easy opportunities, so go ahead and do it." But the further along we got, the more positive the response seemed to be. By the time we released the new dashboard and got feedback from our users, the response from senior leaders was "We're surprised that this has had such a good effect!" I wanted to say, "I've been saying this all along!" But I realized...I actually hadn't been saying it all along. I was embarrassed about what felt like missing evidence and did not yet know how to make a case for using data to measure changes moving forward, rather than looking for data that already exists.

From that experience, I learned how to start with a conjecture and say, "On this basis, we expect these metrics to be affected." How do you measure that something is working? Are you expecting an increase in sales? An increase in conversions? If you look at science—which has existed for much longer than product management—it relies upon the initial conjecture to set up the experiment, that first hypothesis or leap of judgment. **Truly data-driven experiments often involve following** your intuition, then establishing a feedback loop of some sort to test whether your intuition is correct.

Focusing on Metrics That Matter

Just as some product managers struggle with limited access to data, others struggle to make sense of *too much* data. With modern analytics tools and dashboards providing torrents of up-to-the-moment information, you can always find some important-looking spike or dip in some important-sounding metric to spend the rest of your day chasing down.

I spent a good deal of my early product career glued to such dashboards, ready to investigate any pattern or trend that seemed interesting or anomalous to me; after all, isn't that what "data-driven" product management is all about? If I noticed a dip in new user sign-ups, I would immediately begin looking through the last week's marketing materials to see if anything seemed off. If I noticed a spike in any one of the many specific metrics that could be described as "user engagement," I would pass it along to my team along with an encouraging note. Over time, the dashboard started to feel like a slot machine—and I was in it to win it.

It took me a long time to realize that treating product management like a game of chance was probably not the best way to help my team achieve its goals. But it was hard to find a better approach when I had no real sense of what all those numbers and graphs in our dashboard actually had to *do* with my team's goals. Because I had not done the work of figuring out what particular metrics mattered to my team, I spent a lot of time chasing down what *Lean Startup* author Eric Ries describes as "vanity metrics." Vanity metrics are often framed as "whatever is going up and to the right"—in other words, whatever makes it look like your team is doing a good job. But negatively trending metrics can also be vanity metrics when product managers spend an unwarranted amount of time worrying about them. (I have more than once played the part of the Hero Product Manager who fearlessly rescued his team from a noticeable dip in a *completely irrelevant* metric.) If you have not cultivated a strong and specific point of view about what metrics matter to your team and why, then *all* of your metrics are essentially vanity metrics.

Here's a classic example to illustrate this point: imagine that you're a product manager working on a search product. You see a sudden decrease in daily page views. What does this mean? And what do you do about it?

This is a well-known Google product manager interview question, and for good reason. If you are working on a product for which the goal is to get people the right information as quickly as possible, a decrease in page views might be a *good* thing. If you are working on a product whose revenue is directly proportional to its page views, a decrease in page views might be a very, very bad thing. The same metric can mean very different things depending on how it aligns with the overall goals and strategy of your team and organization.

Once we start thinking about how metrics relate to our specific goals and strategy, we might realize that there are some metrics we expect—or even *want*—to trend negatively. Imagine, for example, that your team is tasked with evaluating a price increase for a subscription service. There is a good chance that this increase will drive a commensurate increase in overall top-line revenue. There is also a good chance that this increase will result in a certain number of customers canceling their subscriptions. Identifying this "countermetric" up front can help initiate an important conversation with our stakeholders about just how many customers we are willing to lose—and what to do if we see that number trending beyond our expectations.

To summarize, there is no one-size-fits-all answer to the question, "What should we be measuring?" Take a look at your goals and strategy and do your best to figure out what measurable signals might help you understand where you are and where you're going.

Using Survival Metrics to Set Clear Expectations

Perhaps the question I find myself asking product managers most often is "What did you expect to happen?"

This question is often posed in response to excited declarations such as "We onboarded two hundred new users this week!" or "We're seeing a major uptick in usage of our new feature!"

Depending on how much time and effort went into those onboarding efforts, 200 new users could be a big win—or an unmitigated disaster. And depending on how many highly compensated engineering hours went into that new feature, a "major uptick" in usage could still represent a major loss to the business. It is practically impossible to declare whether a particular outcome is "good" or "bad" unless you were brave enough to proactively capture the outcome you expected to see.

This is another example of the outcomes and output seesaw we discussed in Chapter 10. If we are not specific about the outcomes we expect to see, we are almost certain to fall back into measuring the success of our work as a function of vanity metrics, whether those are "Look, some people are using the product!" or "Look, we shipped the feature on time!"

The best product managers are willing not only to commit ahead of time to what success looks like but also to having a challenging but critically important conversation about what *failure* looks like. Product leader Adam Thomas advocates an approach to this conversation called "survival metrics (*https://oreil.ly/ p962F*)." Survival metrics represent the real-world floor to the blue-sky ceiling of your "success metrics." For example, you may have decided that your new feature will be considered a success if it has a thousand active users within the next three months. But what is the *minimum number of active users* you would expect to see in order to warrant further investment in this feature? Is it a hundred? Fifty? Ten? And what will you do if you don't hit that number?

These conversations are never easy, but you are always better off having them before you launch a new product or feature, rather than scrambling to figure out whether those 150 new users are a good or bad outcome after the fact.

When "Data-Driven" Product Management Leads Us Away from Our Users

Myrtle P.
Product Director, 400-person SAAS startup

A few years ago, I found myself tasked with improving the performance of a feature that loads on users' websites. My engineering counterpart had a juicy hypothesis: they found an analysis on how bounce rates increase dramatically with every millisecond of lag time. We made a compelling case that if we could reduce lag time for our own feature to load, we could increase user interactions by a truly impressive amount. It was the kind of "make a change, move a metric, deliver a big win for the business" scenario that product managers dream about.

The problem was, this feature was a fairly old piece of software, and incremental changes to load time meant major development efforts. My engineering counterpart, whom I'd worked with for years and trusted, was very clear with me: "The only way to do this is to rebuild the whole thing from scratch." So I advocated for this approach, and we estimated that it would take about four months. That's a big time commitment, but, hey, given the enormous impact we thought this would have, it seemed well worth it. A couple of people told me it was a bad idea, but I saw a big win on the horizon and thought we could make it work.

Unsurprisingly, those four months turned into two years. Doing a side-by-side rewrite of a core product is no small feat, and there were a bunch of things we didn't think about until we were well underway. And the worst part is, during the two years we were working on this, we weren't able to deliver *anything* that actually helped our customers. **We went down a path that seemed like a sure thing, but lost track of what our users were actually trying to accomplish.** We didn't really validate that milliseconds of load time were actually a problem for our users—we just found an easy thing to measure with a theoretically huge impact and decided to work on optimizing it.

In retrospect, this approach was so seductive precisely because we didn't have to do what most PMs probably wouldn't admit that they don't want to do—talk to lots of customers. We took the path that involved the *least* amount of actual learning from our customers, which I don't think was an accident. Rather than working to understand the other available user problems we could have solved and then evaluating possible solutions, like in Teresa Torres's Opportunity Solution Tree (*https://oreil.ly/du5IJ*), we skipped a bunch of steps when we found something in the data that seemed compelling and defensible. If we had gotten out ahead of talking to our users, we could have saved ourselves a lot of time and pain.

Experimentation and Its Discontents

The idea of "data-driven experimentation" is core to modern product management, and for good reason. Before we invest enormous amounts of resources and time into building something, it is worth doing whatever we can to learn whether or not that thing is likely to succeed with real-world customers in a real-world market.

In theory, experimentation is supposed to objectively resolve questions that might have otherwise been answered through baseless opinions or organizational politics. In practice, I've often seen it have the exact opposite effect. Instead of using experimentation to settle arguments, many teams wind up *arguing about experimentation*, getting into heated debates about whether experiments are being conducted properly, whether the results of experiments are truly significant, and whether experiments are worth running at all.

For many years, I struggled to understand why this was happening, and what could be done about it. And then, in Tim Casasola's always-excellent newsletter *The Overlap (https://oreil.ly/oJNk3)*, I read five simple words that truly shook my world: "Don't prove value. Create it" *(https://oreil.ly/3dXpM)*. In other words, don't run experiments with the goal of proving to your colleagues that something might *theoretically* provide value to your users; run your experiments with the goal of providing value to your users.

Intrigued by this five-word revelation, I reached out to some product managers whose recent experiments have successfully altered the course of their team's work, as well as some product managers whose recent experiments had fallen flat. Sure enough, a clear pattern emerged: the most impactful experiments were driven by a clear motivation to *actually create value for users*. The motivation behind these successful experiments was not to "ship a small thing and then run a bunch of math to see if we can make the case for whether or not it might be valuable to our users at some point in the future," but rather "ship a small thing that we think will be valuable to our users and see if it is in fact valuable to our users."

Let's return to our earlier example of a team tasked with improving the checkout experience for an ecommerce application. As the product manager on this team, you want to make sure that your team is going in the right direction before you make any major changes to a business-critical workflow. You're *pretty* sure that you can increase conversions by streamlining two steps of the checkout process into a single step. But in order to do so, you need to move the "recommended products" area that is currently shown to users during these two existing steps—an area that, to your chagrin, is overseen by another product manager. This product manager is, to put it mildly, not terribly excited about your idea. So you agree to run an experiment to see whether the streamlined workflow results in more conversions—*and* whether it affects user engagement with the "recommended products" area.

You roll out this experiment to a small group of users and anxiously await the results. As expected, there is a statistically significant increase in conversions! But there is also a statistically significant decrease in users clicking through to recommended products. In a sense, both you *and* the other product manager are "right." You both set about making the case for why your respective metric is the more important one. After months of back-and-forth wrangling with no real progress, the path of least resistance seems more and more appealing. Ultimately, the experiment is deemed "inconclusive" and no change is made.

Now let's imagine you had chosen to take a slightly different approach. When confronted with this other product manager's protestations, you take a step back and once again walk through the checkout experience from a *user's* point of view. Very quickly, it becomes apparent to you that the reason so many users are engaging with "product recommendations" is that they've been stuck smack in the middle of the checkout experience, potentially resulting in a fair number of errant clicks and maybe even some abandoned carts. The more you think about it, the less convinced you are that the placement of these recommendations is really delivering any value to your users at all.

So, you set about to find out exactly how many of the users clicking through on these recommendations wind up completing a purchase. But, as you may remember from our original example, granular instrumentation data is not available. So you reach out to some folks on the support side to see if they have any information they can share with you. And, sure enough, several users have recently complained about accidentally clicking on product recommendations as they try to complete their checkout. In the interest of better understanding users' overall expectations, you spend some time perusing other ecommerce apps and realize that most of them put their product recommendations on the "shopping cart" screen, not two clicks into the checkout workflow. Now you're getting somewhere.

You return to the other product manager with an idea for how to move forward: based on the research you've done, you think it will be more valuable for users all around if product recommendations move to the shopping cart and the checkout experience is streamlined. You're pretty sure that this approach will ultimately benefit your users, your company, and both of your teams: after all, more users checking out means more users buying the company's products—including recommended products. You propose an experiment to see if this updated shopping cart and checkout experience can deliver an increase in conversions, with the understanding that those conversions are ultimately the most meaningful metric for *both* of your teams. Reluctantly, the other product manager agrees.

Setting up this experiment takes a little more time than you had planned and involves some not-terribly-easy collaboration between your team and the product recommendations team. But the updated experience you roll out to a small set of users is, ultimately, an experience that you truly believe will deliver more value all around. Sure enough, you see a statistically significant increase in conversions—and a small but nonnegligible decrease in engagement with recommended products. This time, however, the other product manager is not so quick to declare your experiment a failure. You aligned up front on the most meaningful metric, and the experiment seems to have influenced that metric in a significant and unequivocal way. And, since you worked *with* the product recommendations team on this experiment, they can own a part of its success. You present the results of the experiment to company leadership *together*, with a strong recommendation to roll out the new checkout experience to a wider group of users.

As this example illustrates, the way you communicate around an experiment is often more important than the experiment itself. Long story short: nobody really likes having anything "proven" to them, ever. When you create something that is delivering real value to your users, it is much easier to break political logjams and build momentum. And when you create something that fails to deliver value despite your very best efforts, you can work with your team to better understand the assumptions and misapprehensions that might have contributed to a genuinely disappointing outcome.

The World's Most Useless A/B Test

G. L.
Product Manager, consumer tech startup

Early in my product management career, I found myself at odds with a designer on my team about the color and placement of a button in our app. We were in the middle of doing some minor redesigns, and I was *convinced* that the current form of the button was more appealing than the updated one that our designer had proposed. Knowing that a good "data-driven PM" always resolves such disagreements through data and experiments, I proposed we run a simple A/B test, and our designer agreed.

We had a pretty good system in place for running such tests, and it took less than a day to get everything set up. A few weeks later, we reviewed the results of this test—and, to my great shock and surprise, it turned out that I had been dead wrong. Not only had our designer's variant performed better, it had also done so in a "statistically significant" way, which I understood to mean that we must now immediately deploy the changes she had suggested.

I walked over to her desk feeling humbled, but proud of myself for having settled the argument using real user data. She just laughed and said, "Eh, yeah, I reviewed the results, and I think we should probably just leave it as is and work on something else." What?? "Listen," she said to me, "The results may be statistically significant, but there wasn't a ton of engagement with this button overall. Given what a minor part of the app this is, and given that we've already spent a fair amount of time exploring this, I think our time would probably best be spent elsewhere."

This designer was teaching me an important lesson: just because a test yields a "statistically significant" result doesn't mean it's significant for the business or for its users. **I had been so eager to be "scientific" in my approach that I had completely lost sight of the big picture. I was more focused on something measurable and testable than something that might actually drive the bigger results we needed as a business.** Now, I try to start by understanding the size of the opportunity: how many users are actually interacting with this thing, and how meaningful are those interactions? If it's a really minor thing, then a "data-driven" experiment might be a truly useless exercise.

From "Accountability" to Action

Many organizations seek to drive "accountability" among their product managers by holding those product managers responsible for driving specific changes in specific metrics. In theory, this ensures that product managers will prioritize outcomes and stay focused on what will move the product and the company in the right direction.

In practice, though, I've often seen this backfire pretty badly. When product managers are held directly accountable for hitting a specific quantitative number, they often disengage when they feel that number is out of reach. If you're being held accountable for a certain percentage increase in new user growth, for example, and a competitor launches a product that you know is going to chip away at your market share, you might be tempted to just throw your hands up and get ready for an unpleasant quarterly review. In fact, you might be just as likely to disengage if you realize early on that the metric against which you're being evaluated is on a one-way ride to Successville.

Therein lies one of the most uncomfortable and difficult challenges around data-driven "accountability" for product managers: *how do you ask people to be responsible for something that is ultimately outside of their control?* As we've discussed, the most meaningful outcomes for our business are usually the ones determined by user behavior and market dynamics—both of which are maddeningly complex systems. It is nearly impossible to definitively attribute any changes in these systems to a single factor such as the launch of a new feature. That said, as we discussed in Chapter 10, it is important for product managers and their teams to have specific goals in mind, even as the impact their work has on those goals will often be ambiguous and hard to quantify.

So, how do you balance specific quantitative goals with the understanding that your ability to directly impact these goals will always be somewhat nonlinear and ambiguous? This is a tough question, and there is no obvious or all-encompassing answer to it. Broadly speaking, I have found it helpful to explicitly reframe metrics-driven accountability for product managers not as *hitting* a particular quantitative target but rather as *prioritizing their team's efforts to align with that quantitative target.* I usually break this down into six specific responsibilities:

- Know what metrics you're looking at and how they connect to overall team and company goals.
- Have clear and specific targets for these metrics.
- Know what is going on with these metrics right now.
- Identify the underlying issues that are causing these metrics to do what they are doing.
- Determine which underlying issues can be effectively addressed by you and your team.
- Have a prioritized action plan for addressing these issues.

When taken as a whole, these six bullet points can help product managers stay engaged with their team's goals, regardless of whether those goals seem to be telling a good or bad story. If the numbers for which you are accountable are moving in the right direction, but you don't know why or what to do about it, you are not doing your job as a product manager. And, if the numbers for which you are accountable are moving in the wrong direction, but you have taken the time to understand why and develop a plan of action, you *are* doing your job as a product manager.

Summary: No Shortcuts!

The notion of data-driven product management can promise an almost magical-seeming worry- and risk-free future. If used thoughtfully and thoroughly, data can be a critical tool for understanding your users and your product—but it won't do your job for you. You are still ultimately responsible for understanding the decisions you need to make, finding the best data you can to help inform those decisions, and working with the abjectly qualitative human beings in your organization to actually *make* those decisions.

Your Checklist

- Recognize that a data-driven approach still means that you will have to set priorities and make decisions.
- Avoid using the word *data* to generalize specific information. Say what that information is and how it was gathered.
- Have a clear point of view on which metrics matter to your team and how those metrics are connected to your goals and strategy.
- Be specific about what you *expect* to happen before a product launch or any other action with measurable outcomes.
- Complement your success metrics with "survival metrics" to facilitate an up-front conversation about what outcomes will or will not warrant continued investment in a new product or feature.
- Run experiments with the goal of creating value for your users, not proving yourself to your colleagues.
- Acknowledge that the specific impact your work has on high-level business outcomes, such as growth and revenue, will always be difficult to quantify.
- Use specific quantitative goals and targets to prioritize your team's work, not to assess your own personal success or failure as a product manager.

12

Prioritization: Where It All Comes Together

As we've discussed in the preceding chapters, there are many defensible ways to tread water before making an important decision. You can make big, impressive PowerPoint presentations! You can get into serious, intense debates about the difference between "mission" and "vision"! You can bury yourself in dashboards and insist that you "need more data"!

But sooner or later, there are some important questions you will need to answer with your team: What do you build? How much of it do you build? How will you know if it is successful? What should you *not* build? In fact, what should you stop supporting altogether?

These questions often come to a head during a process broadly referred to as "prioritization." This is when you sit down with your team to figure out what you're actually going to do for the next finite period of time. You may be pulling in user stories from an existing backlog, or you may be working with your team to identify and scope new ideas. But whatever you're doing, you will have to make some important decisions. And you will never feel like you have enough information to make those decisions with the degree of confidence and certainty that you desire.

It is in this process of prioritization that goals, strategy, metrics, experiment results, and just about everything else we've discussed all come together. Unfortunately for you, the picture they form might be a wholly inconsistent, confusing, and contradictory one. Here again, product managers often turn to frameworks for the assurance that they are doing prioritization the "right" way. But every single prioritization framework contains enough ambiguity to break down completely if you don't know where your team is going and how you plan to get there. If you are using an impact-versus-effort matrix, how exactly do you define *impact* if your goals are unclear? If you are using the MoSCoW method of prioritization (in which the *M* stands for "must have"), how do you know what constitutes a must-have if you don't know who you're building for?

No matter what framework you use and how much preparation you've done, there will inevitably be moments in your prioritization process where you realize that a critical question is unanswered or a goal is not as clear as you thought it was. In this chapter, we'll look at how you can move forward and make the best decisions you can, regardless of the formal prioritization framework or process your team uses.

Taking a Bite of the Layer Cake

As you set about making prioritization decisions, you will likely have many different layers and levels of company, team, product, and user goals, strategies, and metrics to keep in mind. In theory, all of these layers should fit together into a tidy cascade of clarity and purpose. In practice, they are much more likely to resemble a big, messy layer cake (Figure 12-1). Not every layer of the cake is necessarily delicious, nor does every layer of the cake complement the adjacent layers. Some layers might be particularly sweet and fluffy; others might be dry and crumbly. It is your job, with every decision you make, to figure out which layers are worth reaching for in this particular bite.

The bigger your company, the taller and more unwieldy the layer cake is likely to be. The smaller your company, the messier and denser. No bite of the cake is ever going to be perfect, but you will still need to put together the best one you can, every single time.

Imagine, for example, that you are working at a large company that has well-defined and well-socialized corporate revenue and user growth goals, plus well-defined and well-socialized strategic initiatives. You nodded along when these things were presented at various all-hands meetings, but when the time comes for your team to prioritize the next quarter of work, you have a hard time reconciling them. The initiatives, though exciting and compellingly worded, don't seem to ladder up directly to the company's revenue goals. You had been planning to make some changes to the company's core product, but the initiatives all seem focused on new products and features. So, what do you do?

Figure 12-1. The layer cake of goals, strategies, insights, and other stuff. Each decision about what you build, how you build it, and how much of it you build is its own unique bite of the layer cake.

In short, you do the best you can. You take a look at all the layers available to you—from high-level company goals to specific user insights and product metrics—and try to take the bite that will be most delicious for your company and your users. You might, for example, look at product instrumentation data and decide that changes to the core product are ultimately much more likely to deliver against both the company's overall revenue goals *and* your individual team's quarterly OKRs. In this case, you might find yourself making a case to company leadership such as "We are choosing to prioritize making improvements to the company's core product because we believe it will most directly impact our company's revenue goals. This is in line with our team's OKRs of creating the best possible experience for our existing customers to drive revenue and retention."

Alternately, you might do some competitive analysis and realize that you have a really interesting opportunity to focus on a new user segment that has been previously underaddressed by the company at large. Focusing your team on finding new solutions for *new* users could very well align both to the company's strategic initiatives *and* to its overall growth goals. In this case, you might find yourself making a case to company leadership such as "We are choosing to prioritize understanding and developing solutions for new user segments that our core product currently does not serve. This is in line with the company's strategic initiatives, and we believe it will ultimately have a positive effect on the company's growth goals."

Neither of these approaches is fundamentally right or wrong. The challenge, as always, is to make the best decision you can with the information you have, even when that information seems incomplete or contradictory—which it usually will.

Every Decision Is a Trade-Off

Every time I log in to Netflix, it asks me whether I am using the product on behalf of "Matt" or "kids." I do not have kids, nor has a kid ever used my account for the decade or so that I have been a Netflix subscriber. So why do I have to complete this extra step before watching the latest episode of *Is It Cake?* while I drift off to sleep?

Full disclosure: I am not and never have been a product manager at Netflix. But I am quite confident that just about any parent I know would be *much* more upset at discovering that their eight-year-old has been bingeing *Squid Game* than I am at having to mindlessly tap the Enter button on my remote one more time.

This now-ubiquitous pattern illustrates a fundamental truth about product development: every decision is a trade-off. When you add new functionality to help one type of user, you will likely frustrate another type of user. When you streamline an experience to remove extraneous-seeming steps, some people will complain loudly about how much they miss those steps. And, when you invest a ton of your team's time and energy into building an exciting-sounding new feature, that feature might come nowhere near to justifying its own cost.

Here are tips for navigating these trade-offs thoughtfully and effectively:

Start small.

Most of the time, you won't know how good or bad a decision really is until *after* you've made it. For that reason, you are often better off prioritizing small steps that allow you to gather some feedback and adjust course. This is where the kind of experimentation we discussed in Chapter 11 can be particularly valuable and where the timeboxes and fixed constraints that come with many Agile development frameworks can be used to your advantage.

Think about different user segments or personas, and prioritize their needs.

As the example above illustrates, different user segments or personas are likely going to have different needs and goals, and what helps one might frustrate another. For example, features that serve a small but high-value group of power users might complicate the experience for a larger but lower-value group of casual users. Figuring out which segment to prioritize, and how best to address their needs, will probably necessitate taking several messy bites out of a big, messy layer cake.

Thinking in terms of different user segments or personas can often help you mitigate the downside of whatever decision you make. You might, for example, be able to roll out some new changes to a particular subset of users based on their existing behavior or preferences. Generally speaking, you are always better off thinking about specific needs of specific users rather than trying to find the best compromise for "everybody."

Document your assumptions.

Even as you work to make informed trade-offs, you *still* must make some assumptions in order to move forward. You might assume that the results of a small experiment will scale to a wider base of users. You might assume that the outliers in a particular dataset your team consulted are not that important. You might assume that your users' fundamental needs will remain unchanged for the amount of time it takes your team to explore and deliver a solution. Rather than minimizing or hiding these assumptions, try documenting and discussing them with your team. This will leave you better equipped to adjust course when new information comes along that may validate—or invalidate—the assumptions you've worked together to catalog and understand.

Remember that everything you build comes at a cost—even if that cost is invisible.

At times, it can seem like a product manager's job is to find the most defensible thing to build at any given moment, work with their team to build that thing, and then move on to the next. But it's always worth keeping in mind that your team's time comes at a cost to the business and, if you are not justifying that cost, you may eventually find yourself having to justify your team's very existence. If none of the things your team is considering building seem all that impactful, think about how you might broaden or refocus your team's goals and strategy to better align with the company's overall ambitions.

Effective product managers do not shy away from communicating the downsides of the trade-offs they are making. In doing so, they help their teams, organizations, and leaders feel more comfortable moving forward with decisions that—like all decisions, ideally—aim for progress, not perfection.

Starting Small to Make Big Changes at a Legacy Company
Geof H.
Product Leader, paper and packaging enterprise

I recently started leading product at a company that does paper and packaging. This is a tremendously exciting space, with enormous potential to improve products that are deeply integrated into the lives of countless people and companies. But, in over a decade working in product, I've learned that you can't just waltz in and say, "Your company is outdated! You should be doing what a digitally native company would do!" To drive real, lasting change, you need to get from idea to results as quickly as possible and show your company that this kind of thing is really possible, not just a far-fetched fantasy flown in from Silicon Valley.

So the first thing I did when I started was get to know the general managers (GMs) on our plant floors—the people who had the most knowledge of our day-to-day goals and challenges. I asked what their biggest challenges were and got a pretty clear and consistent answer: lost pallets. And that answer makes a lot of sense! Imagine if you're putting together a complex merchandising display with a hundred pieces, and a pallet with a dozen of those pieces goes missing. Suddenly, you might need to rerun the entire job, which can substantially slow down production. So I asked one of our GMs, "What if we could tell you where your stuff is all the time?" The answer was a resounding "Yes! If you can do that, you will have free rein to do whatever you need in our facility to make it happen."

From a technical standpoint, this isn't a terribly complex problem to solve. We can use basic, commercially available sensors to prototype a solution that will drive real, immediate results for that GM. And that's really my strategy: make the GM the hero. You may have your own ambitions to "transform" or "disrupt" the business, but the people who make up that business need to understand how this is going to help them achieve their ambitions. **If you can solve a real problem for somebody, they will tell the story to their boss, and their boss's boss, and**

before you know it, you have the whole company advocating for your work.

Keeping the Entire Experience in Mind

Much has been written about how product teams and organizations can easily turn into "feature factories," churning out a bunch of exciting-sounding features that don't really deliver any value to the business or its users. (Here, again, I recommend Melissa Perri's excellent *Escaping the Build Trap*.) Nearly every product manager I know has complained to me at least once that their company is an output-obsessed feature factory that only *pretends* to care about its users. But nearly every product manager I know, myself included, has also contributed to this very problem by prioritizing the features that will be easiest to manage over the features (and nonfeatures) that will be most impactful.

In practical terms, this often means prioritizing the features that are *least* likely to require coordination with other product managers and teams. Nearly every product manager is given implicit or explicit purview over a particular part of the app, success metric, and/or user journey. And nearly every product manager is likely to prioritize the work that can be done within the clear and comfortable boundaries of their own responsibilities and their own team.

The reasoning behind this is not hard to understand: product management is difficult enough when the only stakeholders you really need to align are the designers and developers you work with every day. Once you need to coordinate with other product teams, you will also need to navigate *their* goals, ambitions, expectations, and internal misalignments. Thanks, but no thanks.

The inconvenient truth here is that the very features and improvements that cross multiple teams' areas of responsibility are, almost without fail, the most impactful to the business and its users. A 2013 *Harvard Business Review* article by Alex Rawson, Ewan Duncan, and Conor Jones called "The Truth About Customer Experience" (*https://oreil.ly/mOo97*) makes a critical point that often gets lost in the conversation about product management: from a customer's perspective, the most important part of a product is often not its individual "features" at all but rather how those features come together to create a seamless and cohesive experience.

In summary, the very things that are going to be most impactful for product managers to prioritize are often the ones that are going to be the most frustrating and difficult to execute. This results in many product managers and teams dutifully avoiding any changes to the most interconnected parts of their product, which in turn leaves many modern products feeling like jumbles of disconnected features, rather than seamless and easy-to-navigate experiences.

For real-world examples of this anti-pattern, one need not look farther than the flagship products made by some of the very digital-product companies whose "best practices" often get trotted out in conference talks and whitepapers. I say this not to throw gratuitous shade at these companies, but rather to point out that—truly—*nobody* has this definitively figured out. There is no single operating model or portfolio management framework that can solve for the amount of on-the-ground coordination, collaboration, and thoughtfully facilitated decision-making that goes into keeping all the pieces of a complex product humming together in user-centric harmony.

So what does this mean for working product managers? In short, it means that, no matter where exactly the silos and boundaries fall in your particular organization, you're going to have to do the hard work of reaching beyond those silos and boundaries. Here are some tactical tips for identifying, prioritizing, and executing opportunities beyond your immediate team's purview:

Use your own product regularly to complete entire tasks and journeys.

One way to make sure you are living in your user's reality is to regularly use your own product in a manner that closely resembles the way your actual users do. Rather than doing tightly scoped tests and walk-throughs of your own feature(s), try signing up for a new account and completing the entire suite of tasks or journeys that are most important to a specific user type or persona. You will likely discover that the most meaningful opportunities to improve the experience overall are not definitively scoped to your team's work—or to any single team's work, for that matter.

Start with team goals, not tactical dependencies.

When coordinating across teams, it can be tempting to start by identifying the tactical dependencies that will need to be resolved for work to move forward. But these dependencies are rarely all that motivating, nor do they necessarily speak to the user needs that you will be working together to address. Before getting into the nitty-gritty of dependencies, have a conversation about how you can work together to maximize your impact. Since work that involves multiple features or product areas tends to be of particular value to users (and in turn to the business), you might find that this goal-based conversation shifts the tone of your collaboration from

"Ugh, we have to coordinate so many different little things" to "Wow, we can make a really, really big difference here."

Look at subtractive solutions.

A recent article in *Nature* magazine (*https://oreil.ly/X8QE8*), which was shared widely in the product community, describes how our brains are inclined to pursue additive solutions to problems before we even consider subtractive solutions. For me and many other product managers, this helped explain why the answer to so many problems always seems to be "Let's add another feature," even when that problem is "Our users seem to think we have too many features." One of the benefits to looking across multiple features or product areas is that you can often identify opportunities to *subtract* or streamline functionality in a way that would be much harder if you were strictly limited to your own part of the product.

By way of example, a product leader I worked with once offered a $5,000 cash bounty on any user setting that a product manager could successfully argue should be removed from the app. Of course, removing a setting from the app usually had ramifications for many product managers' and teams' work. But a cash bonus provided an incentive for product managers to do the difficult work of coordinating across teams—even if it meant that the bonus would ultimately need to be split a few ways.

Once again, start small.

The more teams and individuals are involved in something, the higher the stakes can seem. This, in turn, can amplify anxiety and risk aversion. When you are working together to reevaluate bigger parts of the user experience, look for opportunities to start with small changes. Measure those changes, analyze the results, and move forward.

Again, remember that no product organization in the world has this all figured out. Don't give up if it feels like your particular company's operating model or org chart seems purpose-built to discourage collaboration across teams. Keep one foot firmly planted in your user's reality and don't be afraid to step the other one outside of your team or silo in order to deliver the best possible outcomes.

From Shiny Objects to Jewels of Understanding

As you do the hard work of prioritizing what matters to your users and your business, you will likely be constantly barraged with ideas for shiny new features. No perfectly articulated strategy will ever serve as a comprehensive bulwark against this, and you may be tempted to see your job as swatting away as many of these "shiny objects" as possible. But people generally don't like having their ideas swatted away, and your goal is ultimately not to say no to stakeholders, but rather to help them make the best decisions they can.

So, for starters, when somebody comes to you excited about a new idea, don't react in a way that turns that excitement into resentment. Work in partnership with the person suggesting the idea to understand just what makes it so exciting in the first place. Maybe this new idea reflects a change in overall company strategy or priorities that you wouldn't otherwise have known about. Maybe a competitor's new feature has been getting a lot of positive press and warrants further investigation. Maybe somebody just thought something was *really cool* and wanted to share it with you. Rather than fighting the momentum behind shiny and new ideas, see if you can redirect that momentum toward the ideas that will deliver the most value for your users and your business. If you put in the work to understand how a shiny new feature could solve a real problem for your users, you are in a better position to generate excitement around *all* the different ways you might solve that problem.

For example, imagine that a developer on your team is really excited about allowing your users to log in with their credentials from a social platform that, in your discerning opinion, is destined to be a short-lived flash in the pan. This developer arrives at your prioritization meeting having already coordinated with support to find a few examples of users asking to log in with this new platform's credentials. You pause for a moment and try to suppress your frustration. How in the world could this person think that something so marginal is worth prioritizing? In an effort to quickly move past this suggestion by way of a goal-based question, you say, "Interesting...how many of our actual users do you think are currently *unable* to log in because this feature is not available?" The developer nods with resignation. You kept the team on track.

Unfortunately, you also might have missed an important opportunity. Something about this idea had your developer excited enough to dig through user feedback before your prioritization meeting! Perhaps this developer is really passionate about improving the overall login experience for your users, which might open up an important discussion about *less* shiny and new but potentially more impactful ideas, such as improving your password recovery workflow. Perhaps this developer read about how the social platform in question took a truly novel and interesting approach to its authentication workflow, which might open up an important discussion about what makes for a good authentication workflow in the first place. Something about this idea got your developer truly motivated, but you won't be able to harness that motivation if you look for ways to dismiss their suggestion outright.

Taking this approach, you might find yourself open to new ideas that you had not initially thought worthy of exploring. This constitutes yet another critical opportunity to involve your team not just in executing but also in learning, thinking, and experimenting. Unfortunately, these activities will often fall by the wayside if you don't explicitly make them a part of how your team prioritizes its time and effort. In Agile parlance, a finite amount of time devoted to learning, researching, and/or experimenting (as opposed to building or coding) is often called a "spike." In keeping with "The Best Thing About Best Practices" from Chapter 7, using this specific language can be helpful in communicating that you are not haphazardly taking time away from executional work but rather intention-ally prioritizing time for the thoughtful exploration of how best to approach that executional work.

Here, our guiding principle "All efforts in service of outcomes" reminds us that successful execution is not just about *doing lots of stuff* but rather about prioritizing the activities that are most likely to help us achieve our goals. Some of the most important product decisions I've seen made by members of my team have happened when the first item on their to-do list for the next week wasn't "Write a bunch of code to complete this feature," but rather "Research five possible implementation approaches that would help us better understand this feature."

Using Prototypes to Validate or Invalidate Feature Ideas

J.D.

Product Manager, 50-person entertainment startup

When I was working at a 50-person entertainment startup, we had an idea for a really, really cool geolocation-based feature. The idea had been floating around for a while when I started, but I took the lead on

writing up a lightweight spec, getting buy-in from across the organization, and making sure it had a place on our roadmap.

After a few months of planning, we were ready to start building.
During a prioritization meeting with the product team, we discussed a
few potential approaches we could take to getting the product started.
At first, the conversation gravitated toward a fairly technical discussion
about how we would implement a geolocation-based feature. One of our
developers wanted to use an open source option that would require more
work but carry no additional cost. Another developer had a vendor they
preferred, whose service was costly but would require less work on our
end.

Always up for a good technical challenge, the developer who preferred the open source option offered a solution: give her two weeks to see
if she could make a geolocation-aware prototype to test the open source
solution and then make a decision. I was a little nervous about kicking
off this project with a prototype that wouldn't necessarily lead us to our
actual feature, but everybody seemed excited about this, so we agreed to
move forward.

Two weeks later, we set up a time for our developer to demo the prototype she had built. It was, from her perspective, a complete technical
success. She was able to create a basic proof-of-concept app that simply
fired off an alert when any of the geolocation criteria we had written into
the product spec were met. And she was able to do it using the free, open
source solution she favored.

But as she walked us through the solution she had built, a few of us
started to have the same creeping thought: how useful would this feature
actually be to our users? Hearing our developer walk through the way
she had used this prototype left us with some big questions about how
valuable our users might find the full-fledged feature we were imagining.
So, rather than moving forward with building the feature, we decided to
give the prototype app to a few of our colleagues and see whether it
pointed to a feature that would actually be useful.

After just a week, it became very clear to us that this feature was not
actually as valuable as we had imagined. The specific geolocation criteria
we thought we could use to customize an entertainment experience were
not met as often as we had hoped and, furthermore, didn't seem to align

with the actual needs and preferences of my colleagues in the moments when the alerts were triggered.

Yes, ideally you should test a prototype with users from outside your organization. But the biggest risk of testing something internally is that you will validate an idea that isn't valuable for your users, and I'm proud of the fact that we were actually able to invalidate an idea that we had all thought would be great. What we thought was just a technical proof of concept actually turned out to be a critical way for testing whether the feature we planned to build would be valuable for our users. **A two-week prototype probably saved us six months of development time that would not have helped us meet our organizational goals.**

But This Is an Emergency!

In theory, one of the primary functions of a prioritization process is to determine both what will and what will not be built in a given time frame. But in practice, every single organization must deal with "emergency" requests. (We walked through one such request at the end of Chapter 5.) In the spirit of product managers making themselves obsolete, I often suggest handling these requests with a templatized intake form. These questions can be a good place to start:

- What is the issue?
- Who reported this issue?
- How many users is it affecting?
- How does this issue affect our company-level goals, such as revenue?
- What would happen if this issue were not addressed in the next two weeks?
- What would happen if this issue were not addressed in the next six months?
- Who is the contact person for further discussing/resolving this issue?

Depending on the specifics of your organization, you can customize your template to accommodate feature-happy marketing teams, account management teams that request last-minute custom work, and even developers who seem to habitually prioritize a new bug that they discovered over the work they had set out to do in your prioritization meeting. You can also fine-tune the specific questions around the number of users affected and the potential reve-nue ramifications based on how broadly accessible that information is within your organization. (Or, even better, use this template as a starting point for making that information more accessible!)

In many cases, I've found that the mere presence of a template like this makes the volume of emergency requests drop significantly. After all, it's much easier to storm into a (chat) room and say, "THIS NEEDS TO BE FIXED RIGHT NOW" than it is to sit down and figure out the actual impact of the work you're asking somebody else to complete on your behalf.

Prioritization in Practice: Same Options, Different Goals and Strategies

Imagine that you are working as a product manager at an ad-supported video startup. Your company pulls in video from around the web to create "personal-ized video playlists" that people can enjoy at parties, on their commute, or just to kill time. You know that short-form video is *huge* right now, and you know that there's a lot of potential in personalized aggregation as the video market becomes more fragmented.

As you sit down to approach your next prioritization meeting, you see five items on the roadmap slated for the next quarter:

- Connect to new display advertising network.
- Add social sharing feature.
- Build functionality for sponsored video playlists.
- Improve personalization algorithm.
- Launch Android app (currently iOS-only).

Some of these ideas have been kicked around within the company since it started. Some of them were supposed to be built last quarter but were pushed back. And some of them wound up on the roadmap because senior stakeholders kept asking for them and you found it much easier to say, "You've got it—it's going on the roadmap!" than to debate the finer points of something you wouldn't really need to think about for a while.

As is often the case, these things are all very different from one another. It's not entirely clear why you would build one over the other, or even what kind of resourcing they would require. So, you turn to your organization's goals.

Wait, goals? This is a *startup*. You rummage through some old emails from your founder and find something labeled "OUR MISSION." It reads:

Our mission is to completely transform the way that people consume video. By aggregating video from all over the web and using machine learning to create a "personalized playlist," we can disrupt the media industry and create a better experience for our users.

"OK," you think to yourself, "it looks like we have something that resembles a goal (transforming the way that people consume video) and something that resembles a strategy (using machine learning to create personal playlists)." How would you prioritize these five potential ideas against those goals? It's not easy, is it?

Now, suppose that, rather than just winging it, you decide to sit down with the founder and see how effectively this mission can (or cannot) help guide the specific prioritization decisions you are setting out to make with your team. You walk him through the five items on your team's roadmap, and he agrees that the company's mission statement doesn't provide much tactical guidance. So you agree to draft some quarterly goals that will help your team prioritize its efforts moving forward. And you agree to refine these goals by testing them against the actual roadmap your team is about to prioritize.

After going back and forth a few times, you wind up with the following OKR-style goal for the next quarter:

Our high-level goal for the next quarter is to get our product in front of anybody who is currently engaged in the behavior of watching videos across multiple platforms. We will know we are on the right track toward achieving this goal when:

- *Weekly app downloads have increased by 200%.*
- *70% of users who download the app complete account creation.*
- *The average number of connected video platforms per user has increased from 1.3 to 2.*

You know that this goal and its corresponding success metrics are not perfect or 100% comprehensive, but when you went through them with the founder, you were able to strike a few items off your list (especially those that might increase revenue without contributing to user growth). There are a few ideas you need to research a bit more (how many users are you currently losing to not having an Android app?), but at the very least you have a clear sense of how to proceed. Some of the sales folks might be annoyed that you won't be working on their priorities first, but you're not too worried about it because your choices are clearly being driven by company-level goals.

Now, imagine that your conversation with the founder goes very differently. After the meeting, you wind up with the following OKR-style goal for the next quarter:

Our high-level goal for the next quarter is to increase the company's revenue while minimizing the need for customized development work. We will know that we are achieving this goal when:

- *Overall revenue has increased by 30%.*

- *The percentage of revenue coming from automated ad systems has increased from 30% to 60%.*

- *We are able to continue at or exceed our current rate of user growth.*

Again, these are not perfect or 100% comprehensive, and they don't tell you quite as much about who you're building for and what problem you're solving for them. But they provide some clear guidance about what you might want to build right now, as well as some guidance about how you might want to implement some items on the roadmap. (Could you build a "sponsored video playlist" system in a way that would not contribute to increasing customized development work?)

Hopefully, thinking through these scenarios helps to illustrate the importance of keeping strategy and execution aligned—and how goals, strategy, objectives, and metrics all tend to blur together when you have actual prioritization decisions to make. Don't let that stop you from making the best decisions you can, and certainly don't let it stop you from working closely with your team to make those decisions together.

Summary: Think Big, Start Small

Deciding what to build, how to build it, and when to build it can be one of the most overwhelming parts of a product manager's job. Inconsistencies in company strategy, missing bits of data, and misalignments on your own team can all conspire to leave you feeling like *any* decision you make is the wrong one. But, for better or worse, product management rarely ever affords us the luxury of knowing with utmost confidence and certainty that we are making the right decision. Use this uncomfortable reality to your advantage by breaking down big plans and decisions into small enough steps that you can gather feedback, reevaluate, and adjust course as needed.

Your Checklist

- Don't expect your company's and team's goals, strategies, objectives, and metrics to fit together into a tidy cascade. Treat them more like a messy layer cake and try to find the best bite you can with every decision you make.

- Recognize that any formal prioritization framework is still going to rely upon subjective concepts like "impact" and "must-build." No matter which framework you choose, if any, you will still need to navigate the stomach-churning feeling of making an important decision with incomplete information.

- Approach every decision you make as a trade-off, and explain that trade-off as comprehensively and fearlessly as you can.

- Document the assumptions that go into making a decision and bring them to your team, rather than minimizing or ignoring them.

- Think about entire user journeys and tasks, not isolated "features."

- Remember that *subtracting* features and functionality can sometimes be a value-add for your users and business. Not every problem is best solved by adding more features!

- When your colleagues come to you excited about something they want to build, work to understand that excitement rather than reflexively saying no.

- Incorporate "spikes" and other opportunities to explore and learn with your team into your prioritization activities.

- Create a lightweight process for handling "emergency" requests rather than rushing to address them personally.

- Look for every possible opportunity to shorten the distance between strategy and tactics by testing your goals, strategy, and objectives against real-world product prioritization decisions.

- Break down your big plans into small enough steps that you can gather feedback and adjust course.

13

Try This at Home:
The Trials and Tribulations
of Remote Work

Several decades ago in mid-2019, I found myself having a conversation with a few product managers who had made the transition to working remotely. "It's fantastic," one of them said. "I don't have to waste half of my life traveling from place to place, and I think I'm actually getting better at my job!" With an air of self-satisfied contrarian certainty, I responded, "Yeah, I mean, that sounds great, but I can't imagine not being able to spend time face-to-face with people. I actually *love* the amount of travel I'm doing for work, and I don't think I'd be nearly as good at my job if I had to do it remotely."

Whoops.

In the last several years, countless guides to remote and distributed work have been published, each with its own "useful fictions" that may help you think through how best to work with your own distributed or hybrid team. But, just as there is no such thing as a single step-by-step guide to doing product management, there is certainly no such thing as a single step-by-step guide to *remote* product management. If anything, the ever-shifting trends toward and away from remote work only add more variables to an already-overwhelming equation.

In this chapter, we'll discuss some of the common challenges of doing product management remotely, and the tremendous amount of effort and thoughtfulness that goes into doing it well. Note that the word *remote* generally refers to an individual working outside of a centralized office space, while the word *distributed* generally refers to a team operating without a centralized office space. The ideas discussed in this chapter should be relevant for fully distributed teams and for teams that are balancing on-site and remote work.

Building Trust from Far Away

Once upon a time, I held firm to the assumption that it was nearly impossible to build a strong team without a shared physical workspace. After all, how are you supposed to get beyond transactional relationships with your colleagues if you aren't having informal chats over lunch or coffee? How are you supposed to collaborate generatively if you can't work something out on a whiteboard? And how are you supposed to build trust with people if you can't even be in the same room with them?

The answers to that last question, in particular, can be quite surprising. In an excellent article entitled "Remote Work Insights You've Never Heard Before," (*https://oreil.ly/LCohz*) engineering leader Sarah Milstein makes the bold claim that "distributed teams often have higher trust—and thus work better—than colocated teams." Milstein lays out several reasons for why this may be true, but the one that resonates most with me builds upon the notion of "swift trust" (*https://oreil.ly/M7shY*) as articulated by Debra Meyerson in 1996. Meyerson's work explored how trust can be built quickly and decisively on temporary teams, and Milstein points out how such dynamics can play out similarly on distributed teams. In short, if you and your colleagues are not working within the physical and social structures of a formal and long-standing team, *you need to make the choice to trust each other pretty quickly*. You can't look over each other's shoulders or keep score about who is showing up first in the office or leaving last (though you can re-create these low-trust behaviors via digital proxy if you really, really, really want to).

It is worth remembering that, while swift trust may accelerate the speed at which distributed team members must make the decision to trust each other, it is still very much a *decision* made by complex people with their own backgrounds, experiences, and expectations. There is no single recipe or tactical handbook for building trust across different teams full of different people. To truly build trust on any team—and on a distributed team in particular—it is important to look beyond prescriptive "best practices" and instead facilitate a conversation about how the individuals on that team want to work together, and why.

For example, there has been a fair amount of debate lately around whether folks on distributed teams should be required to turn their video cameras on for meetings. Some have argued that this is critical for building trust, while others have argued that it might put undue pressure on people who are dealing with the messy realities of working from home. The very existence of this debate speaks to the single most uncomfortable truth about distributed teams: every person is different, every team is different, and the recontextualization of work from a single shared workplace to a messy amalgam of work and home spaces only adds to that complexity.

Rachel Neasham, an experienced product leader whose colleagues spoke highly of her ability to build trust on remote teams, shared a particularly valuable perspective on this matter: rather than thinking in terms of "Should we or should we not implement a cameras-on rule?" she likes to think in terms of "How do we create a culture where people *want* to be deeply engaged on remote calls?" Neasham pointed out to me that, even if people are mostly following a cameras-on rule, it can become a source of judgment between colleagues, which ultimately erodes trust. "It's fascinating," she told me, "that tactical issues such as whether or not people turn their cameras on are almost always symptoms of deeper issues."

Indeed, once you begin digging into those deeper issues, you realize pretty quickly that there is no one recipe for a high-functioning distributed team. As we discussed in Chapter 8, making small changes and then retrospecting on those changes as a team is generally the most sustainable path forward.

Resolving Conflicts Across Language Barriers on a Distributed Team

Lisa Mo Wagner
Product Coach

Several years ago, I found myself at odds with an engineering counterpart over how to proceed with some refactoring work. I had navigated this conversation many times before, and I was usually able to work in close partnership with developers to understand the importance of this work and prioritize our efforts accordingly. But this time, my engineering counterpart and I were really struggling to communicate with each other. We were both working in a language that was not our first, coming from substantially different cultural backgrounds, and trying to build trust on a geographically distributed team. I couldn't shake the feeling that he thought I was a terrible product manager, and it was making it increasingly difficult for us to do the work we needed to do together.

I sought the advice of a trusted colleague, who suggested that I provide feedback to my engineering counterpart in writing. The hope was that, if I wrote out a few situations where we had struggled to work together and clearly described what they had felt like from my perspective, he would have some time to process this information offline and we would then be able to talk through it more easily. So I wrote up a few examples, sent them through to my engineering counterpart, and we got a half hour on the calendar the next week to talk through them together.

Long story short, we wound up talking for two hours and having an incredible conversation. We went through the feedback I had sent bit by bit, and it was clear that having a shared written record made this conversation *much* easier than it would have been otherwise. As we walked through one of the situations I had documented, he said to me, "I remember this situation—but I don't remember it being so bad at all. Why was it so difficult for you?" I explained to him that it left me feeling like he thought I was a bad product manager, which in turn had left me feeling defensive. He listened for a moment and said, "I don't think you're incompetent. I think you're a really good product manager. I just don't agree with everything you say." In that moment, we realized that we were both making a lot of assumptions about each other, and we agreed to leave those assumptions behind and work together in good faith.

By the end of that call, we were telling Dungeons and Dragons jokes and laughing together! And perhaps more importantly, we both walked away with a profound understanding that our working relationship could have been amazing from the beginning if we had communicated more directly and openly with each other. When you're working on a distributed team, especially a globally distributed team, it's particularly easy to fall back into your own assumptions. **Communicating directly across geographic, language, and cultural divides requires both vulnerability and effort—but that effort is always worthwhile.**

Simple Communication Agreements Create Meaningful Trust

"Trust" is a big and amorphous concept, and many teams struggle to find specific, tactical steps they can take toward building it. Over the last several years, I have been surprised to find that the most immediate impediments to building team trust are often misaligned expectations around day-to-day communication.

When I have prompted teams to describe specific instances that depleted trust, many of them have been as simple as "I thought somebody was going to get back to my email and they didn't," or "I receive more messages from my teammates than I can handle, and I'm afraid that they all think I'm blowing them off."

I went through this firsthand with my own small distributed team several years ago, when one of my business partners was splitting her time between New York and Lima, the other between New York and Madrid, and I had just relocated to Portland, Oregon. Walking around downtown with my wife on a Saturday afternoon, I heard a volley of alert noises emanating from my pocket. Ding! Ding! Ding ding ding! I checked my phone, and it turned out one of my business partners was leaving a flurry of comments on a Google document we were working through together. I froze in my tracks and shook my head. "I'm sorry," I told my wife, "I should probably go home. This looks important."

On the way home, I began to stew with resentment. Who was my business partner to straight-up inundate me with messages like that? What kind of low-trust, transactional, nonsense partnership was this? Was I even a *partner* at all? By the time my wife and I got home, I was positively *fuming*. I picked up the phone, called my business partner, and righteously demanded an explanation for why she was dumping this work on me smack in the middle of my weekend. She responded with genuine bafflement: "I didn't expect you to even look at those comments—this just happened to be the time I was available to work. Why do you even have your phone set to give you alerts on Google Docs comments? That sounds horrible!"

Humbled by this moment, I opened our next partners meeting by apologizing for my own assumptions and asking if there were any other areas where we were struggling to communicate across our different working hours and time zones. We wound up identifying the following issues:

- Misalignment about how quickly a response is expected (e.g., if I receive an email from one of my business partners, I might interpret it as urgent —even if it is decidedly not urgent!).

- Unclear expectations around how long a given task will take (e.g., if I ask one of my business partners, "Can you take a quick look at this?" how much actual time am I asking for?).

- Inbox overwhelm, which makes it difficult to parse and prioritize new messages (e.g., if I email one of my business partners and they have 100 unread messages already sitting in their inbox, how do they know what's important?).

Based on these issues, we aligned on a set of questions that we attempted to answer in a brief set of agreements that we dubbed our "Comms Manual." Those questions are:

- How quickly are you expected to respond to an asynchronous message in each channel (email, text, Slack, etc.)?
- What criteria must we make explicit in any ask of each other (e.g., how long we are asking for, when we need it by, whether it is a blocker or not)?
- What are our individual and team working hours, and how do we handle messages sent and received outside of these working hours?

We put our answers to these questions in a one-page document, which we turned into a template that you can access here (*https://oreil.ly/twnb4*). Every team is different, and every team's Comms Manual can—and should—be different. One place I've found it helpful to start, especially for distributed teams, is simply by asking the question, "When somebody on this team receives a message from somebody else on this team, how quickly do they expect a response?" Unless everybody on your team can immediately rattle off the same answer—and they likely can't—this makes a pretty clear case for why having explicit communication agreements in place is so important.

Navigating Synchronous and Asynchronous Communication

There is an exercise I often run with teams that consists of mapping their existing communication channels and ceremonies on a 2x2 grid. One axis of this grid is labeled from "colocated" (meaning that everybody works in a single shared physical space) to "distributed" (meaning that everybody works from their own separate physical space). The other axis is labeled from "synchronous" (meaning that messages are sent and received at the same time, such as with face-to-face or voice-to-voice conversation) to "asynchronous" (meaning that messages are sent and received at independent times, such as with email and other messaging platforms). As of January 2022, the resulting visual often winds up looking something like Figure 13-1.

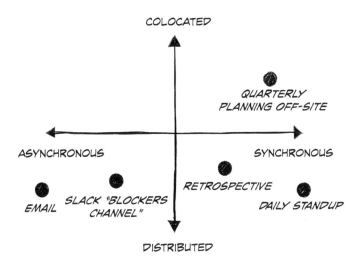

Figure 13-1. A typical team's channels and ceremonies mapped circa January 2022

Having run this exercise with dozens of teams, two interesting patterns have emerged. First, there is often a fair amount of disagreement over which channels are actually synchronous and which channels are actually asynchronous. This debate is often particularly spirited when it comes to chat platforms like Slack and Teams; usually, some people on a team believe that these channels implicitly demand up-to-the-moment attention, while others believe that these channels can be checked once or twice a day. Again, these disconnects speak to the importance of having explicit communication agreements in place.

The second and in many ways more insidious pattern is that many teams are using their synchronous time primarily for activities that could be described as "status updates." And sure enough, for some teams, synchronous status updates can be a valuable way to get people on the same page and coordinate around complex work. For many other teams, though, synchronous status meetings can be a frustrating waste of time.

If you have ever drank out of, or chuckled at, a mug that says, "I SURVIVED ANOTHER MEETING THAT SHOULD HAVE BEEN AN EMAIL," you may very well have experienced this exact thing. For many teams, the widespread adoption of distributed work has simply accelerated the path to a somewhat inevitable reckoning: "Why are we spending our precious time together talking about stuff we already did?" This holds particularly true for teams working across far-flung time zones, where synchronous time can be tremendously hard to come by.

Again, every team's approach to using synchronous and asynchronous time will be different. In the sections that follow, we look at some common approaches to synchronous and asynchronous communication for distributed teams and how some distributed teams have integrated these approaches into a "synchronous sandwich."

Synchronous Communication for Distributed Teams: Choreographing Time and Space

Many of the teams I work with are eager to shift their synchronous time away from status updates and toward collaborative decision-making. That is, until they find themselves trying to get a dozen half-asleep people to make a decision while five of them are checking their email. The word that comes up most frequently in my conversations with distributed product teams navigating synchronous communication is "intentional." As in, "You have to be *really* intentional about the way you structure and facilitate your team's time together." Sure, if you are working in a shared office space, you can throw a whiteboard in the middle of the room and just "jam out" a passable solution (though the quality of that solution may be debatable). But if everybody is Zooming from home with email, ecommerce, and cat videos just one imperceptible click away? Yeah, good luck.

Keeping a distributed product team engaged and active for synchronous collaboration requires a surprising amount of planning, preparation, and discipline. Here are some tips I've found helpful for meticulously choreographing space and time to get the most out of your team's synchronous collaboration:

Keep it brief and keep it focused.

Earlier in my career, I figured that remote team members could simply "call in" for our four-hour sprint-planning meetings. To those remote team members, I offer my sincere and belated apologies. Staying engaged for an hours-long remote meeting—especially when that meeting is open-ended and poorly planned—is not something that should be asked of anybody. These days, I try to limit all remote synchronous meetings to one hour and break down longer meetings into multiple one-hour sessions with their own clear inputs, outputs, and goals. (We'll discuss this more when we get to the "synchronous sandwich" approach later in this chapter.)

Work in shared documents.

One way to bring structure and clarity to your synchronous meetings is to work together in shared documents, rather than tasking a single individual with documenting your conversation. If you are working toward creating a shared document like a roadmap or one-pager, this allows you to keep the meeting's desired outcome tangible and accessible for everybody involved. It also helps foster a sense of shared ownership, rather than positioning one person—usually, let's face it, the product manager—as the document's (gate)keeper.

Use familiar tools.

No synchronous collaboration ever feels like a truly level playing field. There are always some people who are more comfortable speaking up, some more familiar with the subject matter, and so on and so forth. But whenever you introduce a new tool for participants to use, you are introducing not one, but *two* additional levels of discrepancy: people who are more familiar with the particular tool you've chosen and people who are more comfortable navigating new tools in general. I've found it easiest to work in tools like Google Docs (or even Google Slides for whiteboard-style activities) that people are already likely to be using. Whatever trade-offs there are in terms of functionality are often more than made up for in terms of ease of use and familiarity. (Of course, "familiar" tools will vary from team to team—some may very well be deeply familiar with newer collaboration tools and platforms!)

Assume a 3x multiplier for prep and practice time.

Here's the one that I've found most important, but hardest to follow: for every hour of high-value synchronous time you plan to spend with your team, assume that it will take *three hours* of prep and practice to use that time well. In other words, if you are planning a one-hour roadmapping session with your team, put three hours on your calendar in the days beforehand to really think through what the final outcome of the roadmapping session will look like and how you want to structure each step of that session. You may even want to practice the session a few times yourself or with your colleagues, to make sure it runs smoothly.

If there is one theme that runs through the above suggestions, it is that well-spent synchronous time for distributed teams requires a lot of intentional prep and planning. But if you are willing to do that prep and planning, you may very well find your team more engaged and open to collaboration than they would be in a purely colocated environment. Especially when it comes to important shared efforts like prioritization and roadmapping, the ability to work in a centralized digital workspace can maximize engagement and participation. And when your team gets accustomed to working this way, you may very well find it easier to directly include stakeholders who were once kept at arm's length by geographic or organizational distance.

Using a Simple Impact-versus-Effort Matrix to Encourage Collaboration on a Remote Team

Janet Brunckhorst
Director of Product Management, Aurora Solar (*https://oreil.ly/ NZI13*)

We were working with a client who had a remote development team in another time zone. Though they were supposedly working in an Agile way, their process was still very disconnected: the product manager would write out a bunch of user stories in Jira, prioritize those user stories, and throw them over the wall to a remote team of designers and developers. This meant that the product managers were making a lot of assumptions about how easy or difficult it would be to deliver a particular feature, and it left the development team feeling pretty far removed from critical product decisions.

As the team embarked upon a particularly big and important project, it was clear that something had to change. So, we got all the product managers, designers, and developers together and had a very different kind of conversation about what we would build and why. First, before addressing any technical or tactical concerns, we had an open conversation about the core user needs we were trying to address. Then, we asked the open-ended question: "How might we address these needs for our users?" We collected ideas and plotted them on a very simple 2x2 impact-versus-effort matrix (Figure 13-2): how hard is this going to be versus how much of an impact will it have for our users? This gave the developers the opportunity to talk through the effort each idea would involve and the product managers the opportunity to describe the user-facing impact.

By the end of this meeting, we had a major breakthrough. The product manager realized that the solution that they wanted the most—but assumed would be way too difficult—wouldn't actually be any harder to execute than the other approaches they had considered. We were all able to commit to a path forward that delivered the most value to the product's users and made the best possible use of the developers' time. And the developers thought it was awesome too! **They were able to participate in a conversation that defined the product, rather than just being asked to execute against a predetermined set of tasks.**

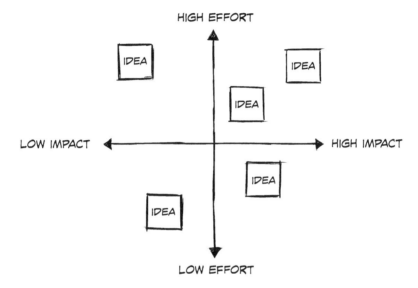

Figure 13-2. An impact-versus-effort matrix

Asynchronous Communication for Distributed Teams: Setting Specific Expectations

Given the difficulty of coordinating synchronous time among distributed teams, many such teams are quick to express a preference for asynchronous communication. And without a doubt, asynchronous communication affords some much-needed flexibility for folks struggling to balance enormous amounts of complex work; that 1 p.m. meeting is going to cut your day in half no matter what, but an email or shared document is something you can respond to on your own time.

In the interest of conserving their collective time and energy, distributed product teams often fall into the habit of communicating via volleys of "quick pings." These are the short "Can you take a look at this" or "Quick Q for you" emails, Slack chats, and other asynchronous messages that often haunt our inboxes during and beyond our working hours.

Each of these quick pings is, in fact, usually quite quick to send. But taken as a whole, these messages and the follow-up messages they spawn can represent a bottomless and unbounded time commitment for the people who must receive, contextualize, and prioritize them. An email thread that takes less than a minute to start can wind up collectively costing days of productive time before it is resolved or abandoned.

Ironically, the asynchronous messages that are fastest and easiest to send are often the most time-consuming and anxiety provoking to answer. In the interest of appearing friendly and not directly asking my colleagues for too much, I have often found myself omitting crucial information (such as, um, the reason I'm sending the message in the first place, what kind of response I need, and when I need it) from my own asynchronous messages. While this approach may have left me feeling like a cool and friendly guy, it also left my colleagues having to *guess* what I needed from them, when I needed it, and how important it really was.

As more and more of my work has been taking place via asynchronous messages, I have been making a more and more concerted effort to be clear and direct in what I am asking for and why I am asking for it. This is, of course, easier said than done. In the hopes of keeping myself honest, I keep the following checklist printed above my desk:

Before hitting SEND, ask yourself:

- Can the reader determine what action(s) this email is requesting within 10 seconds of receiving it?

- Have I directly stated the desired outcome and time frame?

  — "Please review by Friday 3 p.m."

  — "Can we meet before next Tuesday?"

- If I'm sending the same message to multiple recipients, have I clearly communicated what I am asking for from each person?

  — "Adding Abdul and Rachel to cc: as an FYI."

- If I am asking for feedback, am I clear about what kind of feedback I want and why?

  — "Attached is a rough outline for next Tuesday's presentation. Please spend no more than 10 minutes reviewing the overall structure of the outline and let me know if anything major seems to be missing. I will begin building out the deck itself on Thursday morning, so any feedback before then would be greatly appreciated."

- If I am using a generic follow-up phrase like *following up* or *checking in*, am I clearly (re)stating the desired type of response or action?
  - — "Following up on this email to see if you have 15 minutes next week to prepare for our presentation. Tuesday morning is currently wide open for me. Does 11 a.m. work for you?"

Putting more time and effort into the asynchronous messages that you send —whether you are sending them via email, Slack, Teams, or any other channel— will ultimately require *less* time and effort from your colleagues.

Making a "Synchronous Sandwich"

For your highest-stakes distributed work, you may very well want to get the best from both synchronous *and* asynchronous communication. After all, synchronous communication gives you the opportunity to generate and synthesize new ideas with your colleagues, while asynchronous communication gives you and your colleagues the opportunity to sharpen and refine your own thinking outside the pressure of a group setting.

When I'm working with a distributed team to assemble an important deliverable or make an important decision, I usually schedule a meeting that takes the form of a "synchronous sandwich"(Figure 13-3).

3. SUMMARIZE/UPDATE (ASYNCHRONOUS!)

2. DECIDE/CO-CREATE (SYNCHRONOUS!)

1. PREP/PRE-READ (ASYNCHRONOUS!)

Figure 13-3. A synchronous sandwich. Which slice of bread should go "first" in this image has been hotly debated, but I maintain that the bottom slice of bread must be laid down before you can get to the delicious fillings.

Each synchronous sandwich has three fairly straightforward steps:

- Send an asynchronous pre-read at least a day in advance of your meeting. This encourages participation from people who might need a little time to get their thoughts together, and it orients the entire group to the questions and tasks at hand.

- Facilitate a timeboxed, synchronous meeting where you work together to make a decision, co-create a document, or solve a problem as described in the pre-read.

- Send an asynchronous follow-up with next steps and action items no more than one day after your synchronous meeting. This keeps the momentum going and makes sure that everybody who participated in your meeting sees and understands its outcomes—even if they were distracted in the moment.

These three simple steps are a good starting point for making sure that your colleagues have the time to prepare their individual thoughts, the space to synthesize those thoughts into a shared plan or decision, and the opportunity to understand that plan or decision moving forward. Here's a template (*https://oreil.ly/sJyti*) you can use to begin mapping out your own synchronous sandwich.

Over the last year, I've found myself breaking down nearly all of the long meetings I used to conduct in person into several smaller synchronous sandwiches facilitated over video chat with shared documentation. For example, I now kick off roadmapping exercises for early-stage startups with a single, hour-long session to identify the mission-critical business milestones that the business must achieve in the next 3, 6, 9, and 12 months. At the end of that session, I send around the milestones we aligned on and ask participants to start thinking about all the different ways (existing products, new products, service offerings, partnerships) that we might achieve them. From there, we schedule further synchronous sandwiches to explore specific ideas within each of these categories, estimate their impact, and prioritize them against the milestones we set in our first session.

From beginning to end, the entire roadmapping process usually winds up taking place over four hour-long synchronous sandwiches, spaced out over one or two weeks. Following the three-for-one rule we discussed earlier, that adds up to about 16 hours of preparation and facilitation. Yes, 16 hours is a major time commitment—but in my experience, this commitment is well worth it when your team has important decisions to make. The level of engagement and collaboration I've seen across these shorter facilitated sessions has far exceeded what I experienced during longer, less structured in-person meetings.

As with any other communication practice, the synchronous sandwich will be most valuable when you collaborate with your team to make it your own. If, for example, you find that participants are not engaging with those asynchronous pre-reads, consider adding 10 minutes of "look at the pre-read and jot down questions" time at the beginning of your synchronous meetings. As always, stay attuned to the specific needs of your team and work with your team to understand and address those needs.

Creating and Protecting Space for Informal Communication

Back before the days of working from home, I was a huge believer in the 3 p.m. coffee break. Juuuuuust as the afternoon doldrums set in, I would gather up as many folks as I could and lead a motley caravan of designers, developers, marketers, product managers, and executives down the street to the "good coffee place." These coffee breaks often brought together people who would not have otherwise had much reason to communicate directly, and the resulting conversations were probably more valuable to the organization than half of our formal meetings.

When I started working from home, the idea of an *anytime anything* break immediately felt like a far-fetched fairy tale from the distant past. Much of the informal communication that had once served as both a vital information pipeline and a reliable morale booster just...disappeared. And nearly every attempt to re-create it via "Zoom happy hours" and "just for funsies" chat rooms felt unbearably awkward.

In the years since, I've seen many teams make small but meaningful steps toward bringing informal communication back to their teams. Rather than attempting to *re-create* their colocated rituals, they have created new rituals that better reflect the rhythms, constraints, and realities of distributed work. These rituals, of course, vary enormously from team to team. But I have observed a few consistent patterns that might help provide your team with a place to start:

Help people find each other and trust that they are connecting.
One of the best things about those 3 p.m. coffee breaks was that you could actually *see* people talking to each other, creating new bonds, and sharing information that would have otherwise remained siloed. On distributed teams, there is really no equivalent of a communal space that organically breaks down into one-on-one conversations. (Some teams have tried to

re-create this dynamic via Zoom breakout rooms, but I have yet to see it work exactly as intended.)

The teams I've seen most successfully navigate informal communication have, either implicitly or explicitly, shifted the bar from "Let's create a space where everybody can share lots of information with each other in the open" to "Let's create some spaces where people can broadly get to know each other, in the hopes that they will then follow up to share relevant information with each on their own time." I've worked with many product managers who assumed that their Zoom happy hours and just-for-funsies Slack channels were a failure, only because they couldn't actually *see* all the valuable follow-up conversations that were happening outside of those spaces. As always, the best way to find out whether such conversations are happening is to retrospect with your team.

Create opportunities for people to share the things they're already doing outside of work. Many folks I know have tried to engage their teams in group games and exercises that involve their own, shall we say, *work-like activities.* While some teams and individuals take to these with aplomb, others are not so happy to have "forced fun" added to their already-packed calendars. I tend to fall into the latter camp—especially when that "forced fun" feels annoyingly generic and doesn't really tell you all that much about the personalities and interests of your colleagues.

Instead of asking their teams to participate in entirely new activities, many product managers I know have found success creating opportunities for their teams to share the things they're already doing outside of work. One team I work with, for example, has been hosting a "Memories for Mondays" thread in their shared Slack channel, where everybody can start the week by sharing one fun thing they did over the weekend. This small and not-terribly-demanding activity has given that team a chance to get to know each other better as people, and it has even resulted in a few folks meeting up in person to go for a hike or attend a concert. Speaking of which...

If you feel comfortable and safe doing so, find some time to connect in person. When we embrace that informal communication is categorically different in a distributed work environment, we can also recognize the unique value of informal communication in person. Until I was once again able to do so safely and comfortably, I don't think I realized just how much I missed being able to share a meal or a walk with a colleague. Of course, *safely* and *comfortably* are the operative words here. If you are hoping to organize a larger in-person offsite, recognize that everybody has their own personal threshold of safety and comfort and respect their boundaries.

Remember to give yourself some break time too.

Finally, remember that those 3 p.m. coffee breaks were, first and foremost, *breaks*. If you want to have the time and energy to communicate effectively with your colleagues, you need to give yourself time to rest and recharge. If folks on your team are insisting that they are too busy to share a fun memory from their weekend or join a quick Zoom call to welcome a new team member, you might want to inquire gently as to whether they are giving *themselves* the time they need—and if there's anything you can do to help.

The shift to distributed work is neither easy nor linear, and it often requires substantially recalibrating our expectations around what informal communication looks and feels like. But once we truly accept the ways in which distributed work is different—not better or worse, just *different*—we can also accept the incredible opportunity to build strong working relationships with people from all around the world.

Creating Space for Informal Conversations Between Two Offices

Tony Haile
Senior Director of Product, Twitter; former CEO, Scroll (*https:// scroll.com*)

When I was the CEO of Chartbeat, our whole team worked in the same room. This had its downsides in terms of hiring and ambient noise, but there was one major upside: incidental conversations. When you hear about teams performing well, trust is a huge part of that. And trust often develops through conversations outside of formal, scheduled meetings. I like face-to-face interactions, but with a distributed team this isn't always possible.

At Scroll, we have one office in Portland, Oregon, and one office in New York. This left us with an interesting challenge: how can we create room for incidental conversations when the team is distributed between two physical locations?

To help solve this problem and foster a sense of shared space, we created an always-on video link between our two offices. Now, when people show up to work, they can see all of their colleagues in the other office on a big screen right in the middle of the room. And if they have a quick question to ask or thought to share, they can press a button to activate an audio link. Rather than having to reach out and schedule a formal meeting, you can just slap the button and say, "Hey!" much like you would if you were actually working in the same room. Our inspiration came from Gawker Media, who had used a similar approach to connect teams in New York and Hungary.

I don't know how this approach would scale if we had a ton of people in different locations all working remotely. But for us, it has opened up space for conversations that simply would not be happening otherwise. It has made a real difference in terms of building camaraderie and an ease of communication among the team. And when you're building products, that is something you absolutely need.

Hybrid Moments: Balancing In-Person and Remote Work

As of writing this, the only thing that feels certain about the future of remote work is that it is completely uncertain. There have been multiple rushes to prognosticate about the future of "return to work," but they've all proven wrong so far. The future will certainly involve some degree of "hybrid" setups, where some people work from home and some from offices, some days are "in the office" days and some are "work from home" days, etc.

The core idea of this chapter—the idea that the way your team communicates needs to be something you proactively address and nurture together—only holds more true as the distinctions between working in an office and working from home grow more nuanced and intricate. Keep in mind that more complexity requires more communication—and keep communicating.

Summary: Strength Training for Your Communication Practice

Product management is hard, and remote product management can be even harder. But the lack of a shared office space often forces us to be even more thoughtful and deliberate about the way we communicate with our teams. Think of remote work as strength training for your communication practice; it might feel uncomfortable and exhausting in the moment, but you'll be glad you did it the next time you're asked to do some heavy lifting.

Your Checklist

- Recognize that distributed work is no better or worse than colocated work —just different.
- Also recognize that every distributed team is, itself, different. Get to know the individuals on your team and work with them to find the rhythms, cadences, and channels that work best for their particular needs.
- Make sure your team has clear, consistent, and well-documented answers to questions like "How quickly are you expected to respond when you receive a message from one of your colleagues?"
- Co-create a comms manual or other operating agreement that can help your team avoid day-to-day misunderstandings that deplete trust.
- Think carefully about how best to use your team's precious synchronous time, especially if you are working across time zones. If you think a "status update" meeting could just as easily be an email, ask your team what they think about it.
- Remember that effectively running a synchronous meeting with a distributed team requires a lot of preparation and practice. Be prepared to spend three hours planning and preparing for each hour of synchronous meeting time you schedule for your team.
- Take advantage of shared documents and visual platforms to encourage direct participation in remote meetings.
- Resist the urge to send vague and open-ended messages to your team. Be specific about what you need, why you need it, and when you need it.
- Send your colleagues a pre-read and a follow-up before and after any important meeting (a "synchronous sandwich").
- Provide low-lift opportunities for your team to share their extracurricular activities and interests.
- Don't believe anybody who tells you that they've figured out the future of hybrid work. Keep paying attention, adjusting to changes as they come, and communicating openly with your team.

14

A Manager Among Product Managers (The Product Leadership Chapter)

As ill-prepared as I was for the realities of product management, I was even worse prepared for the realities of product leadership. Which is not to say that I didn't *think* I was prepared. After years of navigating the day-to-day indignities of product management, I was sure that I had learned just about everything there was to learn about how to run a product organization—or at least, everything there was to learn about how *not* to run a product organization. "I can't believe the people in charge are making such obvious mistakes," I would say to myself. "If I could just be promoted to the right position, I'd be able to fix this whole mess in no time."

Several promotions later, the "whole mess" remained very much unfixed. And most of the steps I was taking to make it better—steps that had worked quite well when I was a product manager, thank you very much—seemed to be making it worse. Slowly but surely, I began to develop some empathy for the leaders who I had once badmouthed over after-work drinks.

Over time, I began to wonder if people were meeting up for after-work drinks to badmouth *me*. I wanted to be a "cool boss," but I was also terrified that folks in my direct line of reporting would make mistakes that reflected poorly on me personally. When people came to me with problems, I fell back into old habits of commiseration: "I know, right, this company is SO MESSED UP!" Unsurprisingly, that line didn't play terribly well coming from somebody who was ostensibly responsible for making the company *less* messed up.

Long story short, I wish I had understood just how much learning, unlearning, and relearning goes into becoming a manager. There are many great resources for new and aspiring managers, including Richard Banfield, Martin Eriksson, and Nate Walkingshaw's *Product Leadership* (O'Reilly), Julie Zhuo's *The Making of a Manager* (Portfolio), and Camille Fournier's *The Manager's Path* (O'Reilly). You should read all of them, and you should seek frequent guidance from the product leaders in your network. As we will discuss in this chapter, just because you are a good product manager does not in any way guarantee that you will be a good *manager*, or a good leader.

For the purposes of this chapter, I'm using the terms *manager* and *leader* colloquially to refer to "people who are responsible for the work of others, either through a formal organizational structure or through informal credibility they have cultivated." As with all things in product management, this distinction can get unclear and ambiguous—which makes it all the more important for you to understand and deliver against the particular responsibilities you carry in your organization, whether or not they are formally captured in an org chart.

Climbing the Ladder

There comes a time in nearly every product manager's career when they utter four little words that, unbeknownst to them, are about to teach them some hard but valuable lessons: *I deserve a promotion*.

Early in my career, I certainly bought into the idea that a promotion was the shiny prize that would give me the power to make big important changes. I complained to anyone in earshot that I couldn't actualize my brilliant ideas for the company because I didn't have authority over the entire product roadmap. I complained to my colleagues, some of whom had been at the company for much longer than me, that I had been there for a *whole year* and hadn't been promoted yet. (Sorry, former colleagues.) I was embattled, entitled, and kind of a jerk.

Finally, I approached my company's VP of engineering, whom I had always counted on for a balanced and thoughtful perspective. I went off on my point-by-point argument for how great I was. I had been there for a year! I was working all the time—morning, afternoon, and evening! I was doing the jobs of three people! I had shipped a bunch of products! I concluded my persuasive essay with a dramatic "which is why I deserve to be a SENIOR PRODUCT MANAGER."

The VP of engineering smiled. "Thanks for sharing that," he said. "It sounds like you've been doing a lot of great work for the company. Let me ask you—what do you think are the responsibilities of a senior product manager?"

I froze. Somehow, I had never even thought about that. "Um, you know, it's like, a product manager, who, um, has, uh, more, uh...authority...over...more... parts...of...the product?" Again, I was met with a patient smile. "I have a challenge for you," he said. "I want you to write out what you think the job description for a senior PM here would be. Then I want you to put together a list of which of those responsibilities you are fulfilling in your current role and a growth plan for you to step into the other responsibilities."

My face scrunched up. Still riding high on self-righteousness, I blurted out, "What if I'm already doing all of them really well?" Yet again, a patient smile. "You don't even know what they are yet! Besides, there is always room for growth. Whenever somebody tells me that they don't have any room for growth, what I hear is that they don't really understand their role."

That last statement hit me like a punch in the gut. Here I was, a year or so into my product management career, insisting that I was the *world's best product manager* and I had *nothing to learn*. Had all those "I deserve a promotion!" conversations betrayed a lack of the very experience and maturity I was insisting I possessed?

The short answer is *yes*. Those challenging conversations with our VP of engineering gave me a gift that I have had the honor of passing along to many product managers in the years since: the realization that "I deserve a promotion because I've worked really hard and I'm really great" is not the sentiment of a mature and effective product manager.

Throughout this book, we've discussed the importance of starting with the outcomes we seek to drive for our business and its users, before getting into the weeds about all the amazing, difficult, fiddly work we're doing as individuals. This same principle holds true as we seek advancement within or across organizations. David Dewey, a product leader I had the privilege of working with at Mailchimp, shared with me the first question he asks any product manager who approaches him about receiving a promotion: "What could the company accomplish with you in a promoted position that it can*not* accomplish now?" I love this question, because it forces you to think about the potential impact of your desired role and why *you* are the right person for that position. Returning to an idea expressed in Ben Horowitz's "Good Product Manager/Bad Product Manager" (*https://oreil.ly/z3688*), defining and understanding the impact of your role is part of a good product manager's job.

Surprise! Everything You're Doing Is Wrong

So, you put together a job description and a growth plan. You spoke eloquently to the impact of the work you're currently doing—and to the greater impact you could have if you were promoted to a product leadership role. And you got the promotion! You are now managing multiple products, or multiple people, or maybe one person and one *really important* product. (Again, the variability never ceases!)

Your prior performance reviews described you as "a rockstar who gets things *done*." You write beautiful product specs, facilitate phenomenal meetings, and prioritize your time and efforts like a boss. And now, you're going to be able to get even more things done!

But just as you start settling into your new role, a junior product manager on your team brings you *their* pitch for a new product. And it is...certainly less beautiful than your beautiful documents. It doesn't answer all the questions you want it to answer. And, worst of all, it concludes with a recommendation that you aren't sure you fully agree with.

Your team is supposed to present this to executive leadership tomorrow. Your calendar is already booked up. You have a reputation to live up to, you *just* got this promotion, and you don't want to mess it up. But you also don't want to start off your first product leadership role by alienating your own team. So, as kindly and generously as you can, you say, "This is GREAT. Thank you SO MUCH. If you don't mind, I'm just going to take it and make a few changes. THANKS AGAIN!"

At 8 p.m. that night, you open up the document and make a few changes. A few little sentences to edit here, a few data points to clarify there. You rewrite the recommendation at the end of the pitch until it's something you can support. You send it through at about 10 p.m., with an encouraging note telling the junior product manager that you know they're going to do a GREAT job. You close the computer and smile a big smile. Here you are, late at night, putting in the hours to help your team succeed. This whole "product leadership" thing might just work out for you after all.

The next day, you log on for the big presentation and watch your junior product manager stumble through the pitch document you edited. Executive leadership seems pretty disengaged. Not wanting this presentation to be a total bust for you *or* for your junior product manager, you decide to chime in: "Hi, sorry everybody, just wanted to share a bit more of the thinking behind the recommendation here." Executive leadership perks up. They ask a few questions, which you are ready and prepared to answer. Your recommendation is accepted, and everybody seems pretty happy about it.

Everybody, that is, except for your junior product manager, who abruptly logs off without sharing the usual meeting-concluding pleasantries. You follow up with a quick Slack message, "Hey, you OK? I thought you did GREAT! Sorry if I commandeered that meeting a bit, just wanted to make sure that the execs saw that you had my support." Even as you type this, you realize that you're not really *that* sorry. This was a high-stakes presentation, you wanted to make sure it was successful, and it was successful.

In the following weeks, that success begins to fade. Your junior product manager, fighting back tears in your next 1:1 meeting, explains that they had worked with their entire engineering and design team to come up with their initial recommendation and had lost a lot of trust when they presented *your* recommendation instead. To make matters worse, other product managers in the organization are now bypassing your junior product manager entirely and trying to get time on *your* calendar instead. After all, everybody knows that you're the one pulling the strings and making the big decisions. Uh-oh.

In the product world, individual contributors often get promoted for the very behaviors that limit their effectiveness as leaders. And as you step into a product leadership role, the continuation of these behaviors will have two interrelated and equally negative consequences: you will burn out, and your team will feel disengaged and disempowered. Accept the fact that you will need to unlearn some old behaviors and learn some new ones—and that those new behaviors may not come easy for you, no matter how big and fancy your title might be.

The Standard You Set for Yourself Is the Standard You Set for Your Team

Over the last several years, many product leaders have come to me deeply concerned that their teams are on the cusp of burning out. "It's just such a trying time," they say to me, "and I'm really worried about everybody. I keep telling people to take time off, to find a good work-life balance, and to disconnect at the end of the day, but I get the sense that people are still working too long and doing too much."

In response, I ask: "Are *you* taking time off, finding a good work-life balance, and disconnecting at the end of the day?" More often than not, this question is met with a string of qualifiers and excuses. "Well, I mean, I try to, but my team really needs me right now and there's just so much to do. *I'm putting in those extra hours so that folks on my team can disconnect!"*

These product leaders are often surprised to learn that their teams are telling me the exact same thing.

There is simply no way around this one: when you are a product leader, the standard you set for yourself *is* the standard you set for your team. If you are in the office until 8 p.m., your team will think that you expect them to be in the office until 8 p.m., no matter how many times you insist otherwise. If you are sending emails at 3 p.m. on a Saturday, your team will think that they need to respond to emails at 3 p.m. on a Saturday (unless, as we discussed in Chapter 13, you have explicitly stated otherwise in a team comms manual). And if you haven't taken any time off in three years, you can be pretty certain that your team won't be taking advantage of that "unlimited vacation" policy either.

When product leaders tell me that they are too overwhelmed and overworked to take time off or turn off their computers after dinner, I often ask them to do a simple exercise that I also recommend to overwhelmed junior product managers: stack rank *everything you're currently doing* in order of how much it is helping your team achieve its goals. Then draw a line under the amount of stuff you can reasonably do within your actual working hours (Figure 14-1). Anything below the line gets delegated, reshaped, or simply dropped.

Figure 14-1. An annotated, stack-ranked list of activities from highest to lowest impact (your list will likely be much longer!)

When product leaders begin dropping some of the less-impactful activities from their daily to-do lists, they often find that the folks on their team feel more comfortable doing the same. This is both because a good example has been set and because work has a tendency to beget other work; all those things you're doing "for" your team still need to be received, reviewed, and responded to. Ultimately, becoming an effective product leader means learning to measure your value by something other than how late you're staying and how hard you're working.

How Reflexively Saying Yes to Executives Can Destroy Your Team—and Get You Promoted!

Q.S.
Product Manager, technology enterprise

Several years ago, a director-level product leader I worked with secured a rare audience with the company's CEO. To the great delight of this product leader, the CEO really liked what my colleague was working on. "This is great," our CEO said. "Do you think you could ship it by Tuesday?" My colleague responded, without flinching: "Absolutely."

So, emboldened by the CEO's interest, this product leader went back to his team and said, "Cancel your weekend plans. Call your families and tell them you won't be seeing them for a while. The CEO wants this on Tuesday, and we're going to make it happen." They embarked upon a grueling effort to get the product out the door and, sure enough, they *did* get it out the door.

In the weeks that followed, several members of that team straight-up quit. They weren't terribly interested in staying all weekend with zero notice, and I can't blame them. The product leader who led the team, though? He got promoted! He earned a reputation as "the kind of product leader who gets things done" and was quickly made a VP.

Here's the thing that haunts me to this day: Would that director have been promoted if, rather than saying yes to the CEO, he had said, "You know, I'm not sure. I need to check with my team. Can you help me understand why Tuesday is the particular day you have in mind?" It's easy enough for me to speculate that he wouldn't have been promoted—and that uncertainty is probably exactly why he *did* say yes in the moment. But that yes definitely came at a huge cost to his team and to our organization at large, which lost some of its most talented engineers.

I try to keep this in mind now when I find myself facing similar situations. **When senior leaders ask questions, I do my best to give them the benefit of the doubt and treat those questions as real questions, not as cloaked demands. I also try to be aware of the fact that my own questions might be taken as cloaked demands.** The simple task of taking things at face value can require a lot of bravery, and it might not get us the immediate positive recognition we receive from reflexively saying "Yes," but it ultimately leads to happier teams and healthier organizations.

The Limits of Autonomy

If there are two words that have defined the product leadership discourse over the last decade or so, they are *autonomy* and *empowerment*: autonomy as in "Give teams the room to make smart decisions without micromanagement," and empowerment as in "Give teams the information and resources they need to execute effectively against those decisions."

These are noble and sound goals, and they are tremendously difficult to achieve effectively. Books like Marty Cagan's *Empowered* (Wiley) and Christina Wodtke's *The Team That Managed Itself* (Cucina) provide comprehensive and compelling pictures of what empowered teams look like in the real world—and the hard work that goes into creating them.

Unfortunately, many product leaders—myself very much included—have misinterpreted the call to "autonomy" (and the fear of micromanagement) as permission to just "leave teams alone and let them do their best work." This is a compelling fantasy for product leaders who are becoming aware that their old habits will not serve them in their new roles and who are struggling to balance an ever-expanding set of responsibilities.

Having been on both sides of this misconception, I can say definitively that "just do whatever you want" ultimately delivers neither autonomy nor empowerment. Many of us have learned this the hard way when planning a group meal for people who insist that they're "up for anything!" only to reveal a plethora of previously unstated preferences and restrictions when everybody sits down to eat. Most people turn out to be pretty opinionated about food when it comes time to order, and most product leaders turn out to be pretty opinionated about product when it comes time to build something. I've seen many product leaders swing hard from "micromanagement" to "autonomy," only for their teams to suddenly go from *building* what those leaders want to *guessing* what those leaders want. And, much as I did when I accidentally brought a bunch of vegans to a restaurant called PORK, those teams are likely to guess wrong.

In a canonical text about empowered teams (*https://oreil.ly/kOWUB*) (which also includes a thoughtful perspective on the distinction between management and leadership), Marty Cagan makes it very clear that an "empowered" team doesn't mean a disconnected team:

> Truly empowered teams also need the business context that comes from the leadership—especially the product vision—and the support of their management, especially ongoing coaching, and then [to be] given the opportunity to figure out the best way to solve the problems they have been assigned.

In other words, simply "leaving teams alone" is not the same thing as empowering those teams. Effective product leadership is not about disconnecting from on-the-ground teams but rather about finding new ways to support those teams.

Clear Goals, Clear Guardrails, Short Feedback Loops

Supporting product teams without micromanaging them is a challenge for every product leader. And while each product leader has their own approach, I have found three things consistently helpful for striking this balance: clear goals, clear guardrails, and—most importantly—short feedback loops.

The idea of providing your team with clear goals is pretty straightforward and has been discussed at length in this and many other books. If your team doesn't know how you are defining success, then they will not be able to deliver success. As we discussed in Chapter 10, pushing down on the "outcomes" side of the outcomes and output seesaw will often empower your team to fly higher in its executional work.

Providing clear guardrails is a bit trickier, as it often leaves product leaders feeling like they are walking right up to the ledge of micromanagement. But product leaders often have access to important information that their teams do not, and they do their teams no favors by withholding this information. For example, you might know that your CEO is vehemently opposed to a particular solution that one of your teams is currently evaluating, or that a particular technical system is likely going to be deprecated in the coming months due to a pending top-secret acquisition. These are the kinds of real-world constraints and concerns that product organizations must navigate, and it takes courage, discipline, and practice to communicate them in a way that avoids finger-pointing or excuse making.

Finally, and most importantly, effective product leaders work in short feedback loops. Product leaders tend to be busy people with packed calendars, which often leads to long periods of time between conversations with their teams. This leaves their teams with a *lot* of room to misinterpret the goals and guardrails they have been provided, go too far down a road that has already been closed off, or otherwise get far out ahead of themselves before a product leader can look at their work and say, "Oh, whoops, I think our wires got a little crossed here."

Many of my very worst days as a product manager came when I made a big presentation to product leadership, only to be told, "No, that isn't what we wanted at all." But when I became a product leader myself, it took me years to realize that the lesson from these experiences was not "Don't be a jerk," but rather "Don't let a team go for too long without feedback." Now, I advise product leaders to explicitly discourage their teams from spending too long on anything before taking the time to review it together: "Here is what success looks like. Here are some things you need to keep in mind. Please spend no more than one hour drafting something, then bring it back to me in a few days and we'll review it together."

Working in incomplete drafts (like the timeboxed one-pagers we discussed in Chapter 9) and short feedback loops allows you to better align vision and execution at all levels of the organization. It also helps you get out ahead of situations where the guidelines and guardrails you provide get lost or misinterpreted as they are folded into specific product ideas.

Navigating the Inevitable "Your Product Sucks" Email

Michael L.

Product Leader, growth-stage startup

By the time you become a product leader, you likely have a pretty good sense of what your high-level responsibilities are going to be and how to manage them. You're building a team, building a discipline, inspiring your team, and keeping them moving. You're engaging with leadership from other functional areas and making sure they know what's going on and why. And even when you are doing all of those things well, there will still come a time in almost every product leadership role where you are one of many recipients of an email from your CEO that says, in so many words, "Why does your product suck?"

One particular example from my own career comes to mind. In this case, the email from our CEO, which was sent to a number of cross-functional leaders including myself and our CTO, stated that our customer support experience was an unacceptable mess and asked who was responsible for it. Now, we had just rolled out a roadmapping tool, and anybody who wanted to could see that we had pushed back revamping our customer support experience to do some other work that we believed was more closely aligned with our KPIs. But just because it's on the roadmap doesn't mean that anybody—especially your CEO—is actually going to understand how and why it was prioritized, especially when the actual experience within the product is pretty rough.

So, this email comes through, and I'm trying to think of how to respond. Before I can say anything, another leader chimes in with "I stand by my team's decision, and there's only so much we can do." I completely understand the impulse to protect your team in this kind of situation—but that response just kind of blew everything up, resulting in a heated back-and-forth email exchange that played out over an entire weekend. It culminated with the CEO declaring, "This was a bad decision. I don't see any strategic thought behind this, and as a customer, I would never return to an app with this bad an experience."

The thing is...our CEO wasn't necessarily wrong! We may very well have made a poor decision about what we prioritized. Ultimately, a group product manager on my team wound up stepping in and doing what we should have done in the first place: walk the executive team through how we made the prioritization decisions we made and adjust those decisions to better align with our CEO's vision.

It's worth remembering that, even when you've made it to a product leadership role and you're ostensibly doing everything right, you're still going to get that "Why does your product suck?" email. And, in that moment, it's still going to be really difficult for you. You might feel like a fraud or an impostor. You might wonder if your product sucks because *you* suck. But at the end of the day, you still always have things to learn from these experiences. Every product leader has strengths and weaknesses, goes through good days and bad days, and makes mistakes. The real challenge is staying open to learning from those mistakes.

Externalizing Yourself

Somewhat counterintuitively, our guiding principle for the CORE skill of organization, "Make yourself obsolete," holds even more true when you are a product leader. The best product leaders are always working to externalize their own knowledge, wisdom, and experience so that they can guide their teams without having to stay too involved in the day-to-day minutiae of product work.

The short feedback loops we discussed earlier in this chapter often help product leaders identify the areas where such guidance would be most urgent and impactful. For example, I worked with one product leader who found herself consistently giving feedback to teams that the "outcomes" they had defined looked more like a list of features they intended to build. After having the same conversation with multiple product managers, she wrote and shared a checklist of the things she looks for when evaluating whether or not an outcome is actually an outcome, including:

- Is it measurable?
- Is it a little bit outside of our control (i.e., does it require feedback from the market)?
- Does it connect to our company goals for the year?

Similarly, product leader David Dewey (whom we met earlier in this chapter) wrote up a document with his product leadership philosophy after fielding many requests to mediate conflicts between individuals and teams. With his permission, I've included my favorite part of that document here:

> I believe that communication is the key that unlocks the solution to almost all of our problems. Too often people say a thing is happening, or that someone thinks something, and I ask, "Have you talked to them?" And the answer is no. And my response is, "What you just said to me? Go say those exact words to them."

Creating and sharing simple documents like this can help scale your impact while managing your time. As an added bonus, externalizing your own thought process can help you better understand that thought process, providing a great opportunity for you to reflect on your own unique approach to product leadership.

Product Leadership in Practice

Let's look at three common scenarios you are likely to encounter on your product leadership journey. Note that these are not strictly scenarios for formal product leaders but rather scenarios where any working product manager can cultivate their leadership skills. As with the scenarios from prior chapters, take a moment to reflect on how *you* might handle the situation before reading on.

SCENARIO ONE

Engineer: We're just about done with the work we have scoped! What do you think we should move on to next? (Figure 14-2)

Figure 14-2. An engineer asks what to work on next

What's really going on

This can be one of the most gratifying moments for an ascending product manager. Clearly, you've built some trust and credibility on your team—and you're being asked one of those big, important questions that *real* product managers get asked. But, as we discussed in Chapter 2, the fact that folks on your team have to ask you this question at all might be a sign that you've become a bottleneck and failed to cultivate your organization skills. While this can be a boost to your ego, it's a problem for your team.

What you might do

Make sure that everybody on the team is crystal clear about the goals you are working toward and your strategy for achieving those goals. This is one of those critical moments for you to externalize and systematize yourself so that your whole team can level up its decision-making process. Tell your team that you'd like to create a transparent enough prioritization system that they will *always* know what to work on next. Then work with them to create that system together.

Patterns and traps to avoid

Build this particular thing!
> Again, resist the urge to be the Hero Product Manager and answer the question in the moment. Your whole team should be able to answer this question without having to ask you!

Build whatever you want!
> I've seen some product managers run prioritization meetings simply by asking their teams, "What do you want to work on next?" This can feel like the easiest path toward keeping your colleagues engaged, but at the end of the day, your team should be prioritizing against outcomes, not opinions.

Sorry, I'm really busy. Can we talk about this at the next prioritization meeting?
> If an engineer on your team is unsure what to work on between prioritization meetings, then you've got bigger issues to deal with than an overbooked calendar. Rather than shooing away an engineer on your team, take the time to better understand what exactly is going on. Did the engineering team run out of work to do? Are they just trying to get a sense of what comes next? And if so, why? Be patient, ask questions, and listen.

SCENARIO TWO

Other product manager: You know, I think this work is really more in my team's purview than in yours. We'll take it from here and let you know if we need anything from you. (Figure 14-3)

Figure 14-3. Another product manager says, "Got it!"

What's really going on

As you find yourself taking on more responsibilities in more complex organizations, you will almost certainly run up against situations where "ownership" becomes unclear and ambiguous. These situations can quickly escalate into high-stakes custody battles, where product managers and leaders jockey for control over what they consider important parts of the product or the organization. Long story short: these battles can incur a lot of collateral damage and rarely work out well for anybody, even the ostensible winner.

What you might do

Set about to better understand how the work in question fits into the goals of your team, the other product manager's team, and the organization at large. The work in question may very well be more aligned with the other product manager's goals than it is with yours—but you'll never know if you don't take the time to find out. Remember that your job is to deliver outcomes for the business and its users, not to "own" as much of the product as possible. Stay focused on the path that makes the most sense and try to get beyond a binary mindset— "Either you own it or I own it"—as quickly as you can. Consider proposing a follow-up conversation to talk through how both of your teams can work together to best deliver against the business's goals and, if necessary, suggest a standing meeting to keep your teams aligned.

Patterns and traps to avoid

Sure thing, sounds good. [Secretly complains to manager.]
> Nothing says, "You should not trust me" better than acting agreeable in the moment and then immediately complaining to your manager. If you think that the other product manager's team should not move forward with the work in question, it is your responsibility to resolve that with the other product manager directly. If you truly can't reach a resolution, consider asking the other product manager if you can mutually seek mediation from a higher-level manager who might have more information about how the work in question aligns with the company's overall goals.

Sure thing, sounds good. [Secretly begins doing the work with their own team.]
> More than once, I have seen a product manager begin doing the very work they just ostensibly stepped away from, thinking that if they can do it quicker and better, they can reclaim what is rightfully theirs. This creates duplicative work, depletes trust, and generally makes things worse for everybody.

Sure thing, sounds good. [Secretly begins badmouthing other product manager to anybody who will listen.]
> This is perhaps the most common anti-pattern I have seen emerge in this scenario: a defensive reaction is triggered, product martyrdom kicks in, and before you know it, you're sitting at a bar (or backchanneling over Slack) talking about how this other product manager is a *huge jerk* who is *totally out to get you*. As we discussed in Chapter 4, the other product manager's intentions are largely irrelevant; they may in fact be a huge jerk, or they may be a lovely person who is trying to take some work off of your already-overfilled plate. Stay focused on the outcomes you are trying to deliver and resist the urge to speculate and vent about your colleagues.

No, I think my team should handle it, thank you very much. [Other product manager inevitably responds in one of the three ways described here.]

Duck season! Rabbit season! Duck season! Rabbit season! Remember, your job as a product manager is to facilitate a good decision, not to get into an endless back-and-forth with no clear goals. Product leaders, regardless of their formal title, always put business and user goals ahead of their own ambitions.

SCENARIO THREE

Direct report: I'm sorry, I just think that folks on the marketing side have completely unrealistic expectations about what we're going to deliver before our big fall event. (Figure 14-4)

Figure 14-4. A product leader's direct report venting about those clowns in marketing

What's really going on

Statements like this can be minor asides or major requests for help, and there's no way to really know what is behind them unless you dig a little deeper. Many times in my own career, I have taken an excuse for a test-drive with my manager to see if they will give me permission to avoid dealing with a particularly thorny issue. Other times, I have found myself bringing a particularly thorny issue to my manager in the genuine hope that they will help me figure out how best to resolve it.

What you might do

Get specific. Ask your direct report what exactly those expectations are, what about them is unrealistic, and what the potential ramifications of that misalignment might be. Offer to help them set up some time with the relevant stakeholders from marketing, so that *they* (not you!) can work through these issues directly. And let them know that, if they truly cannot reach a resolution with their colleagues in marketing, you are willing to step in to help facilitate that conversation—bearing in mind that facilitating a conversation is very different from *taking over* that conversation.

Patterns and traps to avoid

lol yea marketing sux.
> As you step into positions of product leadership—formal or informal—one of the first and hardest lessons you will learn is that you can't complain about your colleagues in the way you once did. (You may, in fact, realize that you never should have complained about your colleagues in the way you once did!) This holds particularly true when you are speaking to somebody whom you directly manage.

Don't worry. I've got your team's back and I'll defend whatever you wind up delivering.
> While it can be tempting to defend your direct reports from unreasonable or unrealistic expectations coming from other parts of the organization, this approach ultimately "defends" those direct reports from getting better at their job. Learning how to resolve conflict is critical for product managers, and you do your direct reports no real favors by insulating them from such conflict.

Well, listen, we're a marketing-led organization. Our CEO came from marketing. That's just the way it is.

As you climb through the ranks of a product organization, there will be times when, often due to sheer exhaustion, you will be tempted to blame things on "the CEO" or "the organization" or "the board" or even "the bone-crushing engine of late capitalism." Any and all of these may very well constitute real constraints for your team and your organization, but your job is to help your reports thoughtfully navigate these constraints, not to model helplessness and martyrdom.

lol yea being a product manager sux.

A little bit of commiseration about the hard work of product management can be fine. But this commiseration should never serve as a stand-in for actually *doing* the hard work of product management.

Summary: Stepping Into Your Best Self

Regardless of whether or not you are seeking a formal product leadership role, the lessons of product leadership can help you build more trust and drive better outcomes in any product role. Just remember that product leadership will almost certainly require you to give up some of the coping mechanisms and "getting things done" behaviors that may have gotten you recognized and promoted in the first place. Be prepared, as always, to get over your own defensiveness, take a clear-eyed look at your strengths and weaknesses (even the best product leaders have both!), and continuously evolve your own practice.

Your Checklist

- Acknowledge that every aspiring product leader—yes, even you—has strengths and weaknesses. You will always have room to learn and grow.
- When you're pursuing a promotion, think about how that promotion would help the business achieve its goals, not why you "deserve" it!
- Keep in mind that the behaviors that got you promoted to a leadership position are not necessarily behaviors that will serve you well in a leadership position—and be ready to unlearn those behaviors.
- Remember that the standard you set for yourself is the standard you set for your team. If you want people to disconnect from work at night,

disconnect from work at night. If you want people to take time off, take time off.

- If you find yourself overwhelmed and overworked, make a stack-ranked list of all the things you're doing according to how they're contributing to your team's goals. Then delegate or drop anything you can't do within your actual working hours.

- Make sure your team has access to the information they need in order to make good decisions, even if that information might feel constraining or micromanage-y.

- Never let your reports or teams go too long without receiving feedback from you on important projects and deliverables. As we discussed in Chapter 9, work collaboratively in timeboxed incomplete drafts.

- If you find yourself having the same conversation with folks time and time again, look for opportunities to externalize your side of that conversation in a shared document.

- Check your ego when you find yourself being asked a lot of important, strategic questions. Remember that part of your job is to organize your teams to answer those questions themselves as best they can.

- Avoid turf wars over who gets to "own" any particular part of the product; stay laser focused on the outcomes you are driving for the business and its users.

- Take complaints from your direct reports seriously and help provide them the space and guidance to resolve thorny issues as best they can.

- Re-read Chapter 5 of this book from a product leader's perspective. How could the senior stakeholders in that chapter's stories and scenarios have approached things more effectively?

15

In Good Times and Bad

As of early 2022, there were about 1.96 million apps in the Apple App Store and 2.87 million in the Google Play Store according to mobile app agency BuildFire (*https://oreil.ly/YPTde*).

According to that same source, the average smartphone owner uses 10 mobile apps on a daily basis and 30 apps total every month.

That leaves a lot of disappointed product managers.

I cite these statistics not to be fatalistic, but rather to set the expectation that building a product destined for the meteoric success associated with companies like Apple, Netflix, Facebook, or Google is exceptionally rare. Great product managers work on products that fail all the time. There are no "best practices," no perfect prioritization frameworks, no Agile-cadabra magic words that will guarantee the success of your product.

Product managers working on established and successful products face their own set of challenges that can be just as galling. Established companies tend to become risk averse, bureaucratic, and political, at times making it difficult to implement minor changes that have clear user value. Even when the numbers are going in the right direction—*especially* when the numbers are going in the right direction—getting out ahead of fast-changing user needs can prove incredibly difficult.

Product management is not an easy job, but the practice of product management can make everybody's job easier. It can help programmers become better communicators, marketers become more excited about technical work, and executives understand the tactical ramifications of high-level strategic decisions. Great product management turns insidious tension and misalignment into opportunities for learning, sharing, and collaborating—in good times and in bad.

The Soothing Lull of an Organization on Autopilot

In nearly every product organization, particularly more mature product organizations, there are usually stretches of time where teams go into "autopilot" mode. Sometimes, this is because external conditions are so favorable that the numbers are all going in the right direction and nobody is feeling much pressure. Sometimes, this is because people have stopped paying attention to the numbers at all and the product team is operating with minimal accountability and oversight. And yes, sometimes, this is because all the right pieces are in place and you are operating like a well-oiled product machine.

But this autopilot mode comes with substantial risk. When a team has gone too long without a new challenge or a fresh perspective, it can begin to feel like "the way things are" is the only path to success. New ideas that don't support the status quo are watered down or waved away. Teams become more insular and less curious, important questions go unasked, and critical opportunities are missed.

When your team feels like it is on autopilot, it becomes more important than ever for you to seek out challenging ideas and alternate explanations. Talk to users who have abandoned your product, even if there aren't many of them, and try to figure out what went wrong. Explore competing products and document how they are addressing fundamental user needs. (Or, as we discussed in Chapter 6, refresh your user personas to see if those needs have changed.) Bring challenging questions back to your team: What if the direction you're taking is totally wrong? What if the linear growth you're experiencing is a fraction of what's possible? Model openness and curiosity by asking questions that directly challenge the work for which *you* are most directly responsible.

Finally, channel these challenging questions into hands-on collaborative work via timeboxed prototypes (Figure 15-1). What if we reinvented the product from scratch in one week? What if we've built our existing product on a pile of assumptions and historical accidents that are no longer serving the business or its users? Creating tangible prototypes of a wholly reimagined product can help us connect these big questions to the smaller steps we might take to answer them for our users.

One of my favorite ways to approach these prototypes is with an hour-long "reinventing the product" session. The setup is pretty simple: you bring together some cross-functional stakeholders, assign them a user persona and an important task for that user to accomplish, and give them five minutes to put together a rough digital or paper prototype showing how they might *completely reimagine* their product to help that user complete that task. Almost without fail, the resulting artifacts capture streamlined, guided experiences with simple calls to action. These simple experiences often stand in stark contrast to the complicated and feature-jammed screens of the existing product.

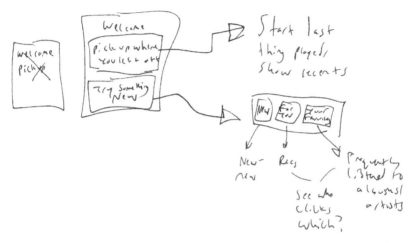

Figure 15-1. The messy but authentic results of a hypothetical five-minute paper prototyping session for a popular music-streaming service, complete with crossed-out first drafts and squiggly arrows. Note how even a messy and low-fidelity prototype can tell us a lot about the kind of experience our users might prefer.

The Good Times Aren't (Always) the Easy Times

So, if a lack of immediate challenges and the resultant autopilot mode are not the signs of truly good times in a product organization, what are? Here are a few general indicators that your work is contributing to the health and success of your team and organization:

Conflicts are discussed in the open.
> A healthy product organization is not marked by a lack of conflict; rather, it is marked by the ability to address and resolve conflict in the open with minimal defensiveness, ego-driven attacks, and passive-aggressive flailing. As we discussed in Chapter 4, disagreement can be a critical tool for making good decisions as a group.

Everybody feels invested in the work that they are doing.
> In a healthy product organization, everybody is invested in the work that their team is doing and in the way that their team is working together. If

you suggest a new product idea or a new process improvement and it's met with a chorus of shrugs, this does not mean that you have the full and unwavering support of your product team. In many cases, disinterest is more dangerous than disagreement.

People see new information (and new people!) as an opportunity, not a threat.
In a healthy product organization, people never shy away from signals that they are on the wrong path. They do not wait until their quarterly review to share that they are unlikely to hit a quantitative goal. They recognize that their mission, per the CORE skills of product management, is to bridge their users' reality with their organization's reality—and any information, people, or ideas that help them do so are seen as a gift.

To summarize, the truly good times as a product manager are not necessarily the easy times. Nor are they necessarily times when the company itself is doing well, though that certainly helps. The times when product management is most successful are those when new challenges are actively sought out and approached with openness, curiosity, and candor.

It is not an accident that these times tend to coincide with major product launches, last-mile pushes to get a new feature out the door, and other high-stakes, high-pressure situations. The moments that require the most collaboration, the most adaptability, and the most willingness to try new things quickly tend to be the moments when product management truly shines. The real challenge is to bring that same level of energy and excitement to your work every single day.

Carrying the Weight of the World

Early in my career, a mentor of mine told me that a product manager's job is "to think about every single little thing that could possibly go wrong, before it goes wrong." I replied, "Well, that's pretty much what I do all the time anyhow, so this job should be perfect for me!"

For people who are inclined to carry the weight of the world on their shoulders, product management can be a little bit *too* perfect. Being a product manager can leave you feeling like every problem you encounter is yours to solve, from new products launched by competitors to personal disagreements among your colleagues. And during moments of organizational turmoil, product management can feel both relentlessly demanding and absolutely futile, like pushing a boulder up a hill while 10 larger, more important boulders roll down past you.

Many of my worst moments as a product manager have occurred during times like this, when the sheer weight of the job felt unmanageable. I have thrown tantrums in front of well-intentioned colleagues, stormed out of meetings with senior leaders, and withheld critical information from my own team out of fear that they would be mad at me. And the vast majority of this bad behavior has been motivated by the same dangerous fallacy: "I am the only thing keeping this team (or this company) from completely falling apart."

This is where the connective nature of product management can serve as an amplifier of organizational discord. As a product manager, you are responsible for connecting people throughout the organization, and the more broken and misaligned these connections are without your direct and constant intervention, the more you can start to feel like you are the only thing standing between your team (or your company) and oblivion. During these times, you might begin to feel like you need to be everywhere at once to put out fires and resolve disputes. You might catch yourself grumbling to your friends, and sometimes even to your colleagues, about what a mess this whole thing is. But it's *your* mess, and you can't even imagine how it would continue to operate without you.

To revisit our bad product manager archetypes, this is where the thin line between the Hero Product Manager and the Product Martyr starts to blur. If you begin to feel like you are the only person who can save your team and your company, you are going down a dangerous path. Here are a few steps you can take to avoid falling on the double-edged sword of product heroism and martyrdom.

Make a list of the things outside of your control.
> Did a tech giant just launch a product that directly competes with yours? Are two senior leaders in your organization embroiled in a battle for the CEO position? While both of these developments might have a serious impact on your job, you can't control another company's roadmap or another person's ambitions. Make a list of the things that are outside of your control to serve as a reminder that it is not your job to solve every problem for everybody.

Look for opportunities to delegate important things.
> One way you can break the cycle of heroism and martyrdom is to delegate truly important things to your colleagues. Rather than trying to insulate your team from organizational dysfunction, ask your team to step up and take on responsibility for something that is mission critical for your shared

success. Delegating important things to your colleagues means that they will likely run up against some of the same friction and frustration that you have been experiencing. While this is not an easy thing, it is often a good thing. It will give you a chance to address these challenges as a group, rather than feeling like you are the only person capable of and responsible for solving them.

Show up for the routines and rituals that bring your team together.

During challenging times, it's easy to let things fall through the cracks— especially things that don't reflect the perceived urgency of the moment. Informal team gatherings (in-person or remote), high-level brainstorming conversations, team show-and-tell sessions—these are usually the first things to disappear from your calendar when the going gets tough. You might assume, as I often have, that your team will be just as happy to gather together minus one stressed-out product manager. But your absence sends a powerful and dangerous message that the time you spend with your team is just not that important. Your colleagues might, in turn, wonder why *they* don't have anything more important to do.

One of the very best things you can do as a product manager is to protect the time that your team spends together doing normal, fun, and routine stuff. Show up, be present, and model for your team that, even in the midst of major challenges, it is of the utmost importance that you find time to step back, communicate, and connect.

Imagine You Work for the Best Company in the World

There will be many times in your career when the "good times" and "bad times" seem to blur into a mélange of medium-beige "OK times." These are the times when you have made peace with the real-world constraints of your organization. You have a pretty good sense of what's possible and what's not possible. You aren't getting everything done that you'd like to, but you're getting *enough* done. Your team isn't exactly on autopilot—there are still fights to be fought and challenges to be overcome—but you have a pretty good sense of which fights you are likely to lose and which challenges are likely to become insurmountable.

Over time, these experiences can calcify into a kind of risk-repellant armor. If you've seen a leader in your organization react poorly to bad news, you might decide to omit a few of the more disappointing numbers from your monthly check-in. If the engineers on your team have reflexively dismissed user insights, you might decide that it's easier to just let them focus on implementation details.

If other product managers in your organization have been rewarded for shipping a bunch of useless features, you might decide that there's little point in focusing too much on the outcomes your team is trying to deliver for the business and its users.

As we discussed in Chapter 7, acknowledging and working within the fixed constraints of your organization is often a smart way to focus on the value you are delivering to your users. But over time, many product managers continue applying these constraints to their own work, even when the constraints themselves may no longer exist. For example, I have seen many product managers continue to withhold "bad news" from company leadership, even when the individual leader with a reputation for reacting poorly to such news is long gone. Similarly, I have seen many product managers insist that their company will *never* be "outcome focused," even as company leaders ask those very product managers to articulate the outcomes their teams are hoping to achieve in the coming months.

In practice, these preemptive self-negotiations are often one of the biggest impediments to achieving team psychological safety, a concept that Harvard organizational behaviorist Amy Edmondson describes in her paper "Psychological Safety and Learning Behavior in Work Teams" (*https://oreil.ly/oT4i2*) as "a shared belief held by members of a team that the team is safe for interpersonal risk taking." While many product managers are quick to blame company leadership for a lack of psychological safety, it is often *those very product managers* whose assumptions and projections about company leadership leave their teams feeling unsafe to take interpersonal risks. If the folks on your team have strong opinions about company leaders with whom they have never directly interacted, those opinions must be coming from somewhere—and that somewhere may very well be you.

Here's a thought experiment I've run with product managers and leaders to help them break out of this pattern: imagine that you are working for the *best company in the world*—whatever that means to you. What action would you take today? What would you tell your leadership if you weren't convinced they "can't handle bad news"? How would you engage with your team if you weren't so sure that they "don't care about user insights"? What would you propose as a next big step for the product you're working on if you weren't sure that "this company only cares about shipping a bunch of meaningless new features"?

Sure enough, you may very well run up against the very constraints and limitations you anticipated. But you may also be surprised. Many times in my own career, I have discovered that the company leader who I've heard "can't handle bad news" actually *can* handle bad news, especially when that bad news is delivered fearlessly and directly. Individuals (and the teams and organizations they constitute) are absolutely capable of change, but they must be given the opportunity to step into that change. Leaving the door open for the people around you to learn and grow is one of the most generous and impactful things you can do as a product manager.

Summary: It's Hard Work, but It's Worth It

From the thrill of a product launch to the frustrations of organizational dysfunction and inertia, product management tends to have some pretty extreme highs and lows. Product management necessitates being smack in the middle of whatever is going on with your team and your organization, which means that if there's a lot of difficult stuff going on, there's going to be a lot of difficult work to do.

It is for this very reason that product managers can have such a profound positive effect on the lives and experiences of their colleagues. Because you are in the middle, the actions you take are likely to be outsized in their impact. As the informal ambassador between your team and the rest of the organization, you can set the tone for how people communicate with one another, listen to one another, and demonstrate respect for one another's time and perspective. And during tumultuous times, you can choose to be the fearless protector of the very best things about your team and your company.

Your Checklist

- Be wary of your organization and team falling into autopilot. Actively bring new ideas and challenging perspectives to your team at all times.

- Use timeboxed prototypes to explore alternate product directions, even when there is no immediate or obvious pressure to change course.

- Remember that a good product organization is not one free of conflict, but rather one in which conflict is handled openly and without personal attacks.

- Try to bring the energy and enthusiasm from your best and most exciting moments as a product manager to every day of your work.

- If you begin to feel like you are the only person keeping your team or your organization from falling apart, take a step back. Make a list of the things you can't control, delegate impactful work to your colleagues, and make sure you are protecting your team's most valued routines and rituals.

- Understand that the "in the middle"-ness of your role carries great responsibility, but also great opportunity. Do everything in your power to protect and embody the very best things about your team and your organization.

- Don't let your past experiences calcify into untested assumptions about your team and your organization. Try things that you aren't sure will work and give the people around you a chance to learn and grow with you.

Whatever It Takes

Over a decade ago, I hoped that simply having the title "product manager" would grant me power and authority. The word *manager* suggested that I would be in charge of something. The word *product* suggested that the thing I was in charge of would be an entire product and, in turn, all the people whose work goes into building that product. Who wouldn't want that job?

But this could not be further from the truth. As a product manager, your title gives you nothing—no formal authority, no intrinsic control over product direction or vision, and no ability to get a single meaningful thing done without the help and support of others. To whatever extent you are able to lead through partnership and trust, you must earn that trust every minute, every day. And you must chart your own path to earning that trust in a role full of irresolvable ambiguity and irreducible complexity.

Without exception, this means that you will make mistakes—glaring, egregious, embarrassing mistakes—as you build your product management practice. You will be evasive when you need to be direct. You will be impulsive when you need to be patient. You will follow "best practices" to the letter, and they will *still* backfire in ways you never could have imagined. The mistakes you make will have real repercussions for yourself, your team, and your organization. You will be humbled by the generosity and forgiveness shown by your colleagues. And over time, you might even become more forgiving toward yourself.

And therein lies the true beauty of product management. No matter how smart you are, product management demands that you learn how to be wrong. No matter how charismatic you are, product management demands that you learn how to back up your words with actions. And no matter how ambitious you are, product management demands that you learn how to respect and honor your peers. Product management does not give you an airtight job description or a veneer of formal authority to hide behind. If you want to succeed, you will need to become a better communicator, a better colleague, and a better person.

A few years ago, I delivered a training session at a large, process-driven enterprise financial services company. When the topic turned to the day-to-day responsibilities of a product manager, a recent hire expressed his frustration at the unexpected ambiguity of his new role: "I feel like every day I show up for work, this is a totally different job." The other product managers in the room just smiled. Eventually, he started smiling too. Like many product managers before him, he had asked the question, "Just what am I supposed to *do* all day?" And without even realizing it, he had already found the answer: *whatever it takes.*

A Reading List for Expanding Your Product Management Practice

The last few years have seen an explosion of high-quality content for working product managers. What follows is a list of the books that have proven most impactful for me in building my product management practice, as well as a few notes about how each book might be helpful to you. Note that this is only a guide to book-length content; there are countless articles, newsletters, Twitter accounts, and videos from conference talks that may prove just as helpful. As always, keep an ear to the ground and never hesitate to ask the working product managers in your network what *they've* been reading lately.

Escaping the Build Trap by Melissa Perri (O'Reilly, 2018)

- *If You're Looking For:* A phenomenal overview of *why* product management matters and how product managers can deliver enormous value to organizations.

- *How It Helped Me:* The way Perri frames product management as the facilitation of a value exchange between a business and its users is still my very favorite take on the discipline writ large. This is a great place to start for any practitioners or executives who want to know what product management is and why it matters.

Inspired (https://oreil.ly/mphIA) by Marty Cagan (Second Edition, Wiley, 2018)

- *If You're Looking For:* The foundational text of modern product management.

- *How It Helped Me:* Your colleagues, your manager, and your manager's manager have all read *Inspired*—and you should too. There are tons of useful concepts and structuring frameworks in this book, and the second edition is particularly concise and clearly written.

Strong Product People: A Complete Guide to Developing Great Product Managers (https://oreil.ly/ziGgE) by Petra Wille (2021)

- *If You're Looking For:* A generous and comprehensive guide to understanding and cultivating your own and others' strengths as a product manager and leader.

- *How It Helped Me:* There are *so many* helpful ideas in this book, it's hard to know where to start. But Wille's thoughtful breakdown of the role of coaching in product leadership has been particularly valuable to me personally. If I could only have one product management book at my disposal as I progress in my own career, I would be very happy for it to be this one.

Mindset: The New Psychology of Success (https://oreil.ly/sJnw8) by Carol S. Dweck (Random House, 2006)

- *If You're Looking For:* A way to work past your overachiever tendencies and open yourself up to being wrong and learning new things.

- *How It Helped Me:* In Chapter 3 of this book, we discussed how cultivating a growth mindset is key to succeeding as a product manager. This book helped me understand how and why I was often operating within a fixed mindset, and it even opened up some space for me to understand how moments that made me feel smart or accomplished might be doing material harm to my team and organization.

Crucial Conversations (https://oreil.ly/q6Cad) by Joseph Grenny, Kerry Patterson, Ron McMillan, Al Switzler, and Emily Gregory (Third Edition, McGraw-Hill Education, 2021)

- *If You're Looking For:* Strategies for having difficult conversations without becoming defensive, shutting down, or freaking out.

- *How It Helped Me:* An absurdly high percentage of the work of product management comes down to suppressing and working through defensive and counterproductive reactions to other people's comments and questions. This book is an incredible resource for avoiding common communication traps for product managers, and it is equally helpful for navigating difficult conversations in a personal context. The idea of "victim stories" as a way of dealing with conflict helped me understand and work through my own tendencies toward being a Product Martyr.

The Trusted Advisor (https://oreil.ly/hU8nE) by David H. Maister, Charles H. Green, and Robert M. Galford (20th Anniversary Edition, Free Press, 2021)

- *If You're Looking For:* Actionable strategies for building trust with customers and senior stakeholders.

- *How It Helped Me: The Trusted Advisor* helpfully describes many counterproductive behaviors that I have been too quick to deploy in my own work. Reading this book for the first time was the very last time I said something like "I'll put my best people on it" when scoping out a consulting gig.

Continuous Discovery Habits (https://oreil.ly/rJ4Nr) by Teresa Torres (Product Talk, 2021)

- *If You're Looking For:* A comprehensive and actionable guide to shortening the distance between entire product teams and the customers they serve.

- *How It Helped Me:* Teresa Torres has made innumerable contributions to the product world, but her clear and straightforward definition of *continuous discovery* (which begins "At a minimum, weekly touchpoints with customers...") is a perfect no-nonsense way to evaluate whether teams and organizations are actually serious about doing the work that goes into learning from their customers.

Customers Included (https://oreil.ly/aD7Ic) by Mark Hurst (Second Edition, Creative Good, 2015)

- *If You're Looking For:* A compelling and thoughtful guide to why, and how, to include customers in your product development process.

- *How It Helped Me:* Mark Hurst is one of my favorite writers and thinkers about the relationship between humans and technology. This book is phenomenally written, to the point, and full of compelling real-world examples.

Just Enough Research (*https://oreil.ly/JNWYi*) by Erika Hall (Second Edition, A Book Apart, 2019)

- *If You're Looking For:* Straightforward and useful guidance on conducting research to learn about stakeholders, competitors, and users.
- *How It Helped Me:* This book provides an incredibly valuable balance of specific research approaches and high-level guidance about *why* and *how* to conduct research. It is both a handy reference and a fun read, concise and useful and engaging through and through. I usually keep it on hand whenever I'm embarking on a project that involves any kind of research, both to read up on specific techniques and to realign my overall approach as needed.

The Scrum Field Guide: Agile Advice for Your First Year and Beyond (*https://oreil.ly/4Vkyo*) by Mitch Lacey (Second Edition, Addison-Wesley Professional, 2016)

- *If You're Looking For:* Practical guidance on implementing Agile frameworks.
- *How It Helped Me:* Early in my career as a product manager, I read a *lot* of books about Agile software development—and this was my favorite. Specifically, this book really helped me understand and navigate the reactions I could expect from my team as we began implementing Agile practices.

Radical Focus (*https://oreil.ly/zrfvG*) by Christina Wodtke (Second Edition, Cucina Media, 2021)

- *If You're Looking For:* More information about the Objectives and Key Results framework or just a fresh take on setting organizational goals overall.
- *How It Helped Me:* Having implemented the Objectives and Key Results framework with varying degrees of success at different organizations, I was thrilled to find a book that describes OKRs in compelling, narrative terms. Nearly every mistake a team can make when implementing OKRs

is brought to light here, and Wodtke's emphasis on focus as a goal serves as an important reminder that the goals we set also provide critical guidance about what *not* to do or build.

Lean Analytics by Alistair Croll and Benjamin Yoskovitz (O'Reilly, 2013)

- *If You're Looking For:* A no-nonsense guide to how analytics can help you understand what's actually going on with your product and business.

- *How It Helped Me:* There are many great books in the *Lean Startup* series, but this one is my very favorite. Even as a person who is deeply wary of overreliance on quantitative metrics, I found this book very helpful in thinking through how and why analytics can be used to improve the way that organizations work.

The Advantage: Why Organizational Health Trumps Everything Else in Business (*https://oreil.ly/HXZxO*) by Patrick Lencioni (Jossey-Bass, 2012)

- *If You're Looking For:* A way to better understand organizational health (and dysfunction).

- *How It Helped Me: The Advantage* is the first business book I recommend to most people, because it describes common patterns of organizational dysfunction with unparalleled clarity and generosity. Reading *The Advantage* helped me understand that many of the patterns of organizational dysfunction I had encountered in my career as a product manager were real and widespread, not just functions of my own inexperience.

Good to Great (*https://oreil.ly/Z5b7P*) by Jim Collins (HarperBusiness, 2001)

- *If You're Looking For:* A meticulous, scientific breakdown of what makes an organization achieve great results.

- *How It Helped Me: Good to Great* is an exhaustively researched, illuminating, and entertaining guide to *why* some companies succeed where others fail. There are great lessons here about organizational leadership that I've found crucial for understanding when, why, and how to provide candid feedback to senior leaders. The follow-up *How the Mighty Fall* (*https://oreil.ly/QDPYG*) is also a great read.

Articles, Videos, Newsletters and Blog Posts Cited in This Book

"Product Management for the Enterprise" by Blair Reeves

- *https://oreil.ly/i3Jk7*

"Product Discovery Basics: Everything You Need to Know" by Teresa Torres

- *https://oreil.ly/iOYm4*

"What, Exactly, Is a Product Manager?" by Martin Eriksson

- *https://oreil.ly/K6MZ3*

"Interpreting the Product Venn Diagram with Matt LeMay and Martin Eriksson"

- *https://oreil.ly/cBEds*

"Leading Cross-Functional Teams" by Ken Norton

- *https://oreil.ly/BN9Ak*

"Getting to 'Technical Enough' as a Product Manager" by Lulu Cheng

- *https://oreil.ly/9xWpa*

"You Didn't Fail, Your Product Did" by Susana Lopes

- *https://oreil.ly/e6BdT*

"Good Product Manager/Bad Product Manager" by Ben Horowitz

- *https://oreil.ly/z3688*

"The Tools Don't Matter" by Ken Norton

- *https://oreil.ly/PUblu*

"The Failure of Agile" by Andy Hunt

- *https://oreil.ly/HuwWb*

"The Heart of Agile" by Alistair Cockburn

- *https://oreil.ly/sUyhQ*

"Incomplete by Design and Designing for Incompleteness" by Raghu Garud, Sanjay Jain, and Philipp Tuertscher

- *https://oreil.ly/JKMoH*

"Why Happier Autonomous Teams Use One-Pagers" by John Cutler

- *https://oreil.ly/FFzbq*

"One Page/One Hour"

- *https://oreil.ly/nYQeP*

"Making Advanced Analytics Work for You" by Dominic Barton and David Court

- *https://oreil.ly/RpgVO*

"What Are Survival Metrics? How Do They Work?" by Adam Thomas

- *https://oreil.ly/p962F*

"Opportunity Solution Trees: Visualize Your Thinking" by Teresa Torres

- *https://oreil.ly/du5IJ*

"Don't Prove Value. Create It." by Tim Casasola

- *https://oreil.ly/3dXpM*

"The Truth about Customer Experience" by Alex Rawson, Ewan Duncan, and Conor Jones

- *https://oreil.ly/mOo97*

"People Systematically Overlook Subtractive Changes" by Gabrielle S. Adams, Benjamin A. Converse, Andrew H. Hales, and Leidy E. Klotz

- *https://oreil.ly/X8QE8*

"Empowered Product Teams" by Marty Cagan

- *https://oreil.ly/kOWUB*

Index

A

accountability, data-driven, 178-179

Adams, Gabrielle S., 259

The Advantage: Why Organizational Health Trumps Everything Else in Business (Lencioni), 255

Agile
  ceremonies, conversations about, 129
  common myths, 122
  compared to Waterfall, 127-128
  daily standup meetings, 131-132
  failure of, 124
  four actions, 125
  objections to, 132-134
  process changes, documenting, 130-131
  product management, 121
  product strategy, 155
  retrospective, 128-130
  sloganization, 125

Agile Manifesto, 123, 124

Agile Retrospectives: Making Good Teams Great (Derby and Larsen), 128

Ambiguously Descriptive Product Roles (ADPRs), 11

anti-personas, 97

anxiety, managing, 35, 242-244

apologies

danger of inappropriate, 59-60
danger of overwrought, 47

arguments, disadvantages versus options, 35

assume positive intent, 48-50

asynchronous communication
  compared to synchronous, 204-206
  distributed teams, 209-211

autonomous teams, 226-227

autopilot mode, avoiding, 240-241

B

Bad Science (Goldacre), 126

Banfield, Richard, 220

Barton, Dominic, 168, 258

best practices
  advantages, 119
  dangers of, 103-104
  human issues and, 112
  introducing change, 116-118
  introducing from other organizations, 113-116
  recruiting propaganda, 105

best-in-class companies, recruiting propaganda, 105

blame, danger of accepting, 48-49

business goals, user needs, 79

About the Author

Matt LeMay is an internationally recognized product leader, author, and keynote speaker. He is cofounder and partner at Sudden Compass, a collective of world-class strategists, product leaders, data analysts, and network-builders that has worked with companies like Spotify, Google, and Intuit. Matt has built and scaled product management practices at companies ranging from early-stage startups to Fortune 50 enterprises, and has developed and led digital transformation and data strategy workshops for GE, American Express, Pfizer, McCann, and Johnson & Johnson. Previously, Matt was a senior product manager at music startup Songza (acquired by Google) and head of consumer product at Bitly. Matt is also a musician, recording engineer, and the author of a book about singer-songwriter Elliott Smith. He lives in London, England, with his wife, Joan.

Colophon

The cover illustration is by Jose Marzan Jr. The cover font is Guardian Sans. The text font is Scala Pro; the heading and sidebar font is Benton Sans.